# THE LURE OF THE
# LABRADOR
# WILD

# THE LURE OF THE LABRADOR WILD

By Dillon Wallace

With an Introduction by
Lawrence Millman

*A Torngat
Adventure Classic*

Nimbus Publishing Limited

Copyright © 1990 by Chelsea Green Publishing Co.
Introduction copyright © 1990 by Lawrence Millman
Map copyright © 1990 by Chelsea Green Publishing Co.
Illustration copyright © 1990 by Michael McCurdy

First published in 1905 by Fleming H. Revell Company

Printed in Canada
Published by arrangement with Chelsea Green, June 1990


Canadian Cataloguing in Publication Data

Wallace, Dillon, 1863-1939
  The lure of the Labrador wild
  ISBN 0-921054-58-0
  1. Wallace, Dillon, 1863-1939.    2. Hubbard, Leonidas, 1872-1903.
  3. Explorers — Newfoundland — Labrador — Biography.
  4. Labrador (Nfld.) — Discovery and exploration.    I. Title.
FC2193.4.W34   1990        917.18'2042        C90-097632-2
F1140.W18   1990

L. H.
Here, b'y, is the issue
of our plighted troth.
Why I am the scribe
and not you, God knows:
and you have His secret.
D. W.

"There's no sense in going further—it's the edge of
    cultivation,"
So they said, and I believed it . . .
Till a voice, as bad as Conscience, rang interminable changes
On one everlasting Whisper day and night repeated—so:
"Something hidden. Go and find it. Go and look behind
    the Ranges—
Something lost behind the Ranges. Lost and waiting for
    you. Go!"
                              —Kipling's "The Explorer."

# Contents

# Introduction

As with so many adventures, this story begins with a map. More precisely, it begins with no map at all. For the Labrador Peninsula, at the end of the last century, was still very much *terra incognita*, its boundaries unsurveyed, its lakes largely hypothetical, and its rivers subject to dispute. Those few visitors it did receive, such as John J. Audubon and the American scientist A. S. Packard, were mostly content to wander its coastal fringes. And for good reason, too. Labrador's interior had (and still has) a well-earned reputation for being one of the great inhospitable places on earth, a patchwork of Canadian Shield granites and sphagnum moss, labyrinthine caribou trails and desolate subarctic barrens, all set amidst glacier-scoured hills stretching to an apparently limitless horizon.

Enter A. P. Low, of the Canadian Geological Survey. In Labrador today Low is chiefly remembered for a daring winter trip he made on snowshoes from the Hudson's Bay post at North West River to the city of Montreal. But he was also responsible, between 1892 and 1895, for exploring and mapping the elaborate network of waterways in the peninsula's interior. One of the lakes Low explored—rather, partially explored—was Michikamau, a body of water sacred to the Naskapi Indians. I say *partially* because Low relied on the hearsay of his Indian guides to draw up Michikamau's western shores (the lake itself he made both too long and too narrow). This wasn't the only feature on his map that was either simplified or indeed omitted. To cite another, one of unfortunate significance to our story, Low drew just one river flowing into Grand Lake from the interior. In fact, there are five rivers.

There's nothing like a map for inspiring a man to turn his back on hearth and family and light out for the Territory. So you can imagine the excitement of Leonidas Hubbard, a New York writer, when he chanced on Low's Labrador map, which had just enough detail to suggest an itinerary and just enough blank space to suggest genuine exploration. Hubbard was then churning out articles for *Outing Magazine*; articles that did not, he felt, give adequate scope to his talents. He needed something big, something bold, something like one of Robert Peary's polar assaults—Peary was himself a contributor to *Outing*—to ignite those talents. Thus he decided to lead an expedition to Labrador. He'd follow the old Indian route from the North West River Post to Michikamau, then paddle across the lake and proceed northward, until he located the headwaters of the George River. Continuing down the George, he would arrive at Indian House Lake by late September, in time to witness the annual Naskapi caribou kill. At this point, he would proceed along the river to its mouth, at Ungava Bay, or retrace his steps to North West River, whichever the advance of winter made the more practicable. (This itinerary, by the way, could never be followed today, since the Smallwood Reservoir has drowned much of its terrain.)

It was a quite ambitious plan, especially for a man not yet thirty whose previous wilderness experience consisted of a few weekend camping forays, a brief excursion to James Bay, and a snowshoe trek on the north shore of the St. Lawrence. But Hubbard's incurable optimism gave this plan the quality of a lark, a boy's outing writ wonderfully large and bereft of any real danger. Doubtless Hubbard could have persuaded the Pope, if necessary, to join him in Labrador. Actually he did manage to persuade someone almost as improbable as the Supreme Pontiff—his friend Dillon Wallace. "It's always the way, Wallace," he said. "When a fellow starts on the long trail, he's never willing to quit. It'll be the same with you if you go with me to Labrador. . . ." A bit overweight and already forty, Wallace was a New York attorney with virtually no wilderness experience at all.

Hubbard asked his editor Caspar Whitney to sponsor the trip in return for, at the very least, "a bully article." That's Theodore Roosevelt talk (Roosevelt was also a contributor to *Outing*); but then this was 1903 and the reigning President lent his lingo as well as his bravado to not a few enterprises of the time. As for Whitney, he was author of *On Snowshoes to the Barren Grounds* and no mean outdoorsman himself, though by all accounts a rather mean man. He agreed to be nominal sponsor of the Hubbard expedition, but he made it clear that if Hubbard failed, if his canoe capsized or something like that, the novice explorer would receive no sympathy from the magazine—and maybe no publication, either. Whitney's begrudging approval freed Hubbard to enlist the services of George Elson, a mixed-blood Cree, as the third and final member of his expedition. George had a native's canny knowledge of the bush, but he came from the Missanabie region of James Bay and had never once set foot in Labrador. He would act as guide and general factotum.

And so it was that on July 15, 1903 our unlikely trio of adventurers paddled off into the Great Unknown from the North West River Post. Locals shook their black-fly-tormented heads. For this seemed to them an unusually late date to begin a trip of northern exploration.

\* \* \*

The Hubbard expedition discovered no new features in the Labrador firmament, resulted in no new maps being drawn up, and did not even make contact with the Naskapi or the migrating caribou. In short, it accomplished nothing—nothing, that is, except the retelling of its own story in *The Lure of the Labrador Wild*.

All three men left accounts of the trip for posterity. Hubbard and Elson left diaries that read, for the most part, like field notes: what they ate, where they camped, what the weather was like, and so on. But it was Dillon Wallace who ended up being the expedition's Dante, the intrepid chronicler of its ever-increasing descent into Hell. Here was a man who had been a telegrapher on the Long Island Railroad, a secretary with the American Leather Company, a law office clerk, and finally a junior partner in the law firm of McLaughlin & Stern. In photographs he looks a little like the middle-aged Albert Einstein strangely transported to the Labrador outback. You'd hardly expect this sort of person to survive that sort of outback, but not only did Wallace survive it, he went back for more, as if some deeply-buried aspect of himself were at last liberated by his ordeal.

Close on the heels of this ordeal, Wallace journeyed to Labrador again in 1905 to undergo a second, albeit less harrowing trip, which he describes in his second book, *The Long Labrador Trail*. In 1908 he was selected by the Arctic and Explorers clubs to lead an expedition in search of the explorer Frederick Cook, who was then somewhere in the vicinity of the North Pole and presumed lost; only Cook's miraculous appearance at the eleventh hour kept Wallace at home. In 1913, at the age of fifty, he returned to Labrador and mapped the Beaver River as well as a number of small lakes. Once again the world gave him up for lost; once again he resurfaced, scarcely the worse for wear, after yet another hair-raising trip.

A true survivor, Wallace eagerly passed on his savvy to others. He was an early sponser of the Boy Scouts of America and spent his last years lecturing Scouts on the art of wilderness survival. He died in Beacon, New York, September 28, 1939.

But what of *The Lure of the Labrador Wild* itself? Holed up in a barn in North Adams, Massachusetts, Wallace wrote the book with the help of a journalist named Frank Barkley Copley. The two men alternated sessions of writing and wood chopping, the latter activity working off steam and possibly some pretty awful memories, too. Upon publication in 1905, the book was an instant success and went through six printings in its first year. This success is not surprising, given such a rousing and dramatic narrative, along with a cliff-hanger ending every bit as suspenseful as a good thriller. But what's surprising is how contemporary the book seems today. Perhaps this is because it's written in such a taut, clean style (Copley's influence?); more likely, it's because the well-nigh overwhelming experience of the Labrador wild touched a very deep nerve in Wallace, obliging him, nay, *compelling* him to bring forth a book that would last a long, long time.

I'll sign off now with a little story of my own. In my travels in Newfoundland and Labrador I've noticed that nearly every outport dwelling seems to come equipped with the same two books—the Bible and *The Lure of the Labrador Wild*. Once I asked a grizzled old outporter which of the two he preferred. With a wicked glint in his eye, he replied: "I'll tell ye, my b'y. For sex, I'll take the Good Book. But for everything else, I'll take *The Lure of the Labrador Wild*. It's the most interestin' book in the world. . . ." Well, maybe not the *most* interesting. But no other book I know is so eloquent about the ways a raw and unforgiving Nature can humble the human species.

Lawrence Millman

Cambridge, Massachusetts
January 1990

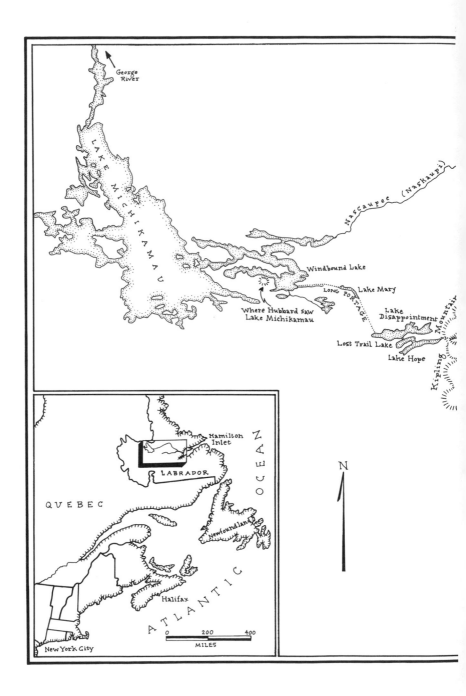

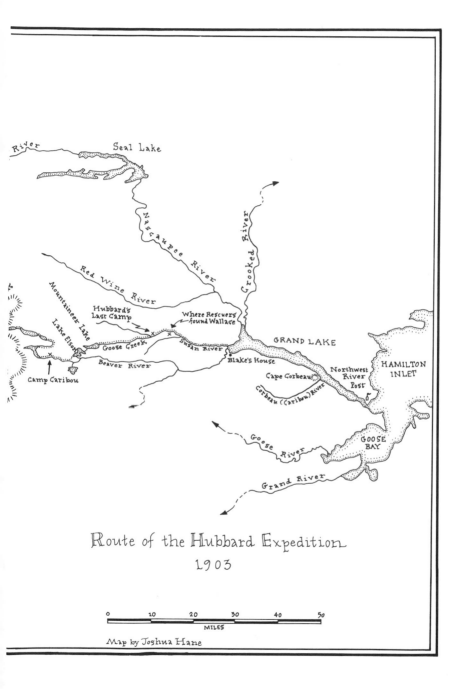

River

Seal Lake

Nascaupee River

Crooked River

Red Wine River

Mountaineer Lake

Lake Elson

Hubbard's Last Camp

Where Rescuers found Wallace

Goose Creek

Swan River

GRAND LAKE

HAMILTON INLET

Camp Caribou

Beaver River

Blake's House

Cape Corbeau

Corbeau (Caribou) River

Northwest River Post

Goose River

GOOSE BAY

Grand River

Route of the Hubbard Expedition
1903

0    10    20    30    40    50

MILES

Map by Joshua Hane

# THE LURE OF THE
# LABRADOR
# WILD

CHAPTER ONE

# *The Object of the Expedition*

"**H**ow would you like to go to Labrador, Wallace?"
It was a snowy night in late November, 1901, that
my friend, Leonidas Hubbard, Jr., asked me this question. All
day he and I had been tramping through the snow among the
Shawangunk Mountains in southern New York, and when the
shades of evening fell we had built a lean-to of boughs to shelter
us from the storm. Now that we had eaten our supper of bread
and bacon, washed down with tea, we lay before our roaring
campfire, luxuriating in its glow and warmth.

Hubbard's question was put to me so abruptly that it rather
startled me.

"Labrador!" I exclaimed. "Now where in the world is Labrador?"

Of course I knew it was somewhere in the northeastern part
of the continent; but so many years had passed since I laid away
my old school geography that its exact situation had escaped my
memory, and the only other knowledge I had retained of the
country was a confused sense of its being a sort of Arctic wilderness. Hubbard proceeded to enlighten me, by tracing with his
pencil, on the flyleaf of his notebook, an outline map of the
peninsula.

"Very interesting," I commented. "But why do you wish to
go there?"

"Man," he replied, "don't you realize it's about the only
part of the continent that hasn't been explored? As a matter of
fact, there isn't much more known of the interior of Labrador
now than when Cabot discovered the coast more than four
hundred years ago." He jumped up to throw more wood on the
fire. "Think of it, Wallace!" he went on, "a great unknown land
right near home, as wild and primitive today as it has always

1

been! I want to see it. I want to get into a really wild country and have some of the experiences of the old fellows who explored and opened up the country where we are now."

Resuming his place by the blazing logs, Hubbard unfolded to me his plan, then vague and in the rough, of exploring a part of the unknown eastern end of the peninsula. Of trips such as this he had been dreaming since childhood. When a mere boy on his father's farm in Michigan, he had lain for hours out under the trees in the orchard poring over a map of Canada and making imaginary journeys into the unexplored. Boone and Crockett were his heroes, and sometimes he was so affected by the tales of their adventures that he must needs himself steal away to the woods and camp out for two or three days.

It was at this period that he resolved to head some day an exploring expedition of his own, and this resolution he forgot neither while a student nor while serving as a newspaper man in Detroit and New York. At length, through a connection he made with a magazine devoted to out-of-door life, he was able to make several long trips into the wild. Among other places, he visited the Hudson Bay region, and once penetrated to the winter hunting ground of the Mountaineer Indians, north of Lake St. John, in southern Labrador. These trips, however, failed to satisfy him; his ambition was to reach a region where no white man had preceded him. Now, at the age of twenty-nine, he believed that his ambition was about to be realized.

"It's always the way, Wallace," he said; "when a fellow starts on a long trail, he's never willing to quit. It'll be the same with you if you go with me to Labrador. You'll say each trip will be the last, but when you come home you'll hear the voice of the wilderness calling you to return, and it will lure you away again and again. I thought my Lake St. John trip was something, but while there I stood at the portals of the unknown, and it brought back stronger than ever the old longing to make discoveries, so that now the walls of the city seem to me a prison and I simply must get away."

My friend's enthusiasm was contagious. It had never previously occurred to me to undertake the game of exploration; but, like most American boys, I had had youthful dreams of going into a great wild country, even as my forefathers had gone, and Hubbard's talk brought back the old juvenile love of adventure. That night before we lay down to sleep I said: "Hubbard, I'll go with you." And so the thing was settled—that was how Hubbard's expedition had its birth.

More than a year passed, however, before Hubbard was able to make definite arrangements to get away. I believe it was in February, 1903, that the telephone bell in my law office rang, and Hubbard's voice at the other end of the wire conveyed to me the information that he had "bully news."

"Is that so?" I said. "What's up?"

"The Labrador trip is all fixed for this summer," was the excited reply. "Come out to Congers tonight without fail, and we'll talk it over."

In accordance with his invitation, I went out that evening to visit my friend in his suburban home. I shall never forget the exuberance of his joy. You would have thought he was a boy about to be released from school. By this time he had become the associate editor of the magazine for which he had been writing, but he had finally been able to induce his employers to consent to the project upon which he had set his heart and grant him a leave of absence.

"It will be a big thing, Wallace," he said in closing; "it ought to make my reputation."

Into the project of penetrating the vast solitudes of desolate Labrador, over which still brooded the fascinating twilight of the mysterious unknown, Hubbard, with characteristic zeal, threw his whole heart and soul. Systematically and thoroughly he went about planning, in the minutest detail, our outfit and entire journey. Every possible contingency received the most careful consideration.

In order to make plain just what he hoped to accomplish and the conditions against which he had to provide, the reader's patience is asked for a few minutes while something is told of what was known of Labrador at the time Hubbard was making preparations for his expedition.

The interior of the peninsula of Labrador is a rolling plateau, the land rising more or less abruptly from the coast to a height of 2,000 or more feet above the level of the sea. Scattered over this plateau are numerous lakes and marshes. The rivers and streams discharging the waters of the lakes into the sea flow to the four points of the compass—into the Atlantic and its inlets on the east, into Ungava Bay on the north, Hudson Bay and James Bay on the west, and the Gulf of St. Lawrence on the south. Owing to the abrupt rise of the land from the coast, these rivers and streams are very swift and are filled with a constant succession of falls and rapids; consequently, their navigation in canoes—the only possible way, generally speaking, to navigate them—is most difficult and dangerous. In this, to a large extent, lies the explanation as to why only a few daring white men have ever penetrated to the interior plateau; the condition of the rivers, if nothing else, makes it impossible to transport sufficient food to sustain a party for any considerable period, and it is absolutely necessary to run the risk of obtaining supplies from a country that may be plentiful with game one year and destitute of it the next, and in which the vegetation is the scantiest.

The western part of the peninsula, although it, too, contains vast tracts in which no white man has set foot, is somewhat better known than the eastern, most of the rivers that flow into Hudson and James Bays having been explored and correctly mapped. Hubbard's objective was the eastern and northern part of the peninsula, and it is with this section that we shall hereafter deal. Such parts of this territory as might be called settled lie in the region of Hamilton Inlet and along the coast.

Hamilton Inlet is an arm of the Atlantic extending inland about one hundred and fifty miles in a southwesterly direction. At its entrance, which is two hundred miles north of Cape Charles, the inlet is some forty miles wide. Fifty miles inland from the settlement of Indian Harbour (which is situated on one of the White Bear Islands, near the north coast of the inlet at its entrance), is the Rigolet Post of the Hudson's Bay Company— the "Old Company," as its agents love to call it—and here the inlet narrows down to a mere channel; but during the next eighty miles of its course inland it again widens, this section of it being known as Groswater Bay or Lake Melville.

The extreme western end of the inlet is called Goose Bay. Into this bay flows the Grand or Hamilton River, one of the largest in Labrador. From its source among the lakes on the interior plateau, the Grand River first sweeps down in a southeasterly direction and then bends northeasterly to reach the end of Hamilton Inlet. The tributaries of the lakes forming the headwaters of the Grand River connect it indirectly with Lake Michikamau (Big Water). This, the largest lake in eastern Labrador, is between eighty and ninety miles in length, with a width varying from six to twenty-five miles.

The Grand River, as well as a portion of Lake Michikamau, some years ago was explored and correctly mapped; but the other rivers that flow to the eastward have either been mapped only from hearsay or not at all. Of the several rivers flowing into Ungava Bay, the Koksoak alone has been explored. This river, which is the largest of those flowing north, rises in lakes to the westward of Lake Michikamau. Next to the Koksoak, the George is the best known of the rivers emptying into Ungava Bay, as well as the second largest; but while it has been learned that its source is among the lakes to the northward of Michikamau, it has been mapped only from hearsay.

On the map of Labrador made by Mr. A. P. Low of the Canadian Geological Survey, the body of water known as Grand Lake is represented thereon merely as the widening out of a large river, called the Northwest, which flows from Lake Michikamau to Groswater Bay or Hamilton Inlet, after being joined about twenty miles above Grand Lake by a river called the Nascaupee. Relying upon this map, Hubbard planned to reach early in the summer the Northwest River Post of the Hudson's Bay Company, which is situated at the mouth of the Northwest River, ascend the river to Lake Michikamau, and then, from the northern end of that lake, beat across the country to the George River.

The Geological Survey map is the best of Labrador extant, but its representation as to the Northwest River (made from hearsay)

5

proved to be wholly incorrect, and the mistake it led us into cost us dear. After the rescue, I thoroughly explored Grand Lake, and, as will be seen from my map, I discovered that no less than five rivers flow into it, which are known to the natives as the Nascaupee, the Beaver, the Susan, the Crooked, and the Cape Corbeau. The Nascaupee is the largest, and as the inquiries I made among the Indians satisfied me that it is the outlet of Lake Michikamau, it is undoubtedly the river that figures on the Geological Survey map as the Northwest, while as for the river called on the map the Nascaupee, it is in all likelihood nonexistent. There is a stream known to the natives as Northwest River, but it is merely the strait, one hundred yards wide and three hundred yards long, which, as shown on my map, connects Groswater Bay with what the natives call the Little Lake, this being the small body of water that lies at the lower end of Grand Lake, the waters of which it receives through a rapid.

Hubbard hoped to reach the George River in season to meet the Nenenot or Nascaupee Indians, who, according to an old tradition, gather on its banks in late August or early September to attack with spears the herds of caribou that migrate at that time, passing eastward to the sea coast. It is reported that while the caribou are swimming the river the Indians each year kill great numbers of them, drying the flesh for winter provisions and using the skins to make clothing and wigwam-covering. Hubbard wished not only to get a good story of the yearly slaughter, but to spend some little time studying the habits of the Indians, who are the most primitive on the North American continent.

Strange as it may seem to some, the temperature in the interior of Labrador in midsummer sometimes rises as high as 90 degrees or more, although at sunset it almost invariably drops to near the freezing point and frost is liable at any time. But the summer, of course, is very short. It may be said to begin early in July, by which time the snow and ice are all gone, and to end late in August. There is just a hint of spring and autumn. Winter glides into summer, and summer into winter, almost imperceptibly, and the winter is the bitter winter of the Arctic.

If the season were not too far advanced when he finished

studying the Indians, Hubbard expected to cross the country to the St. Lawrence and civilization; otherwise to retrace his steps over his upward trail. In the event of our failure to discover the Indian encampment, and our finding ourselves on the George short of provisions, Hubbard planned to run down the swift-flowing river in our canoe to the George River Post at its mouth, and there procure passage on some fishing vessel for Newfoundland; or, if that were impossible, to outfit for winter, and when the ice formed and the snow came, return overland with dogs.

Hubbard knew that by ascending the Grand River he would be taking a surer, if longer, route to Lake Michikamau; but it was a part of his project to explore the unknown country along the river mapped as the Northwest. I have called this country unknown. It is true that in the winter of 1838 John McLean, then the agent of the Hudson's Bay Company at Fort Chimo, a post situated on the Koksoak River about twenty miles above its mouth, passed through a portion of this country in the course of a journey he made with dogs from his post to Northwest River Post. His route was up the Koksoak and across country to the northern end of Lake Michikamau, which he followed for some little distance. After leaving the lake he again travelled eastward across country until at length he came upon the "Northwest" or Nascaupee River at a point probably not far above Grand Lake, from which it was easy travelling over the ice to the post. The record left by him of the journey, however, is very incomplete, and the exact route he took is by no means certain.

Whatever route it was, he returned over it the same winter to Fort Chimo. His sufferings during this trip were extreme. He and his party had to eat their dogs to save themselves from starvation, and even then they would surely all have perished had it not been for an Indian who left the party fifty miles out of Chimo and fortunately had strength enough to reach the post and send back relief. Later McLean made several summer trips with a canoe up the George River from Ungava Bay and down the Grand River to Hamilton Inlet; but never again did he attempt to penetrate the country lying between Lake Michikamau and Hamilton Inlet to the north of Grand River. The fact was that he found his Grand River trips bad enough; the record he has left of them is a story of a continuous struggle against heartbreaking hardships and of narrow escapes from starvation.

It is asserted that a priest once crossed with the Indians from Northwest River Post to Ungava Bay by the Nascaupee route; but the result of my inquiries in Labrador convinced me that the priest in question travelled by way of the Grand River, making it certain that previous to Hubbard's expedition no white man other than McLean had ever crossed the wilderness between Hamilton Inlet and Lake Michikamau by any route other than the aforesaid Grand River. As has been pointed out, McLean made but a very incomplete record of his journey that took him through the country north of the Grand River, so that Hubbard's project called for his plunge into a region where no footsteps would be found to guide him. Not only this, but the George River country, which it was his ultimate purpose to reach, was, and still remains, *terra incognita*; for although McLean made several trips up and down this river, he neither mapped it nor left any definite descriptions concerning it.

Here, then, was an enterprise fully worthy of an ambitious and venturesome spirit like Hubbard. Here was a great, unknown wilderness into which even the half-breed native trappers who lived on its outskirts were afraid to penetrate, knowing that the wandering bands of Indians who occasionally traversed its fastnesses themselves frequently starved to death in that inhospitable, barren country. There was danger to be faced and good "copy" to be obtained.

And so it was ho for the land of "bared boughs and grieving winds!"

CHAPTER TWO

# *Off at Last*

Labrador's uncertain game supply presented more than one vexed problem for Hubbard to solve. Naturally it would be desirable to take with us sufficient provisions to guard against all contingencies; but such were the conditions of the country for which we were bound, that if the expedition were at all heavily loaded it would be impossible for it to make any headway. Hubbard, therefore, decided to travel light. Then arose the question as to how many men to take with us. If the party were large—that is, up to a certain limit—more food might possibly be carried for each member than if the party were small; but if game proved plentiful, there would be no danger from starvation whether the party were large or small; for then short stops could be made to kill animals, dry the flesh and make caches, after the manner of the Indians, as supply bases to fall back upon should we be overtaken by an early winter. And if the game should prove scarce, a small party could kill, on a forced march, nearly, if not quite, as much as a large party; and requiring a proportionately smaller amount of food to maintain it, would consequently have a better chance of success. Taking all things into consideration, Hubbard decided that the party should be small.

To guard against possible disappointment in the way of getting men, Hubbard wrote to the agent of the Hudson's Bay Company at Rigolet, asking whether any could be obtained for a trip to the interior either at that post or at Northwest River. The agent replied that such a thing was highly improbable, as the visits of the Indians to these posts had become infrequent and the other natives were afraid to venture far inland. Hubbard then engaged through the kind offices of Mr. S. A. King, who was in charge of the Hudson's Bay Company Post at Missanabie,

Ontario, the services of a Cree Indian named Jerry, that we might have at least one man upon whom we could depend. Jerry was to have come on to New York City to meet us. At next to the last moment, however, a letter from Mr. King informed us that Jerry had backed down. The Indian was not afraid of Labrador, it appeared, but he had heard of the dangers and pitfalls of New York, and when he learned that he should have to pass through that city, his courage failed him; he positively refused to come, saying he did not "want to die so soon."

We never had occasion to regret Jerry's faintheartedness. Mr. King engaged for us another man who, he wrote, was an expert canoeman and woodsman and a good cook. The man proved to be all that he was represented to be—and more. I do not believe that in all the north country we could have found a better woodsman. But he was something more than a woodsman—he was a hero. Under the most trying circumstances he was calm, cheerful, companionable, faithful. Not only did he turn out to be a man of intelligence, quick of perception and resourceful, but he turned out to be a man of character, and I am proud to introduce him to the reader as my friend George Elson, a half-breed Cree Indian from down on James Bay.

The first instance of George's resourcefulness that we noted occurred upon his arrival in New York. Hubbard and I were to have taken him in charge at the Grand Central Station, but we were detained and George found no one to meet him. Despite the fact that he had never been in a city before, and all was new to him, his quick eye discovered that the long line of cabs in front of the station were there to hire. He promptly engaged one, was driven to Hubbard's office and awaited his employer's arrival as calm and unruffled as though his surroundings were perfectly familiar.

Our canoe and our entire outfit were purchased in New York, with the exception of a gill net, which, alas! we decided to defer selecting until we reached Labrador. Our preparations for the expedition were made with a view of sailing from St. John's, Newfoundland, for Rigolet, when the steamer *Virginia Lake*, which regularly plies during the summer between the former port and points on the Labrador coast, should make her first trip of the year. A letter from the Reid-Newfoundland Company, which operates the steamer, informed us that she would probably make her first trip to Labrador in the last week in June, and in order to connect with her, we made arrangements to sail from New York to St. John's on June 20, 1903, on the Red Cross Line steamer *Silvia*. On the nineteenth Hubbard personally superintended the placing of our outfit on board ship, that nothing might be overlooked.

As the *Silvia* slowly got under way at ten o'clock the next morning, we waved a last farewell to the little knot of friends who had gathered on the Brooklyn pier to see us off. We were all very lighthearted and gay that morning; it was a relief to be off at last and have the worry of the preparation over. Mrs. Hubbard was a member of the party; she was to accompany her husband as far as Battle Harbour, the first point on the Labrador coast touched by the *Virginia Lake*.

June 24 was my birthday, and early that morning, before we sailed from Halifax, at which port we lay over for a day, Hubbard came into my stateroom with a pair of camp blankets that he had been commissioned by my sisters to present to me. He had told me he had enough blankets in his outfit and to take none with me. How strangely things sometimes turn out! Those blankets which Hubbard had withheld in order that I might be agreeably surprised, were destined to fulfill an office, up there in the wilds for which we were bound, such as we little suspected.

We reached St. John's on the morning of Friday, the twenty-sixth, and promptly upon our arrival were introduced to the mysterious ways of the Reid-Newfoundland Company. The *Virginia Lake*, we were told, already had gone north to Labrador, was overdue on her return trip and might not be in for several days. Hubbard, however, set immediately to work purchasing the provisions for his expedition and supervising their packing. The following day, on the advice of the general passenger agent of the Reid-Newfoundland Company, we took the evening train on their little narrow-gauge railroad to Whitbourne, en route to Broad Cove, where we were informed we should find excellent trout fishing and could pleasantly pass the time while awaiting the steamer.

The Reid-Newfoundland Company failed to carry out its agreement as to our transportion to Broad Cove, and we had considerable trouble in reaching there, but we found that no misrepresentation had been made as to the fishing; during the two days we were at Broad Cove we caught all the trout we cared for. Having received word that the *Virginia Lake* had returned to St. John's, and would again sail north on Tuesday, June 30, Hubbard and Mrs. Hubbard on the morning of that day took the train to St. John's, to board the steamer there and see that nothing of our outfit was left behind. George and I broke camp in time to take the evening train on the branch road to Harbour Grace, where, it was agreed, we should join the others, the steamer being scheduled to put in there on its way north.

When I had our camp baggage transferred next morning to the wharf, and George and I had arrived there ourselves, we found also waiting for the steamer several prospectors who were going to "The Labrador," as the country is known to the New-foundlanders, to look for gold, copper, and mica. All of them apparently were dreaming of fabulous wealth. None, I was told, was going farther than the lower coast; they did not attempt to disguise the fact that they feared to venture far into the interior.

Around the wharves little boats were unloading caplin, a small fish about the size of a smelt. I was informed that these fish sold for ten cents a barrel, and were used for bait and fertilizer. My astonishment may be imagined, therefore, when I discovered that on the *Virginia Lake* they charged thirty-five cents for three of these little fish fried.

At ten o'clock our boat came in, and a little after noon we steamed out of the harbour, Hubbard and I feeling that now we were fairly on our way to the scene of our work. Soon after rejoining Hubbard, I learned something more of the mysterious ways of the Reid-Newfoundland Company. The company's general passenger agent, avowing deep interest in our enterprise, had presented Hubbard with passes to Rigolet for his party. Hubbard accepted them gratefully, but upon boarding the steamer he was informed that the passes did not include meals. Now such were the prices charged for the wretchedly-cooked food served on the *Virginia Lake* that a moderately hungry man could scarcely have his appetite killed at a less expense than six dollars a day. So Hubbard returned the passes to the general passenger agent with thanks, and purchased tickets, which did include meals, and which reduced the cost considerably.

The *Virginia Lake* is a steamer of some seven hundred tons burden. She is subsidized by the Newfoundland Government to carry the mails during the fishing season to points on the Labrador coast as far north as Nain. She is also one of the sealing fleet that goes to "the ice" each tenth of March. When she brings back her cargo of seals to St. John's, she takes up her summer work of carrying mail, passengers, and freight to The Labrador—always a welcome visitor to the exiled fishermen in that lonely land, the one link that binds them to home and the outside world. She has on board a physician to set broken bones and deal out drugs to the sick, and a customs officer to see that not a dime's worth of merchandise of any kind or nature is landed until a good round percentage of duty is paid to him as the representative of the Newfoundland Government, which holds dominion over all the east coast of Labrador. This customs officer is also a magistrate, a secret service officer, a constable, and what not I do not know—pretty much the whole Labrador Government, I imagine.

The accommodations on the *Virginia Lake* were quite inadequate for the number of passengers she carried. The stuffy little saloon was so crowded that comfort was out of the question. I had to use some rather impressive language to the steward to induce him to assign to me a stateroom. Finally, he surrendered his own room. The ventilation was poor and the atmosphere vile, but we managed to pull through. Our fellow passengers were all either prospectors or owners of fishing schooners.

There was much ice to be seen when the heavy veil of grey fog lifted sufficiently for us to see anything, and until we had crossed the Strait of Belle Isle our passage was a rough one. It was on the Fourth of July that we saw for the first time the bleak, rock-bound coast of Labrador. In all the earth there is no coast so barren, so desolate, so brutally inhospitable as the Labrador coast from Cape Charles, at the Strait of Belle Isle on the south, to Cape Chidley on the north. Along these eight hundred miles it is a constant succession of bare rocks scoured clean and smooth by the ice and storms of centuries, with not a green thing to be seen, save now and then a bunch of stunted shrubs that have found a foothold in some sheltered nook in the rocks, and perchance, on some distant hill, a glimpse of struggling spruce or fir trees. It is a fog-ridden, dangerous coast, with never a lighthouse or signal of any kind at any point in its entire length to warn or guide the mariner.

The evening was well upon us when we saw the rocks off Cape Charles rising from the water, dismal, and dark, and forbidding. All day the rain had been falling, and all day the wind had been blowing a gale, lashing the sea into a fury. Our little ship was tossed about like a cork, with the seas constantly breaking over her decks. Decidedly our introduction to Labrador was not auspicious. Battle Harbour, twelve miles north of Cape Charles, was to have been our first stop; but there are treacherous hidden reefs at the entrance, and with that sea the captain did not care to trust his ship near them. So he ran on to Spear Harbour, just beyond, where we lay to for the night. The next day I made the following entry in my diary:

"Early this morning we moved down to Battle Harbour, where Mrs. Hubbard left us to return home. It was a most dismal time and place for her to part from her husband, but she was very brave. It was not yet six o'clock, and we had had no breakfast, when she stepped into the small boat to go ashore. A cold, drizzling rain was falling, and the place was in appearance particularly dreary; no foliage nor green thing to be seen—nothing but rocks, cold and high and bleak, with here and there patches of snow. They pointed out to us a little house clinging to the rocks high up. There she is to stay until the steamer comes to take her home, to spend a summer of doubts and hopes and misgivings. Poor little woman! It is so hard for those we leave behind. I stood aside with a big lump in my throat as they said their farewell." Up there in the dark wilderness for which we were bound Hubbard talked with me frequently of that parting.

On July 6, the day after we left Battle Harbour, the captain informed us for the first time that the boat would not go to Rigolet on the way up, and gave us the option of getting off at Indian Harbour at the entrance to Hamilton Inlet or going on to Nain with him and getting off at Rigolet on the way back. Hubbard chose the former alternative, hearing which the customs officer came to us and hinted that nothing could be landed until we had had an interview with him. The result of the interview was that Hubbard paid duty on our entire outfit.

The next morning, Tuesday, July 7, we reached Indian Harbour. Amid a chorus of "Good-bye, boys, and good luck!" we went ashore, to set foot for the first time on Labrador soil, where we were destined to encounter a series of misadventures that should call for the exercise of all our fortitude and manhood.

# CHAPTER THREE

# On the Edge of the Wilderness

The island of the White Bear group upon which is situated the settlement of Indian Harbour is rocky and
barren. The settlement consists of a trader's hut and a few fishermen's huts built of frame plastered over with earth or moss, and
the buildings of the Royal National Mission to Deep Sea Fishermen, a nonsectarian institution that maintains two stations on
the Labrador coast and one at St. Anthony in Newfoundland,
each with a hospital attached. The work of the mission is under
the general supervision of Dr. Wilfred T. Grenfell, who, in summer, patrols the coast from Newfoundland to Cape Chidley in
the little floating hospital, the steamer *Strathcona*, and during
the winter months, by dog team, visits the people of these inhospitable shores. The main station in Labrador is at Battle Harbour,
and at this time Dr. Cluny Macpherson was the resident physician.

Dr. Simpson, a young English physician and lay missionary,
was in charge of the station in Indian Harbour. This station,
being maintained primarily for the benefit of the summer fishermen from Newfoundland, is closed from October until July. Dr.
Simpson had a little steamer, the *Julia Sheridan*, which carried
him on his visits to his patients among the coast folk. We were
told by the captain of the *Virginia Lake* that the *Julia Sheridan*
would arrive at Indian Harbour on the afternoon of the day we
reached there; that she would immediately steam to Rigolet and
Northwest River with the mails, and that we undoubtedly could
arrange for a passage on her. This was the reason that Hubbard
elected to get off at Indian Harbour.

The trained nurse, the cook, and the maid-of-all-work connected with the Indian Harbour hospital ("sisters," they call
them, although they do not belong to any order) boarded the

16

*Virginia Lake* at Battle Harbour and went ashore with me in the ship's boat when I landed with the baggage. Hubbard and George went ashore in our canoe. A line of Newfoundlanders and "livyeres" stood ready to greet us upon our arrival. "Livyeres" is a contraction of live-heres, and is applied to the people who live permanently on the coast. The coast people who occasionally trade in a small way are known as "planters." In Hamilton Inlet, west of Rigolet, all of the trappers and fishermen are called planters. There the word livyere is never heard, it having originated with the Newfoundland fishermen, who do not go far into the inlet.

The "sisters" who landed with us had difficulty in opening their hospital, as the locks had become so rusted and corroded that the keys would not turn. We offered our assistance, and after removing the boards that had been nailed over the windows to protect them from the winter storms, we found it necessary to take out a pane of glass in order that Hubbard might unlatch a window, crawl through and take the lock off the door. The sisters then told us that Dr. Simpson might not arrive with the *Julia Sheridan* until the following day, and extended to us the hospitality of the station, which we thankfully accepted, taking up our temporary abode in one of the vacant wards of the hospital.

Our first afternoon on Labrador soil we spent in assorting and packing our outfit, while the Newfoundlanders and livyeres stood around and admired our things, particularly the canoe, guns, and sheath knives. Their curiosity was insatiable; they inquired the cost of every conceivable thing.

The next afternoon (Wednesday) Dr. Simpson arrived on his steamer, and, to our great disappointment, we learned that the *Julia* would not start on the trip down the inlet until after the return of the *Virginia Lake* from the north, which would probably be on Friday or Saturday. The Labrador summer being woefully short, Hubbard felt that every hour was precious, and he chafed under our enforced detention. We were necessarily going into the interior wholly unprepared for winter travel, and hence must complete our work and make our way out of the wilderness before the rivers and lakes froze and canoe travel became impossible. Hubbard felt the responsibility he had assumed, and could imagine the difficulties that awaited us should his plans miscarry. Accordingly, he began to look around immediately among the fishermen and livyeres for someone with a small boat willing to take us down the fifty miles to Rigolet. Finally, after much persuasion and an offer of fifteen dollars, he induced a young livyere, Steve Newell by name, to undertake the task.

Steve was a characteristic livyere, shiftless and ambitionless. He lived a few miles down the inlet with his widowed mother and his younger brothers and sisters. For a week he would work hard and conscientiously to support the family, and then take a month's rest. We had happened upon him in one of his resting periods, but as soon as Hubbard had pinned him down to an agreement he put in an immediate plea for money.

"I'se huntin' grub, sir," he begged. "I has t' hunt grub all th' time, sir. Could 'un spare a dollar t' buy grub, sir?"

Hubbard gave him the dollar, and he forthwith proceeded to the trader's hut to purchase flour and molasses, which, with fat salt pork, are the great staples of the Labrador natives, although the coast livyeres seldom can afford the latter dainty. While we were preparing to start, Hubbard asked Steve what he generally did for a living.

"I hunts in winter an' fishes in summer, sir," was the reply.

"What do you hunt?"

"Fur an' partridges, sir. I trades the fur for flour and molasses, sir, an' us eats th' partridges."

"What kind of fur do you find here?"

"Foxes is about all, sir, an' them's scarce; only a chance one, sir."

"Do you catch enough fur to keep you in flour and molasses?"

"Not always, sir. Sometimes us has only partridges t' eat, sir."

We started at five o'clock in the evening in Steve's boat, the *Mayflower*, a leaky little craft that kept one man pretty busy bailing out the water. She carried one ragged sail, and Steve sculled and steered with a rough oar about eighteen feet long. An hour after we got under way a blanket of grey fog, thick and damp, enveloped us; but so long are the Labrador summer days that there still was light to guide us when at eleven o'clock Steve said:

"Us better land yere, sir. I lives yere, an' 'tis a good spot t' stop for th' night, sir."

I wondered what sort of an establishment Steve maintained, and drawing an inference from his personal appearance, I had misgivings as to its cleanliness. However, anything seemed better than the chilling fog, and land we did—in a shallow cove where we bumped over a partly submerged rock and maneuvered with difficulty among others, that raised their heads ominously above the water. As we approached, we made out through the fog the dim outlines, close to the shore, of a hut partially covered with sod. Our welcome was tumultuous—a combination of the barking of dogs and the shrill screams of women demanding to know who we were and what we wanted. There were two women, tall, scrawny, brown, with hair flying at random. The younger one had a baby in her arms. She was Steve's married sister. The other woman was his mother. Each was loosely clad in a dirty calico gown. Behind them clustered a group of dirty, half-clad children.

Steve ushered us into the hut, which proved to have two rooms, the larger about eight by ten feet. The roof was so low that none of us could stand erect except in the center, where it came to a peak. In the outer room were two rough wooden benches, and on a rickety table a dirty kerosene lamp without a chimney shed gloom rather than light. An old stove, the sides of which were bolstered up with rocks, filled the hut with smoke to the point of suffocation when a fire was started. The floor and everything else in the room were innocent of soap and water.

George made coffee, which he passed around with hardtack to everybody. Then all but Steve and our party retired to the inner room, one of the women standing a loose door against the aperture. Steve curled up in an old quilt on one of the benches, while Hubbard, George and I spread a tarpaulin on the floor and rolled in our blankets upon it.

We were up betimes the next morning after a fair night's

sleep on the floor. We again served hardtack and coffee to all, and at five o'clock were once more on our way. A thick mantle of mist obscured the shore, and Hubbard offered Steve a chart and compass. "Ain't got no learnin', sir; I can't read, sir," said the young livyere. So Hubbard directed the course in the mist while Steve steered. Later in the day the wind freshened and blew the mist away, and at length developed into a gale. Finally the sea rose so high that Steve thought it well to seek the protection of a harbour, and we landed in a sheltered cove on one of the numerous islands that strew Hamilton Inlet, where we then were—Big Black Island, it is called.

George had arisen that morning with a lame back, and when we reached the island he could scarcely move. The place was so barren of timber we could not find a stick long enough to act as a center pole for our tent, and it was useless to try to pitch it. However, the moss, being thick and soft, made a comfortable bed, and after we had put a mustard plaster on George's back to relieve his lumbago, we rolled him in two of our blankets under the lee of a bush and let him sleep. Then, as evening came on, Hubbard and I started for a stroll along the shore. The sun was still high in the heavens, and the temperature mildly cool.

A walk of a mile or so brought us to the cabin of one Joe Lloyd, a livyere. Lloyd proved to be an intelligent old Englishman who had gone to Labrador as a sailor lad on a fishing schooner to serve a three-years' apprenticeship. He did not go home with his ship, and year after year postponed his return, until at last he married an Eskimo and bound himself fast to the cold rocks of Labrador, where he will spend the remainder of his life, eking out a miserable existence, a lonely exile from his native England.

After he had greeted us, Lloyd asked: "Is all the world at peace, sir?" He had heard of the Boer War, and was pleased when we told him that it had ended in a victory for the British arms. His hunger for news touched us deeply, and we told him all that we could recall of recent affairs of public interest. I have said that his hunger for news touched us. As a matter of fact, few things have impressed me as being more pathetic than that old man's life up there on that isolated and desolate island, where he spends most of his time wistfully longing to hear something of the great world, and painfully recalling the pleasant memories of his childhood's home and friends, and the green fields and spring blossoms he never will know again. And Lloyd's story is the story of perhaps the majority of the settlers on The Labrador.

The old man had a fresh-caught salmon, and we bought it from him. We then sat for a few minutes in his cabin. This was a miserable affair, not exceeding eight by ten feet, and, like Steve's home, so low we could not stand erect in it. The floor was paved with large, flat stones, and the only vent for the smoke from the wretched fireplace was a hole in the roof. Midway between the fire and the hole hung a trout drying. In this room Lloyd and his Eskimo wife live out their life. During our visit the wife sat there without uttering a word. Her silence was characteristic; for, somewhat unlike our women, the women of Labrador talk but little.

When we had bidden Lloyd farewell, we carried the salmon we had obtained from him back to camp, where Hubbard tried to plank it on a bit of wreckage picked up on the shore. It fell into the fire, and there was great excitement until, by our united efforts, we had rescued it, and had seen part of it safely reposing in the frying pan, while Steve set to work boiling the remainder in our kettle with slices of bacon. As the gale continued to blow, it was decided that we should remain in camp until early morning. Hubbard directed Steve to pull the boat around to a place where it would be near the water at low tide. He and I then threw down the tent, lay on it, pulled a blanket over us and prepared for sleep. It was about eleven o'clock, and darkness was just beginning to fall. Out in the bay a whale was blowing, and in the distance big gulls were screaming. It was our first night out in the open in Labrador, and all was new and entrancing; and as slumber gradually enwrapped us, it seemed to us that we had fallen upon pleasant times.

At one o'clock (Friday morning) we awoke. By the light of the brilliant moon we made coffee, called George and Steve and ate our breakfast of cold salmon and hardtack. George's lumbago was very bad, and he was unable to do any work. The rest of us portaged the outfit two hundred yards to the boat, which, owing to Steve's miscalculations as to the tide, we found high and dry on the rocks. Working in the shallow water, with a cloud of mosquitoes around our heads, it took us until 4:30 o'clock to launch her, by which time daylight long since had returned.

Once more afloat, we found that the wind had entirely died away, and Steve's sculling pushed the boat along but slowly. Grampuses raised their big backs everywhere, and seals, upon which they prey, were numerous. The water was alive with schools of caplin. At eleven o'clock we made Pompey Island, a mossy island of Laurentian rock about thirty-five miles from Indian Harbour. Here we stopped for luncheon, and after much looking around, succeeded in finding enough sticks to build a little fire. I made flapjacks, and Hubbard melted sugar for syrup.

While were were eating, I discovered in the far distance the smoke of a steamer. We supposed it to be the *Julia Sheridan*. Rushing our things into the boat, we put off as quickly as possible to intercept her. We fired three or four shots from our rifle, but got only a salute in recognition. Then Hubbard and I scrambled into the canoe, which we had in tow, and began to paddle with might and main to head her off. As we neared her, we fired again. At that she came about—it was the *Virginia Lake*. They took us on board, bag, baggage, and canoe, and Steve was dismissed.

In an hour we were in sight of Rigolet, and I saw a Hudson's Bay Company Post for the first time in my life. As our steamer approached, a flag was run up in salute to the top of a tall staff, and when it had been caught by the breeze, the Company's initials, H. B. C., were revealed. The Company's agents say these letters have another significance, namely, "Here Before Christ," for the flag travels ahead of the missionaries.

The reservation of Rigolet is situated upon a projection of land, with a little bay on one side and the channel into which Hamilton Inlet narrows at this point on the other. Long rows of whitewashed buildings, some of frame and some of log, extend along the water front, coming together at the point of the projection so as to form two sides of an irregular triangle. A little back of the row on the bay side, and upon slightly higher ground, stands the residence of the agent, or factor as he is officially called, this building being two stories high and otherwise the most pretentious of the group. It is commonly called the "Big House," and near it is the tall flagstaff. Between the rows of buildings and the shore is a broad board walk, which leads down near the apex of the triangle to a small wharf of logs. It was at this wharf that our little party landed.

Hubbard presented his letter of introduction from Commissioner Chipman of the Hudson's Bay Company to Mr. James Fraser, the factor, and we received a most cordial welcome, being made at home at the Big House. We found the surroundings and people unique and interesting. There were lumbermen, trappers, and fishermen—a motley gathering of Newfoundlanders, Nova Scotians, Eskimos and "breeds," the latter being a comprehensive name for persons whose origin is a mixture in various combinations and proportions of Eskimo, Indian, and European. All were friendly and talkative, and hungry for news of the outside world.

Lying around everywhere, or skulking about the reservation, were big Eskimo dogs that looked for all the world like wolves in subjection. We were warned not to attempt to play with them, as they were extremely treacherous. Only a few days before a little Eskimo boy who stumbled and fell was set upon by a pack and all but killed before the brutes were driven off. The night we arrived at Rigolet the pack killed one of their own number and ate him, only a little piece of fur remaining in the morning to tell the tale.

Within an hour after we reached the post, Dr. Simpson arrived on the *Julia Sheridan*; but as he had neglected to bring the mail for Northwest River Post that the *Virginia Lake* had left at Indian Harbour, he had to return at once. Dr. Simpson not being permitted by his principles to run his boat on Sunday, unless in a case of great necessity, we were told not to expect the *Julia Sheridan* back from Indian Harbour until Monday noon; and so we were compelled to possess our souls in patience and enjoy the hospitality of Mr. Fraser. I must confess that while I was anxious to get on, I was at the same time not so greatly disappointed at our enforced delay; it gave me an opportunity to see something of the novel life of the post.

While at Rigolet we of course tried to get all the information possible about the country to which we were going. No Indians had been to the post for months, and the white men and Eskimos knew absolutely nothing about it. At length Hubbard was referred to "Skipper" Tom Blake, a breed, who had trapped at the upper or western end of Grand Lake. From Blake he learned that Grand Lake was forty miles long, and that canoe travel on it was good to its upper end, where the Nascaupee River flowed into it. Blake believed we could paddle up the Nascaupee some eighteen or twenty miles, where we should find the Red River, a wide, shallow, rapid stream that flowed into the Nascaupee from the south. Above this point he had no personal knowledge of the country, and advised us to see his son Donald, whom he expected to arrive that day from his trapping grounds on Seal Lake. Donald, he said, had been farther inland and knew more about the country than anyone else on the coast.

Donald did arrive a little later, and upon questioning him Hubbard learned that Seal Lake, which, he said, was an expansion of the Nascaupee River, had been the limit of his travels inland. Donald reiterated what his father had told us of Grand Lake and the lower waters of the Nascaupee, adding that for many miles above the point where the Nascaupee was joined by the Red we should find canoe travel impossible, as the Nascaupee "tumbled right down off the mountains." Up the Nascaupee as far as the Red River he had sailed his boat. He had heard from the Indians that the Nascaupee came from Lake Michikamau, and he believed it to be a fact. This convinced us that that Nascaupee was the river A. P. Low, of the Geological Survey, had mapped as the Northwest. The Red River Donald had crossed in winter some twenty miles above its mouth, and while it was wide, it was so shallow and swift that he was sure it would not admit of canoeing. He could not tell its source, and was sure the Indians had never travelled on it. In answer to Hubbard's inquiries as to the probability of our getting fish and game, Donald said there were bears along the Nascaupee, but few other animals. He had never fished the waters above Grand Lake, but believed plenty of fish were there. On Seal Lake there was a "chance" seal, and he had taken an occasional shot at them, but they were very wild and he had never been able to kill any.

Strange as it may seem, none of the men with whom we talked mentioned that more than one river flowed into Grand Lake, although they unquestionably knew that such was the case. Their silence about this important particular was probably due to the fact, that while the Labrador people are friendly to strangers, they are somewhat shy and rarely volunteer information, contenting themselves, for the most part, with simple answers to direct questions. Furthermore, they are seldom able to adopt a point of view different from their own, and thus are unable to realize the amount of guidance a stranger in their country needs. In fact I discovered later that Skipper Blake and his son, who have spent all their lives in the vicinity of Hamilton Inlet, never dreamed anyone could miss the mouth of Nascaupee River, as they themselves knew so well how to find it.

We were sitting in the office of the post on Sunday, comfortably away from the fog that lay thick outside, when we were startled by a steamship whistle. Out we all ran, and there, in the act of dropping her anchor, was the *Pelican*, the company's ship from England. In the heavy fog she had stolen in and whistled before the flag was raised, which feat Captain Grey, who commands the *Pelican*, regarded as a great joke on the post. Once a year the *Pelican* arrives from England, and the day of her appearance is the Big Day for all the Labrador posts, as she brings the year's supplies together with boxes and letters from home for the agents and the clerks. From Rigolet she goes to Ungava, then returns to Rigolet for the furs there and once more steams for England.

We found Captain Grey to be a jolly, cranky old seadog of the old school. He has been with the Hudson's Bay Company for thirty years, and has sailed the northern seas for fifty. He shook his head pessimistically when he heard about our expedition. "You'll never get back," he said. "But if you happen to be at Ungava when I get there, I'll bring you back." "Sandy" Calder, the owner of lumber mills on Sandwich Bay and the Grand River, who came from Cartwright Post on Sandwich Bay with Captain Grey on the *Pelican*, also predicted the failure of our enterprise. But Hubbard said to me that he had·heard such prophesies before; that they made the work seem all the bigger, and that he could do it and *would*.

At noon on Monday Dr. Simpson came with the *Julia Sheridan*, and we said good-bye to Rigolet. The voyage down the inlet to Northwest River Post was without incident, except that the good doctor was much concerned as to the outcome of our venture, saying: "Don't leave your bones up there to whiten, boys, if you can possibly help it." We reached Northwest River at two o'clock on Tuesday afternoon, and found the post to be much the same as Rigolet, except that its whitewashed buildings were all strung out in one long row. The welcome we received from Mr. Thomas Mackenzie, the agent there in charge, was most gratifying in its heartiness. Mr. Mackenzie is a bachelor, tall, lean, high-spirited, and the soul of hospitality. Hubbard promptly dubbed him a "bully fellow." Probably this was partly due to the fact that he was the first man in Labrador to give us any encouragement. We had not been there an hour when he became infected with Hubbard's enthusiasm, and said he would pack up that night and be ready to start with us in the morning, if he only were free to do so.

To our great disappointment and chagrin, we found that Mackenzie had no fish nets to sell. We had been unable to obtain any at Rigolet, and now we were told that none was to be had anywhere in that part of Labrador. Hubbard realized fully the importance of a gill net as a part of our equipment and had originally intended to purchase one before leaving New York; but he was advised by Mr. A. P. Low of the Canadian Geological Survey that it would be better to defer its purchase until we reached Rigolet Post or Northwest River, where he said we could get a net such as would be best adapted to the country. Hubbard had no reason to doubt the accuracy of this information, as Mr. Low had previously spent several months at these posts when engaged in the work of mapping out the peninsula. Conditions, however, had changed, unfortunately for us, since Mr. Low's visit to Labrador. Seeing the quandary we were in, Mackenzie got out an old three-inch gill net that had been lying in a corner of one of his buildings. He said he was afraid it was worn out, but if we could make any use of it, we might take it. We, too, had our doubts as to its utility; but, as it was the best obtainable, Hubbard accepted it thankfully and Mackenzie had two of his men unravel it and patch it up.

During the afternoon we got our outfit in shape, ready for the start in the morning. Following is a summary of the outfit taken from an inventory made at Indian Harbour: Our canoe was 18 feet long, canvas covered, and weighed about 80 pounds. The tent was of the type known as miner's, 6½ x 7 feet, made of balloon silk and waterproofed. We had three pairs of blankets and one single blanket; two tarpaulins; five duck waterproof bags; one dozen small waterproof bags of balloon silk for notebooks; two .45-70 Winchester rifles; two 10-inch barrel .22-caliber pistols for shooting grouse and other small game; 200 rounds of .45-70 and 1,000 rounds of .22-caliber cartridges; 3¼ x 4¼ pocket folding kodak with Turner-Reich Verastigmat lens; thirty rolls of films of one dozen exposures each, in tin cans, waterproofed with electricians' tape; a sextant and artificial horizon; two compasses and our cooking utensils and clothing.

At Indian Harbour we had four 45-pound sacks of flour, but Hubbard gave one sack to the pilot of the *Julia Sheridan*, and out of another sack he had given the cook on the *Julia* sufficient flour for one baking of bread and we had also used some of this bag on our way from Indian Harbour to Rigolet. This left us two 45-pound bags and about 30 pounds in the third bag, or 120 pounds in all. There were, perhaps, 25 pounds of bacon, 13 pounds lard, 20 pounds flavored pea meal, 9 pounds plain pea flour in tins, 10 pounds tea, 5 pounds coffee, 8 pounds hardtack, 10 pounds milk powder, 10 pounds rice, 8 pounds dried apples, 7 pounds salt, 7 or 8 pounds tobacco and 30 pounds sugar.

This outfit, it will be remembered, was designed for three men. Hubbard tried to hire some of the natives to accompany us a few miles into the interior and carry additional provisions that we might cache, but failed; they were all "too busy."

Mackenzie treated us royally during the evening we spent at his post, and we enjoyed his hospitality to the utmost, knowing that it was to be our last night under shelter for weeks to come. Now we were on the very edge of the wilderness. Tomorrow we should enter the unknown.

# CHAPTER FOUR

# The Plunge into the Wild

It was nine o'clock on Wednesday morning, July 15, that we made the start. Our canoe, laden deep with our outfit, was drawn up with its prow resting snugly on the sandy bottom of the little strait that is locally known as the Northwest River. Mackenzie and a group of swarthy natives gathered on the shore to see us off. All but the high-spirited agent were grave and skeptical, and shook their heads at our persistency in going into a country we had been so frequently warned against.

The atmosphere was crisp, pure, and exhilarating. The fir trees and shrubs gave out a delicious perfume, and their waving tops seemed to beckon us on. The sky was deep blue, with here and there a feathery cloud gliding lazily over its surface. The bright sunlight made our hearts bound and filled our bodies with vigour, and as we stood there on the edge of the unknown and silent world we had come so far to see, our hopes were high, and one and all were eager for the battle with the wild.

"I wish I were going with you; good-bye and Godspeed!" shouted Mackenzie, as we pushed the canoe into deep water and dipped our paddles into the current. In a moment he and the grave men that stood with him were lost to view. Up through the strait into the Little Lake we paddled, thence to the rapid where the waters of Grand Lake pour out. With one end of a tracking line, Hubbard sprang into the shallow water near the shore below the swift-running stream, and with the other end fastened to the bow of the canoe, pulled it through the rapid. A "planter's" family in a cabin nearby watched us wonderingly.

Then we were in Grand Lake. Hubbard remarked that it looked like Lake George, save that the hills were lower. For a few miles above its outlet the shores on both sides of the lake are low. Then on the south come bluffs that rise, stern and grand

grand in their nudity, almost perpendicularly from the deep, clear water, while on the north come lower hills, for the most part wooded, that retreat more gently from the rocky shore. Heading for the extreme upper end of the lake, where Low's map and the natives had led us to expect we should find the Northwest or Nascaupee River, we paddled along the north shore to a point where we stopped among the rocks for a luncheon of flapjacks and syrup.

We were away without waste of time, paddling diagonally across the lake to the south shore. The fleecy clouds had now thickened, and a few drops of rain had fallen. In our course across the lake we passed Cape Corbeau (Raven), but were so far out that the mouth of the river of that name, which is just east of it, escaped our attention. Cape Corbeau, it had been named by a French missionary, because the ravens build their nests on its rocky top, and, perched high up, croak at you warningly from afar. Always the ravens are there. Involuntarily, as one croaked above our heads, "Nevermore" echoed through my mind. "And my soul from out that shadow shall be lifted nevermore." There were dark shadows ahead of us among the rocks and the forests, and—but in a moment the thought was drowned and forgotten in the beauties of the scenery. Beauties?—yes; for bleak and desolate Labrador has a beauty and a charm all its own.

Two hours after passing Cape Corbeau the rain began to pour, and at 7:30 o'clock, when we made camp on the south shore, we were well soaked. We resumed our journey at 5:30 in the morning. A stiff breeze was blowing, but by keeping in the lee of the shore we made good progress. At ten o'clock, when we found it necessary to cross to the north shore so as to shorten the distance, there was a rising sea, and we had to lighten the canoe and ferry the cargo over in two loads.

It was soon after one o'clock that we reached the upper end of the lake, where we found a stream about 125 yards wide that flowed with a swift current from out a little lake. Into this lake after luncheon we paddled, and when we reached its upper end, there was the mouth of a river, which we immediately hailed as the Nascaupee, the stream that was to lead us up to Lake Michikamau. Its mouth was wide, and it seemed to answer so well all the descriptions we had heard of the river for which we were searching that the possibility of our being mistaken never once entered our heads; in fact, we remained under the impression that it was the Nascaupee until the last.

But we *were* mistaken. We had passed the Nascaupee five miles below, where it empties, together with the Crooked River, into a deep bay extending northward from Grand Lake. At its mouth the Nascaupee is divided by an island into two streams, and this island is so thickly covered with trees, and the streams on either side of it are so narrow, that when we crossed along in front of the bay no break in the line of woods at the mouth of the river was perceptible. Perhaps it will be said we should have explored the bay. I know now myself that should have been done, but in justice to Hubbard it must be remembered that none of us then had any reason to suppose we should find a river at any place other than the extreme upper end of the lake. Time and time again Hubbard had asked the few natives who had been there if the Nascaupee entered Grand Lake at its extreme upper end, and the answer invariably had been: "Yes, sir; he do." Furthermore, it will have to be taken into consideration how hard pressed Hubbard was by the fear that the short summer would end before he had completed his work, and by the consequent necessity of pushing on with all possible speed.

The river up which we started to ascend with light hearts was the Susan, a river which was to introduce us promptly to heart-breaking hardships, a river which is to me associated with the most tragic memories.

On the southerly side of the little lake Porcupine Hill raises its spruce-covered head a thousand feet above the water. Proceeding up the Susan, we found that the river valley was enclosed by low ridges covered with spruce and a few scattering white birch and aspen trees. For the most part the banks of the river were steep and high; where they were low the river formed little pond expansions. For a mile above its mouth we had good canoeing. Up to this point the river was not more than thirty yards wide, and was deep, with little current. Then it began gradually to widen and become shallow and swift, with a boulder-strewn bottom. Soon we had to jump into the water, and with Hubbard at the end of the tracking line, and George and I at either end of the canoe, haul, lift, and push the heavily laden boat up the river, while we floundered over the boulders. Sometimes we would be able to get into the canoe and pole, but never for long. Around the worst places we portaged the whole outfit, canoe and all. It was desperately hard work, and when night came on and we went into camp, we were only two miles above the little lake.

Hard as it was, we should not have minded our work in the rapids so much had it not been for the flies. For the first time we now realized the full force of what had been told us about the fly pest of Labrador. We had considered them annoying at Rigolet and Northwest River, but as soon as we began to buck the rapids they came upon us in clouds. They got into our nostrils, into our ears, into our mouths, into our eyes even, and our faces and hands were streaked with blood from their bites. They were villainous, hellish. Hubbard frequently remarked that the mosquitoes seemed friendly in contrast—and the mosquitoes were by no means considerate of our feelings and comfort either. We had purchased some cheesecloth at Rigolet for face nets, but the trial we had given it during the afternoon had proved that it was too closely woven for us to see through it and do our work, and it was useful only as some measure of protection for our ears and necks. On our faces we also tried some "fly dope" that we had purchased in New York, but it kept the pests away for a few minutes only.

The ordinary Labrador fly is smaller than a pinhead. You do not feel it until after it has had its bite, and then the sensation is like that of a fiery itch. In addition to this kind, we had to withstand the attacks of flies called by the natives "bulldogs." These beasts are about the size of the top joint of one's thumb. They are well named. When they bite, you feel it immediately beyond a doubt. We used to say they bit out pieces of our flesh entire and flew up into the trees to eat them, and we used frequently to beg George to try his luck at shooting the brutes. However, it must be said to the credit of both kinds of flies that they have one good habit—they "knock off" work at the approach of the cool of evening, thus giving you a chance to bathe as well as sleep.

The rain was still pouring when we pitched our tent that first night, but we had a good supper and were reasonably cheerful. There were flapjacks dripping with the syrup of melted sugar, and bacon, and hot bread, and coffee.

"With this sort of work before us," said Hubbard, "we must keep well fed."

"The river," said I, "certainly is the limit. If the Indians have to travel on it much, I feel sorry for them."

"Well," said Hubbard, "we've surely got our work cut out. At this rate we're going to make pretty slow progress."

"Blake told us," I ventured, "we could paddle up the river eighteen or twenty miles, and that he had sailed his boat up that far. I'd be willing to bet he never sailed it up this stream."

"Oh," replied Hubbard, "he was mistaken in the distance. This must be the place where he said the river tumbled off the mountain. What do you say, boys," he added, "to throwing away some of the outfit? We'll never make any progress if we attempt to carry it all."

"Let's stick to it a little longer," suggested George.

However, we decided to abandon some clothing and a pail containing about four pounds of lard; and as George, particularly, was opposed to leaving behind us any provisions, it was decided to eat of them lavishly and pay no attention to the hunt for the present.

All night it continued to rain, and we broke camp and started forward on Friday morning, July 17, in a drenching downpour. George thought this was rather hard. While Hubbard was out of hearing, he told me that the Indians never travelled in the rain, and that he had never been expected to do so before. The fact was that George had never before been on an expedition where there was so much necessity for haste.

We found the river on the second day to be even worse than our worst fears had pictured it, and it kept growing worse as we ascended. The water was so swift and shoal that we could take only a part of the outfit in the canoe, which meant that we had to return at intervals for the rest and track all the way, Hubbard pulling on the line while George and I waded and pushed. Sometimes we were scarcely knee deep in the water, and at other times we would sink up to our armpits. Frequently we were swept off our feet. Once or twice we forced the canoe and outfit through the thick willows and alders that lined the river, and dragged them up the steep bank and attempted to portage; but the country here had been burned and fallen trees were piled high in every direction, so that we were compelled to return to the river and resume our efforts in the raging torrent.

The work was awful, it was heartrending; and though we exerted ourselves to the utmost from six o'clock in the morning until eight at night, we advanced our camp only two miles that day. And when we gathered around the fire at night, how we did "cuss" that river! None of us, however, was discouraged, nor flinched at the prospect. Our oil-tanned, cowhide moccasins and woollen trousers were beginning to show the result of the attacks of bush, rock, and water, but our blue flannel shirts and soft felt hats were still quite respectable. Our coats we had left behind us as an unnecessary encumbrance.

While George was cooking breakfast on Saturday morning (July 18), a red squirrel barked at us from a nearby tree. Drawing his pistol from its holster, Hubbard said:

"Wallace, let's see who shall have the honor of bringing to George the first game of the trip."

I acquiesced, and walking around the tree, caught the first glimpse of the squirrel. At it I carefully aimed my pistol, and down it came. It made a tiny morsel for three men, but as the "first game of the trip," we hugely enjoyed it when George served it in a pot of soup.

At six o'clock we broke camp and labored on, facing the same desperate conditions that we had met the day before. It is true that the rain had ceased to fall, but the good weather brought out the flies in increasing swarms. We fairly breathed flies, and we dreaded them far more than the hard work. Since they attacked us first, we had left our faces unwashed so as to retain the "dope," and they were streaming with a mixture of grease, dirt, blood, and perspiration.

The return of the sun also sent the mercury soaring. At noon that Saturday it registered 90 degrees in the shade. Always at sunset, however, the temperature dropped with startling suddenness, and a variation of from fifty to sixty degrees between the maximum and minimum record for one day was not an unusual thing as long as summer lasted.

Floundering up the boulder-strewn river that Saturday, we found the heat so oppressive that it seemed to us we had got into the torrid zone instead of up to within a few hundred miles of the Arctic Circle. We resolved, however, that the obstacles interposed against our advance by the unfeeling wild should make us fight only the harder, George and I receiving much inspiration from Hubbard, to whom difficulties were a blessing and whose spirit remained indomitable up to the very end. And when we sat down to our evening meal by a cozy fire, we had the satisfaction of knowing that we had doubled our previous day's record and were four miles further up the river.

On our first Sunday out we remained in camp to rest. We were all pretty tired, and enjoyed the long sleep in the morning. The day was fine, but very warm. In the morning Hubbard caught about twenty small trout, and after luncheon he and George went up the river on a scouting trip. When they returned in the evening, they reported important discoveries. First they had come upon a small, rocky stream flowing into our river from the south, which stream Hubbard felt sure must be the Red River the Blakes had told us about, and a mile above that a "two-mile stretch of good water." But the discovery that pleased Hubbard the most was some old cuttings that apparently had been made by Indians; he was of the opinion, as were all of us, that they indicated we really were on the Mountaineer Indian trail to Michikamau, and that we undoubtedly soon should come upon lakes and other good water that would carry us through; and the discoveries of the scouting trip buoyed up our spirits wonderfully.

On Monday morning (July 20) George took an axe and cut

us a portage route from our camp through a swamp a mile and a half to the foot of a steep hill. This route we covered three times. It was impossible for one man alone to carry the canoe through the swamp, and in addition to it and the firearms we had at this period to transport about five hundred pounds of baggage made up into packs of about seventy-five pounds each. At first Hubbard and I found seventy-five pounds a pretty good load to carry, and neither of us could get even that on his back without help from George; but later on we learned to back and carry with comparative ease a hundred pounds or more. In packing we never used either shoulder or chest straps, relying solely upon the head strap, which passes across the forehead.

When, after much groaning and sweating, we finally arrived with all of our outfit at the foot of the hill, it took the combined efforts of all three of us to get the canoe to the top, whence we followed an old caribou trail for a mile along the summit, camping just above the smooth water that Hubbard and George had seen on Sunday. We were all completely exhausted when we reached camp. While staggering along with the canoe a hundred yards from the tent, I became so weak that I suddenly sank to the ground and the others had to come to my rescue and bring in the canoe. But the night was cool and starry, and we sat long by our fire and talked and drank pea soup and tea, and when it came time for us to turn in to our soft bed of fragrant spruce boughs, our troubles had been quite forgotten.

The good water that Hubbard and George thought was two miles long shortened down, when we actually came to it the next morning, to less than half a mile, affording us only a meager opportunity to make use of the canoe. For a little distance we again bucked the rapids, and then left the river for a rough portage of a mile and a half over the hills on the shore. Again at night we were exhausted, but again we had a fine camp on a point overlooking the river. The crisp air came laden with the perfume of spruce and balsam. On the surrounding hills the fir trees were darkly silhouetted against the sky, radiant with its myriads of stars. The roar of the river could be heard dying away into a mere murmur among the hills below.

"Boys," said Hubbard, after we had made a good supper of a mess of trout I had caught at midday, "this pays for all the hard work."

Undoubtedly Hubbard was in fine fettle that evening, and as we lay before the fire with that delicious feeling of languor which comes from conscientious toil, he entertained George and me with quotations from his favorite author, Kipling, while we puffed comfortably upon our pipes. One verse he dwelt upon, as it seemed particularly appropriate to our position. It was:

> When first under fire, if you're wishful to duck,
> Don't look or take heed of the man that is struck;
> Be thankful you're living and trust to your luck,
> And march to your front like a soldier.

CHAPTER FIVE

# *Still in the Awful Valley*

T he next day (Wednesday, July 22) was by far the most disheartening of our journey up the valley of the Susan. We portaged all day through gullies and swamps and over rough ridges, covering in all about two miles and a half. All of us were overcome by the hard work in the burning sun and the poisonous bites of the flies. I was the most susceptible to the attacks of the flies; for ten days I was fairly sick from the poison they instilled. The faces, hands, and wrists of all of us were badly swollen and very sore. My face was so swollen I could scarcely see.

In the morning when we started forward the temperature was down to 33 degrees, but at noon it had risen to 92. Hubbard was attacked with diarrhea, and I with vomiting. We were all too exhausted to eat when we stopped for luncheon, and lay on the moss for an hour's rest, with the tent drawn over us to protect us from the flies.

On a low, barren knoll we cached that day 80 rounds of .45-70 cartridges and 300 rounds of .22's, George marking the spot with a circle of stakes. That left us 120 rounds of .45-70's and 500 rounds of .22's. It had become strictly necessary to lighten our packs, and we had begun to drop odds and ends every day.

In the afternoon Hubbard shot with his pistol a spruce partridge (grouse); it was the first seen by us on the trip. Together with a yellowlegs George had shot, it seasoned a pot of pea soup. We camped that night on a bluff, barren point, and Hubbard named it "Partridge Point" in honor of our first bird.

On Thursday (July 23) Hubbard lay in the tent all day sick. All he was able to eat was some hardtack dipped in tea. At his request George and I scouted for trails. Each of us carried a rifle and wore at his belt a pistol and a cup in addition to the sheath knife we never were without. In our pockets we placed a half-pound package of pea meal. George started westward up the river, and I put for a high, barren hill two miles to the north. As I climbed the hill I heard gulls on the other side, which told me water lay in that direction, and when I reached the top, there at my feet, like a silver setting in the dark green forest, lay a beautiful little shoe-shaped lake. For miles and miles beyond the ridge I was on, the country was flat and covered with a thick spruce growth.

To the northeast of the lake at my feet I could see the glimmer of other water among the trees, and I decided to go on and investigate. In doing so, I managed to get myself lost. Descending the hill to the lake, I made my way through the thick spruce growth in the swamp along the shore. A splash in the water startled me, and soon I found the fresh tracks of a caribou. As he had winded me, I knew it was useless to try to follow him. Pressing my way on to the northeast, I came upon another small lake and several small creeks. At midday I built a fire and made a cup of pea meal porridge. While waiting for my meal to cook, I read a letter that a friend had given me in New York, "to be opened after one week's canoeing in Labrador." It was like a letter just received from home.

In the afternoon the sun became obscured by gathering clouds, and in the thick underbrush through which my course led me I could see scarcely twenty yards ahead. I attempted to get my direction with the compass, but the needle would not respond. Trusting, however, to my ability to find my course without it, I made my way on past two more lakes. A grouse fluttered up before me, and I brought it down with a pistol shot. After tying it to my belt, I decided it was time to turn back home, as we called our camp, and struck off by what I hoped would be a shortcut through the swamp. Then it was that I lost my bearings, and at dusk, when I hoped to reach the first lake I had seen in the morning, I found myself on the shore of a lake I had never seen before.

Too weary to cook the grouse, or even build a fire and make

a cup of porridge, I threw myself on a flat rock, pillowed my head on the trunk of a fallen spruce tree, drew a handkerchief over my face to keep away the clouds of mosquitoes, and slept soundly. At dawn I arose, built a fire, repaired my compass, and ate a cup of porridge. I was not frightened, because with my compass again in working order I knew I should have no difficulty in finding the river, which must be somewhere to the south and which must lead back to camp. So to the southward I took my course, pushing my way through thick brush and over marshes where the ground under my feet went up and down like the waves of the sea.

Towards noon I reached a barren hill, and from its summit saw the river just beyond and the site of one of our old camping places that I knew was eighteen miles below our last camp. Down to the shore of the river I hurried, and built a fire for luncheon. The partridge at my belt had been torn into shreds by the bushes, and again a cup of porridge had to serve me for a meal. It was dark when I reached camp, to find Hubbard greatly worried and George away looking for me.

There had been some good-natured arguments between Hubbard and me as to the merits of our respective compasses, and as he now appeared to have the better of it, he took advantage of the occasion to chaff me unmercifully. Then when George returned they both had fun with me for getting lost.

"That's all right," I said, "your turn, Hubbard, will come later. You haven't been lost yet, because you haven't been out of sight of camp alone. Anyway, I just stayed out for a quiet evening by myself."

My absence on Friday did not delay our progress any; for Hubbard was still unable to travel. On Saturday (July 25) he had not yet fully recovered, but he decided to push forward. A drizzling rain was falling as we started. Each of us carried a load some four miles up the valley and returned; and then Hubbard, with a second load, went ahead to make camp, while George and I, with the remainder of the baggage, endeavored to drag the canoe upstream. Darkness came on when we were two miles below camp. While fording the river, I was carried off my feet by the current and nearly swept over the fall with a pack around my neck.

Then George and I left the canoe on the bank for the night, and each with his pack proceeded to push his way through the thick willows and alders and over the rocks. It was so dark we could not see each other. Falling down constantly and struggling to our feet again, we stumbled on through the pitchy blackness and down-pouring rain, until suddenly we discerned the glowing light of our campfire and came upon Hubbard frying bacon. George and I were too tired to eat; we were glad to lie down in our wet clothes on the bed of spruce boughs that was ready for us and forget our troubles in sleep.

We rested on Sunday—and ate. A partridge I had shot the day before was served stewed with rice and bacon for dinner, while for supper we had twenty-two trout that Hubbard caught in the morning, served with apple sauce and hot bread. This high living fully recompensed us for our hard fight against nature and the elements, and once more full of hope we lay down to sleep.

In the morning (Monday, July 27) Hubbard arose with a feeling of depression, but fair progress during the day brightened him up. A typical fall wind blew all day, and we were very wet and very cold when we went into camp at night. But with the coming of evening the clouds were driven away before the wind, affording us an occasional glimpse of the new moon hanging low in the heavens; and this, together with the sound of the river and the roaring campfire, soon cheered us up. No matter how weary and discouraged we were during the day, our evening fire invariably brought to us a feeling of indescribable happiness, a sweet forgetfulness of everything but the moment's comfort.

Our fire that Monday night was no exception to the general rule, but after supper, while we were luxuriantly reclining before it on a couch of boughs, Hubbard gave expression to a strange feeling that had been growing on him and me in the last few days. It was almost as if the solitude were getting on our nerves. Hubbard was munching a piece of black chocolate, which he dipped at intervals in a bit of sugar held in the palm of his left hand, when he said:

"It's queer, but I have a feeling that is getting stronger from day to day, that we are the only people left in the world. Have you fellows experienced any such feeling?"

"Yes," said I; "I have. I have been feeling that we must forever be alone, going on, and on, and on, from portage to portage, through this desolate wilderness."

"That's it exactly," said Hubbard. "You sort of feel, that as you are now, so you always have been and always will be; and your past life is like a dream, and your friends like dream-folk. What a strange sensation it is! Have you felt that way, George?"

George took the pipe from his mouth, blew out a cloud of tobacco smoke to join the smoke of the fire, and spat meditatively over his shoulder.

"Don't know as I have," he grunted. "I know there's mighty good huntin' down the bay; and I've been thinkin' of Rupert's House [the Hudson's Bay Company Post on James Bay where he was born], and what the fellus I know there are doin' these days. I can't say they seem like dream-folks to me; they're real enough, all right."

Hubbard and I laughed. Solitude was an old story to our friend, the English-Indian, and our "feelings" must have seemed to him highly artificial, if not affected.

Our progress on Tuesday and Wednesday (July 28 and 29) was the old story of hard tracking in the river and difficult portaging. The weather was cloudy and a chill wind blew. On Tuesday we advanced our camp a little more than three miles, and on Wednesday a little more than four. This continued slow work gave Hubbard serious concern, and the condition of our larder and wardrobe was not reassuring. Our bacon and sugar were going fast. Fish had become an absolute necessity, and our catches had been alarmingly small. There was also a lamentable lack of game. Far below we had heard the chatter of the last red squirrel, and seen the last bear signs and the last tree barked by porcupines. There were caribou trails a-plenty, but seldom a fresh track. A solitary rabbit had crossed our trail since we entered the valley, and there were no more rabbit runs visible. We could only hope that as we neared the "height of land," we should find more game—find plenty of caribou, at least, on the moss-covered barrens. We had also noted a change in the timber growth; neither birch nor aspen had we seen for a week.

Our moccasins were breaking through the bottoms, and this was a serious matter; for while George had an extra pair, Hubbard and I had only those on our feet. Hubbard's feet were very sore. Two of his toenails came off on Wednesday night, and a wide crack, which must have made walking very painful, appeared in one of his heels. The nearest thing we had to adhesive plaster was electrician's tape, and with this he bandaged his heel, and tied it and his toes up with pieces of cotton rags we had brought for cleaning rifles.

It was on Thursday, July 30, that we reached the point where another good-sized stream comes into the Susan, or where the river may be said to divide into two branches. We found that the southerly branch came over a low fall from the west, while the other, or northerly branch, flowed down from the northwest. The southerly branch was fully as large as the northerly—narrower but deeper— and not nearly so swift and rocky.

We were very uncertain as to which branch to follow, and Hubbard sent George on a scouting trip up the southerly stream, which we shall call Goose Creek, while he himself climbed a knoll to get a look at the country. A half mile or so up Goose Creek George found a blaze crossing the stream from north to south, which he pronounced a winter blaze made by trappers, as the cuttings were high up on the trees and freshly made. Half a mile above the blaze George came upon the rotten poles of an old Indian wigwam, and this discovery made Hubbard happy; he accepted it as evidence that Goose Creek was the river mapped as the "Northwest" and the Indian route to Michikamau. Accordingly it was decided to follow the southerly branch, and to leave the main stream at this point.

I was glad to leave the valley of the Susan. Our whole course up the valley had been torturous and disheartening. We had been out fifteen days from Northwest River Post and had covered only eighty miles. Hubbard had been ill, and I had been ill. Always, as we pressed onward, I dreaded the prospect of retracing our steps through the Susan Valley. I hated the valley from end to end. I have more reason to hate it now. To me it is the Valley of the Shadow of Death.

# CHAPTER SIX

# Searching for a Trail

When we portaged into Goose Creek on Friday, July 31, Hubbard had quite recovered from his illness, I, too, was well again, and our appetites had returned. It is true that my legs and feet were much swollen from the continuous work in the cold river, but the swelling caused me no inconvenience. All of us, in fact, were in better shape for the fight against the wild than at any time since the start.

For three or four miles up Goose Creek the rapids were almost continuous, and we had to portage for practically the whole of the distance. On August 1 and 2 the weather was cold, with a raw wind and a continuous downpour of rain. At night the rain kept up a steady drop, drop, drop through our tent. On the second, owing to the inclemency of the weather, we did not travel; but the morning of the third brought brilliant sunshine and with the perfume of the forest in our nostrils we pushed on, soon reaching a flatter and a marshy country, where the creek deepened and narrowed with a sluggish current. Here the paddling was good, and for a little way we made rapid progress.

In this marshy stretch by the creek's bank we saw a beaver house, and George stepped out of the canoe to examine it.

"They're livin' here," he remarked. "If we're not too far away when we camp tonight, I'm comin' down with a rifle and watch for 'em. They come out to play in the water in the evenin' and it's not hard to get 'em."

"What's the use of killing them?" I asked. "What could you do with a beaver if you got him?"

"I'd cook it, and we'd have a good snack of beaver meat," said George. "They're the finest kind of eatin', and I'd go a good way for a piece of beaver tail; it's nice and greasy, and better than anything you ever ate."

As we paddled on, George continued to extol the virtues of beaver meat, expatiating on many a "good snack" of it that he had consumed. However, he did not return to the beaver house, for more important things that evening claimed our attention.

It was on this day that we reached a point where our branch creek itself separated into two branches. Upon scouting them, we discovered that each of these branches had for its origin a lake, the two bodies of water from which they flowed being close together some three miles to the westward. Apparently they were small lakes, but we hoped to find that they belonged to a chain that would carry us into the country, and their discovery encouraged us to push on.

This hope was strengthened by Indian wigwam poles that we found in the vicinity. The poles, it is true, were old, indicating that the Indians had not been there for several years; but as it had been a long time since they had ceased to visit regularly Northwest River Post, we thought we had reason to believe that the poles marked what had been a permanent trail rather than the course of a hunting expedition. Hubbard was particularly observant of these old Indian signs. He was anxious to find them, and delighted when he did find them. "Here are the signs," he would say, "we are on the right trail." But we were not on the right trail. The right trail—the Nascaupee route—was miles to the northward. We eventually did stumble upon a trail to Michikamau, but it was another one—a very old one—and we found it only to lose it again.

While we were following up Goose Creek the condition of our commissariat troubles us not a little. The scarcity of game had forced us to draw heavily upon our stores. Only a little of our lard and a small part of our twenty-five pounds of bacon remained. "We must hustle for grub, boys," Hubbard frequently remarked. Our diet, excepting on particular occasions, was bread and tea, fish when we could get them, and sometimes a little pea soup. The pea meal, plain and flavored, was originally intended as a sort of emergency ration, but we had drawn on our stock of it alarmingly. Our flour, too, was going rapidly, and the time was drawing near when we felt that the ration of bread must be cut down.

The only thing, perhaps, that we really craved was fresh meat. For several days after leaving the post we had experienced a decided craving for acids, but that craving had been partially satisfied when, on the barren hills that border the Valley of the Susan, we found a few cranberries that had survived the winter. Every day while we were on Goose Creek we caught a few small trout. When we halted for any purpose, Hubbard always whipped the stream. He was a tireless as well as an expert fisherman. He would fish long after I had become discouraged, and catch them in pools where they positively refused to rise for me. The trout thus obtained were relished, but a fish diet is not strengthening, neither is it satisfying, and as we had had no fresh meat since the day we landed at Indian Harbour a month before, our longing for it had become importunate.

Imagine our joy, then, when on August 3, the day we discovered the petering out of Goose Creek, some fresh meat came our way. Most unexpectedly was the day turned into one of feasting and thanksgiving. As we were preparing, soon after passing the beaver house, to pack at the foot of a rapid just below a little pond expansion, Hubbard saw four geese swimming slowly down the stream. He and George had just lifted their packs from the canoe, while I, some little distance off, had mine on my back. Hubbard had his rifle in his hands. George, who caught sight of the geese almost as soon as Hubbard, grabbed my rifle from the canoe. "Drop!" cried Hubbard, and down we all fell behind the little bank over which the birds had been sighted. There was fresh meat swimming towards us, and while we lay waiting for it to come in sight around the little head of land the excitement was intense.

Soon the leader appeared, and Hubbard and George fired almost simultaneously. If ever there was a goose that had his goose cooked, it was that poor, unfortunate leader. One of the bullets from the .45-70 rifles that were aimed at him went through his neck, cutting the bone clean and leaving his head hanging by two little bits of skin. The other bullet bored a hole

47

through his body, breaking both wings. I did not blame him when he keeled over. The leader disposed of, Hubbard and George again fired in quick succession, and two of the other geese dropped just as they were turning back upstream and vainly trying to rise on their wings, which were useless so soon after the moulting season. The second shot emptied George's rifle. He threw it down, grabbed a paddle and went after one of the birds, which, only slightly wounded, was flopping about in the water.

Meanwhile Hubbard had fired twice at the fourth goose and missed both times. His rifle also being empty now, he cast it aside, seized his pistol, ran around the bank and jumped into the water in time to head off the remaining goose as it was flopping upstream. That brought the goose between him and George, and the bird was so bewildered that Hubbard had time to fire at him twice with his pistol and kill him, while George effectually disposed of the wounded goose by swatting him over the head with the paddle. Thus all four birds were ours, and our exultation knew no bounds. We shouted, we threw our hats in the air and shouted again. Lifting the birds critically, we estimated that we had on hand about fifty pounds of goose meat.

More luck came to us that same day when we halted for luncheon at the foot of some rapid water. As soon as we stopped, Hubbard, as usual, cast a fly, and almost immediately landed a half-pound trout. Then, as fast as I could split them and George fry them, another and another, all big ones, fell a victim to his skill. The result was that we had all the trout we could eat that noon, and we ate a good many.

It was late in the afternoon when we reached the point where the two brooks joined to form Goose Creek. Our scouting was finished in less than two hours, and we went into camp early: for, as Hubbard expressed it, we were to have a "heap big feed," and George reminded us that it would take a good while to roast a goose. Our camp was pitched at the foot of a semi-barren ridge a half-mile above the junction of the brooks. George built a big fire—much bigger than usual. At the back he placed the largest green log he could find. Just in front of the fire, and at each side, he fixed a forked stake, and on these rested a cross pole. From the center of the pole he suspended a piece of stout twine, which reached nearly to the ground, and tied the lower end into a noose.

Then it was that the goose, nicely prepared for cooking, was brought forth. Through it at the wings George stuck a sharp wooden pin, leaving the ends to protrude on each side. Through the legs he stuck a similar pin in a similar fashion. This being done, he slipped the noose at the end of the twine over the ends of one of the pins. And lo and behold! the goose was suspended before the fire.

It hung low—just high enough to permit the placing of a dish under it to catch the gravy. Now and then George gave it a twirl so that none of its sides might have reason to complain at not receiving its share of the heat. The lower end roasted first. Seeing which, George took the goose off, reversed it and set it twirling again. After a time he sharpened a sliver of wood, stuck it into the goose and examined the wound critically.

"Smells like a Christmas goose when one goes through the kitchen dead hungry before dinner," said Hubbard.

"Um-m!" I commented.

In a little while George tried the sharp splinter again. Hubbard and I watched him anxiously. White juice followed the stick. Two hours had passed, and the goose was done!

Events now came crowding thick and fast. First, George put the steaming brown goose in his mixing basin, and deftly and rapidly disjointed it with his sheath knife. Meanwhile, with nervous haste, Hubbard and I had drawn our knives, and with the tin basin of goose before us, all three of us plumped down in a half-circle on the thick moss in the light of the bright-blazing fire. Many of the rules of etiquette were waived. We stood not on the order of our falling to, but fell to at once. We eat and we eat, at first ravenously, then more slowly. With his mouth full of the succulent bird, George allowed he would rather have goose than caribou. "I prefer goose to anything else," said he, and proceeded to tell us of goose hunts "down the bay," and of diverse big Indian feasts. At length all the goose was gone but one very small piece. "I'll eat that for a snack before I sleep," said George, as he started to put the giblets to stew for breakfast.

The fire died down until nothing remained save a heap of glowing embers. For a long time we sat in the darkness over an extra pot of tea. At first, silence; and then, while George and I puffed complacently on our pipes, Hubbard, who never smoked, entertained us with more of Kipling. "The Feet of the Young Men" was one of his favorites, and that night he put more than his usual feeling into the words:

> Now the Four-way Lodge is opened, now the Hunting
>     Winds are loose—
> Now the Smokes of Spring go up to clear the brain;
> Now the Young Men's hearts are troubled for the
>     whisper of the Trues,
> Now the Red Gods make their medicine again!
> Who hath seen the beaver busied? Who hath watched
>     the black-tail mating?
> Who hath lain alone to hear the wild-goose cry?
> Who hath worked the chosen water where the ouana-
>     niche is waiting,
> Or the sea-trout's jumping—crazy for the fly?

> *"He must go—go—go away from here!*
>     *On the other side the world he's overdue.*
> *'Send your road is clear before you when the old Spring-*
>     *fret comes o'er you*
>     *And the Red Gods call for you!"*

Again the silence. The northern lights flashed and swept in fantastic shapes across the sky, illuminating the fir tops in the valley and making the white lichens gleam on the barren hill above us. We thought of the lake ahead with its old wigwams, and the promise it held out of an easy trail to Michikamau made us feel sure that the worst part of our journey was ended. Thus we sat supremely happy and content until long past midnight, when we went to our tent and our bed of fragrant spruce boughs, to be lulled asleep by the murmuring waters of the creek below.

The brooks into which Goose Creek divided near our camp of course would not permit of canoeing, and the morning after our feast (August 4) we portaged through a swamp into the lake that fed the southerly one. We called this small body of water Mountaineer Lake, because the Mountaineer Indians had been there. Besides numerous cuttings and the remains of wigwams, we found the ruins of a drying stage where they had cured meat or fish. From Goose Camp to the lake shore George carried the canoe, and Hubbard and I each a pack. Then while George and I returned for the remaining packs, Hubbard waited by the lake. As he sat there alone, a caribou waded into the water less than a hundred feet away, stopped and looked fearlessly at him for a few moments, and then walked leisurely off into the woods.

"It seemed as if he wanted to shake hands with me," Hubbard said when he told us of the incident. He had to let the deer depart in peace, because both rifles were back with the last loads at Goose Camp, and his pistol was in his bag. Needless to say, we were bitterly disappointed at losing the first deer we had seen, and it taught us the lesson always to take one rifle forward with the first load on a portage.

We spent the afternoon scouting in different directions, and discovered that the only inlet to Mountaineer Lake ended in a bog a mile or so up. A mile or more to the westward, however, George discovered another and much larger lake, which in honor of him we shall call Lake Elson. An old trail led from Mountaineer Lake to Lake Elson, which George pronounced to be a caribou trail, but which Hubbard believed to be an old portage, because it led from lake to lake by the most direct course. There were no axe cuttings, however, to indicate that the Indians had followed it.

We tried the troll in Mountaineer Lake, but caught nothing. Apparently there was nothing there but trout, of which fish I caught eight at the inlet. I shot with my pistol a muskrat that was swimming in the lake, but George did not cook it, as he said the flesh would be too strong at that season. It was raining again and the mosquitoes were out in millions, but with three geese still on hand and a good lake ahead we were indifferent to such troubles as that, although our clothing was not now in a condition successfully to withstand much bad weather.

Rags, in fact, were beginning to appear upon us all. One of Hubbard's trouser legs was ripped clear down the front, and it was continually streaming behind in the wind and getting caught in the bushes despite his efforts to keep it in place with pieces of twine. At length he patched it with a piece of white duffel, and exhibited his tailoring feat to us with much pride.

About noon on August 5, after a two-mile portage, we reached Lake Elson. On the way Hubbard sighted two caribou. He dropped his pack and grabbed his rifle. They were 250 yards away and partially hidden by the timber, and as they were approaching him, he waited, believing he would get a better shot. But, while he was waiting, what he called a "cussed little long-legged bird" scared them off, by giving a sharp, shrill cry of alarm, which the deer evidently were clever enough to construe as meaning that something out of the ordinary was happening.

Lake Elson proved to be about three and a half miles long and a half mile wide. It lay in a basin surrounded by wooded hills. The northerly portion was dotted with low, mound-like islands of drift, with two or three irregular, rocky islands, all completely wooded. It was a beautiful sheet of water, and, like all the lakes in Labrador, as clear as crystal and very cold. On the northerly side there were narrow straits and inlets, doubtless connecting the lake with others to the northwest that were hidden by the growth.

The outlet was at the southern end. It flowed through a pass in a low ridge of hills that extended for a great distance east and west, and emptied into a small lake, the waters of which were discharged through a creek that flowed through a pass in another low ridge that ran parallel with the first as far as we could see. Between the two ridges was a marsh that extended westward for many miles. The ridges and the hills surrounding the lakes were covered with spruce and balsam. Nowhere along our route since we left Northwest River Post, however, had we seen any timber of commercial value; the largest trees did not exceed eight inches in diameter, the generality being much smaller.

We were somewhat disconcerted upon finding no further

signs of Indians, and feared we had lost the trail. Neither trapper's blaze nor trapper's cutting was to be seen; for now we were beyond their zone and in a country that apparently no white man and no breed had ever viewed. We selected a site for our camp near the outlet at the southern end of the lake. In the afternoon Hubbard and George went to some bluffs that could be seen two or three miles to the southward, to scout for a route to Michikamau and find the Indian trail if possible. I remained behind to make camp.

The days were now shortening rapidly; it was dark before eight o'clock. In the grey of the twilight George returned. When he hailed me, I was fishing in the outlet just below the camp, standing on a rock in midstream to which I had waded.

"Come 'long up to camp," he called. Once in the wilderness, we made no distinctions as to master and servant; we were all companions together. Hence George's familiar manner of address.

"When I land two more trout," I shouted back.

"You've got enough; come 'long now," he pleaded.

There was that in his tone that excited my curiosity; he seemed all of a sudden to have acquired an unusual fondness for my society. "What's the matter, George?" I asked.

"I've been about lost," he returned. "Come on and I'll tell you."

I was astonished. I had seen George drop a pack in the bush, where everything for miles around looked alike to me, and without marking the spot or apparently taking note of any guiding signs, he would go directly to it again. I was with him one pitch-dark night when he left a pack among alders and willows in the depth of a marsh, and in the morning he went back two miles straight to the very spot. How a man that could do this could get lost was beyond my understanding. I hurried up to camp.

"How did it happen, George?" I asked.

"I just got turned 'round," he replied. "I didn't have any grub, and I didn't have a pistol, or a fishhook, or any way to get grub, and I didn't have a compass, and I was scared."

"But don't you know how you got lost?" I persisted.

"No, I don't," said George. "I just got lost. But I found myself pretty quick. I never got lost before."

The only way I could account for it was that he had permitted his thoughts to wander. I asked him what he would have done if he had not been able to find his way back.

"Gone to the highest hill I could see," he answered with a grin, "and made the biggest smoke I could make at its top, and waited for you fellus to find me."

While we were talking George was busily engaged in making the fire, putting a goose to boil and preparing water for tea. The twilight deepened, and ere we realized it darkness had come. Every moment we expected to hear Hubbard, but he did not appear.

"Another man lost," said I, with a forced lightness that illy concealed the anxiety George and I both felt; we knew that Hubbard not only had nothing to eat, but no matches to make a fire.

Frequently we stopped our work and talk, to peer into the gathering night and listen for the breaking of a twig. At length I took my rifle and fired at intervals half a dozen shots; but the reports echoed and died away without a reply. A damp north wind chilled the air, and the gloom seemed particularly oppressive.

"Hubbard will have a hard night out there in the bush," said George.

"Yes," I replied; "I don't suppose we can expect him back now before morning; and when a man is lost in this wild country it's pretty hard to find a little tent all by itself."

I was thinking of my own experience farther back, and what might happen should Hubbard fail to find us or we him. He was not so fortunate as I had been, in that there was no river to guide his return. However, at five o'clock in the morning he appeared. He had spent a miserable night on a ridge two miles to the southward, wet and shivering, with no fire, and tormented by mosquitoes. He reported that from the ridge he could hear the roar of a rapid. Darkness had prevented him from going on, and he had not seen the rapid, but he was sure it was a part of a big river.

At first he was loath to admit he had been lost, doubtless remembering how he and George had "guyed" me when I had been out all night and my prediction that his turn would come; but when George confessed to having gone astray also, he made a clean breast of it, telling us he was "lost good and plenty, and scared some, too." Now I had my innings, and I must confess I took great delight in returning some of the chaff they had given me.

Hubbard decreed, in consequence of these experiences—getting lost—that thereafter each man at all times should have on his person an emergency kit, to consist of matches, a piece of fish line, some hooks and two or three flies, enclosed in a film box waterproofed with electrician's tape.

We remained in our camp on Lake Elson for two days in order to scout and dry fish. It was the best fishing place we had yet come to. During our stay we had all the trout we could eat, and we dried and smoked forty-five large ones. The scouting proved that Hubbard's "big river" was an important discovery. It lay two miles to the south of us, flowing to the southeast. Hubbard sent George to look at it, and he reported that it certainly came from large lakes, and it was big, deep and straight. Could it come from Lake Michikamau?

While George was away Hubbard and I took a trip in the canoe around the lake and through some inlets. At the northeast we discovered a creek flowing into the lake, and as there were some old Indian wigwams and cuttings near it, indicating the possibility of its being part of a trail, we seriously considered the advisability of following it up. From a knoll nearby we could see to the northwest other lakes into which the creek might possibly lead us; but, after returning to camp, we considered the situation fully in the light of George's report of the big river, and we decided that to the big river we should go.

This decision was not to prove an error of judgment; for the big river was none other than the Beaver—an important part of an old trail of the Indians to Lake Michikamau.

# CHAPTER SEVEN

# On a Real River at Last

W e broke camp in the forenoon of August 7, and a few hours later, after making two trips back and forth, we arrived with our baggage on the bank of our new river. At last we had a real river to travel on, its average width being between 100 and 150 yards. None of us, of course, then knew that our real river was the Beaver, and that in taking to it we had stumbled upon an old Indian route to Lake Michikamau. If we had known this, it would have made a great difference in our fortunes.

Immediately below the point where we portaged into the river, wooded ridges on either side hugged it close, forming a narrow valley. Just above us the valley broadened, and a mile or so up a big hill reared its barren summit above the black spruce trees at its base, standing there like a lonely sentinel among the little hills that bordered the widening river basin. Despite the fact that we had reached a real river, we still had rapids to encounter, and we had to make so many short portages that after we had ascended the river two miles it was time to camp.

We pitched our tent on a rising plateau just below a stretch of rushing water. As soon as we stopped, Hubbard tried to fish, and while I made camp he landed fifteen trout averaging nearly half a pound each. They were most welcome, as the time had come when we had to live off the country. Our bread ration was now cut down to one-third of a loaf a day for each man. As we had no lard, it was made simply of flour, baking powder, and water. It was baked in our frying pan, and a loaf was about eight inches in diameter and one inch thick, so that our daily ration was but a morsel. We also decided that from now on we should use pea meal only on rare occasions, and to reserve our other provisions, with the exception of a few dried apples, tea, coffee and a little chocolate and cocoa, to give us a start should we at any time find it necessary to make a sudden dash for the Post.

Our clothing was rapidly disintegrating. The front of Hubbard's trouser leg was all torn open again, and once more he had to resort to pieces of twine. We had frequent discussions at this period as to whose appearance was the most beautiful. For a time Hubbard and I would claim the distinction each for himself, but it usually ended by our conceding the distinction to George. As a matter of fact, with our unkempt hair and beards and our rags, we now formed as tough looking a party of tramps as ever "came down the pike." That night in camp I cut up my canvas leggings and used pieces of the canvas to rebottom my moccasins, sewing it on with shoemaker's thread.

It was a glorious evening. A big moon rising over the bluffs beyond us transformed the river into a silvery thread stretching far down through the dark valley. Behind us the black spruce forest made our roaring fire seem more cheerful in contrast. A cold east wind had driven away the flies and the mosquitoes. Supper eaten, our cup of contentment was full to the brim. After all, the wilderness was not so inhospitable. Who would be anywhere else, if he could? Not one of us.

With the sensation that we were the only people in Labrador, a fancy struck me and I suggested to my companions that we ought to organize some sort of government.

"We'll make you, Hubbard," I said, "the head of the nation and call you the Great Mogul. Of course you will be commander-in-chief of the army and navy and have unlimited power. We're your subjects."

"I suspect," replied Hubbard, "you are looking for a political job. However, I, of course, stand ready, like our politicians at home, to serve the country when duty calls—if there's enough in it. As the Great Mogul of Labrador, I appoint you, Wallace, Chief Justice and also Secretary of State. George I shall appoint Admiral of the Navy."

"Where are my ships?" asked George.

"Ships!" exclaimed Hubbard. "Well, there will be only one for the present. But she's a good staunch one—eighteen feet long, with a beam of thirty-three and a half inches. And she carries two quick-fire rifles."

With these and other conceits we whiled away the beautiful evening hours. What a difference there was in the morning! We awoke—it was Saturday, August 8—to find that the east wind had increased in force and was accompanied by a driving, chilling rain. Reluctantly we broke camp, and began a day of back-breaking, disheartening work. The wind soughed dismally through the forests, and it was as though late autumn had overtaken us in a night. The spruce boughs, watersoaked, seemed to hang low for no other purpose than to strike us in the face at every step, and the willows and alders along the river that now and again obstructed our way appeared to be thicker and wetter than ever.

Under these conditions we had made six portages, the longest of which was about three-quarters of a mile, and covered in all about four and a half miles, when one o'clock came and we gave up the fight for the day, to make our Sunday camp and try to get fish. We were ravenously hungry, and ate even the heads of the dried trout we had for luncheon, these being the last of those we caught and smoked on Lake Elson. During the afternoon we put out for the first time the old gill net Mackenzie had given us, and by hard work with the rod caught a few more trout for supper.

It still poured on Sunday morning. Hubbard fished all day, and I the greater part of the forenoon. The net product of our labor was forty-five trout, most of them little fellows. The gill net yielded us nothing. In the afternoon George and I took the rifles and started out in different directions to look for caribou. Neither of us found any fresh tracks. I returned at dusk, to find George already in camp and our supper of boiled fish ready to be eaten. Our sugar was all gone by this time, and our supply of salt was so low that we were using hardly any. In spite of us the salt had been wet in the drenching rains we had encountered all up the Susan Valley, and a large part of it had dissolved.

While we all craved sugar and other sweets, I believe Hubbard suffered the most from their absence. Perhaps the fact that

George and I used tobacco and he did not, was the explanation. He was continually discussing the merits of various kinds of cake, candies, and sweet things generally. Our conversation too often turned to New York restaurants, and how he would visit various ones of them for particular dishes. Bread undoubtedly was what we craved the most. "I believe I'll never refuse bread again," Hubbard would say, "so long as there's a bit on the table."

Monday (August 10) brought with it no abatement of the driving rain and cold east wind. Working industriously for half an hour before breakfast, Hubbard succeeded in landing a single small trout, which fell to me, while he and George ate thick pea meal porridge, of which they were very fond. We made several short portages during the morning, and, despite the dismal weather, our spirits brightened; for we came upon old wigwam poles and axe cuttings, which we accepted as proof that we were now surely on the Indian trail to Michikamau. Towards noon Hubbard said:

"Well, boys, we're on the right road, we've covered three miles this morning, and this rain is killing, so we'll pitch camp now, and wait for the weather to clear and try to get some fish ahead. There are fish here, I know, and when the wind changes we'll get them."

After warming ourselves by a big fire and eating luncheon, Hubbard and I took our rods and fished the greater part of the afternoon, catching between us twelve or fifteen trout.

"You had better cook them all for supper, George," said Hubbard. "This is my mother's birthday, and in honor of it we'll have an extra loaf of bread and some of her dried apples. And I tell you what, boys, I wish I could see her now."

On the following day (Tuesday, August 11) the weather had somewhat moderated, but the east wind continued, and the rain still fell during all the forenoon. We could get no fish at our camp, and at two in the afternoon started forward, all of us hungry and steadily growing hungrier. Hubbard whipped the water at the foot of every rapid and tried every pool, but succeeded in getting only a very few trout. While he fished, George and I made the portages, and thus, pushing on as rapidly as possible, we covered about four miles.

While George and I were scouting on Sunday, we had each caught sight of a ridge of rocky mountains extending in a northerly and southerly direction, which we estimated to be from twenty to twenty-five miles to the westward. Previous to Tuesday, these mountains had not been visible from the river valley, but on that day they suddenly came into view, and they made us stop and think, for they lay directly across our course. However, we did not feel much uneasiness then, as we decided that our river must flow through a pass in the mountains far to the north, and follow them down before turning east.

Our camp on Tuesday night was rather a dreary one; but before noon on Wednesday (August 12) the clouds broke, big patches of blue sky began to appear, and with a bit of sunshine now and again, our hearts lightened as we proceeded on our journey.

At the foot of a half-mile portage Hubbard caught fourteen trout, and our luncheon was secure. Three more portages we made, covering in all about three miles, and then we shouted for joy, for there ahead of us lay open water. Along it for five miles we gaily canoed before stopping for luncheon. Hungry? Yes, we were hungry even after devouring the fourteen trout and drinking the water they were boiled in—I could have eaten fifty like them myself—but our spirits were high, and we made merry. For the first time since leaving Grand Lake there was good water behind us and good water before us.

At the last rapid we portaged the country had flattened out. Wide marshes extended along the south bank of the river, with now and then a low hill of drift. The north side was followed by a low ridge of drift, well wooded. We landed for luncheon on the south bank, at the foot of a wooded knoll, and there we made an interesting discovery, namely, the remains of an old Indian camp and the ruins of two large birch-bark canoes. In November, at Northwest River Post, I heard the story of those canoes.

Twelve years before, it appears, the band of Indians that had camped there, being overtaken by early ice, was forced to abandon its canoes and make a dash for the Post. Game was scarce, and the fish had gone to deeper waters. The Indians pushed desperately on overland, but one by one they fell, until at last the gaunt fiend, Starvation, had claimed them all. Since that time no Indian has ever travelled that trail—the route to Michikamau upon which we had stumbled was thereupon abandoned. The Indians believe the trail is not only unlucky, but haunted; that if while on it they should escape Starvation—that terrible enemy which nearly always dogs them so closely—they are likely to encounter the spirits of them that died so many years ago.

Not knowing anything of this tragic story, we merrily ate our luncheon on the very spot where others in desperation had faced death. It was to us an old Indian camp, and an additional reason for believing we were on the right trail, that was all. While we ate, the sun came out brilliantly, and we resumed our paddling feeling ready for almost anything that might happen. And something did happen—something that made the day the most memorable so far of the trip.

No rapids intercepted our progress, and in an hour we had paddled three miles, when, at a place where the river widened, a big woodland stag caribou suddenly splashed into the water from the northern shore, two hundred yards ahead. I seized my rifle, and, without waiting for the canoe to stop, fired. The bullet went high. The caribou raised his head and looked at us inquisitively. Then Hubbard fired, and with the dying away of the report of his rifle, George and I shouted: "You hit 'im, Hubbard; you've got 'im!" The wounded caribou sank halfway to his knees, but struggled to his feet again. As he did so, Hubbard sent another shot at him, but missed. Slowly the big deer turned, and began to struggle up the bank. Again Hubbard and I fired, but both shots went low.

We ran the canoe to shore, and while I made it fast, Hubbard and George ran breathlessly ahead to where the caribou had disappeared. I followed at once, and soon came upon them and the caribou, which had fallen thirty yards from the river with a bullet hole through his body just back of the left shoulder. A trail of blood marked his path from the river to where he lay. As the animal floundered there in the moss, Hubbard, with the nervous impetuosity he frequently displayed, fired again against George's protest, the bullet entering the caribou's neck and passing down through his tongue the full length. Then George caught the thrashing animal by the antlers, and while he held its head down Hubbard cut its throat.

We made our camp right where the caribou fell. It was an ideal spot on the high bank above the river, being flat and thickly covered with white moss. The banks at this point were all sand drift; we could not find a stone large enough to whet our knives. George made a stage for drying while Hubbard and I dressed the deer. Our work finished, we all sat down and roasted steaks on sticks and drank coffee. The knowledge that we were now assured of a good stock of dried meat, of course, added to the hilarity of the feast. As we thought it best to hoard our morsel of flour, it was a feast of venison and venison alone.

While waiting for our meat to dry, we had to remain in camp for three or four days. On the next afternoon (Thursday, August 13) Hubbard and I paddled about three miles up the river to look for fish, but we got no bites, probably because of the cold; in the morning there had been a fringe of ice on the river shore.

"We'll take it easy," said Hubbard while we were paddling upstream, "and make a little picnic of it. I'm dead tired myself. How do you feel, Wallace?"

"I feel tired, too," I said. "I have to make an extra effort to do any work at all."

Hubbard was inclined to attribute this tired feeling to the freedom from strain after our nerve-racking work of the last few weeks, while I hazarded the opinion that our purely meat diet had made us lazy. Probably it was due to both causes.

As Hubbard was anxious to obtain definite knowledge as to what effect the high ridge of rocky mountains had upon our river, George and I, with the object of ascertaining the river's course, left camp in the canoe on Friday morning (August 14), taking with us, in addition to our emergency kits, our cups, some tea, and enough caribou ribs for luncheon. We portaged around a few short rapids, and then, about eight miles above our camp, came upon a lake expansion of considerable size with many inlets. On the northerly side of the lake was a high, barren hill, which afforded us a splendid view of the surrounding country.

Winding away to the southeast was the river we had ascended. To the west was a series of lake expansions connected by narrow straits, and beyond them were the mountains, which we estimated rose about 2,500 feet above the country at their base. In sheltered places on their sides, patches of ice and snow glistened in the sunshine. Barren almost to their base, not a vestige of vegetation to be seen anywhere on their tops or sides, they presented a scene of desolate grandeur, standing out against the blue sky like a grim barrier placed there to guard the land beyond. As I gazed upon them, some lines from Kipling's "Explorer" that I had often heard Hubbard repeat were brought forcibly to my mind:

> Something hidden. Go and find it. Go and look behind
>    the Ranges—
> Something lost behind the Ranges. Lost and waiting for
>    you. Go!

Let us call these ranges the Kipling Mountains.

To the north, hill after hill, with bald top rising above the stunted trees on its sides, limited our range of vision. Far away to the south stretched a rolling, wooded country. To the eastward the country was flatter, with irregular ranges of low hills, all covered with a thick growth of spruce and balsam fir. Beyond the point where the water flowed from it southeasterly into the river we had ascended, the lake at the foot of our hill seemed to extend directly eastward for four or five miles; but the thick wood of the valleys and low-lying hills made it difficult to see just where it ended, so that from where we stood it was impossible to tell what course the river took—whether it came from the east, bending about in the lake expansion below us, or flowed from the west through the lake expansions beyond. Away off to the northeast an apparently large lake could be discerned, with numerous mound-like islands dotting its surface.

For a long time we stood and gazed about us. Far to the southeast a tiny curl of smoke rose heavenward in the clear atmosphere. That was Hubbard's campfire—the only sign of life to be seen in all that wide wilderness. The scene was impressive beyond description. It gave me a peculiar feeling of solemnity and awe that I shall never forget.

We found on our hill a few dead twigs of sub-Arctic shrubbery with which to make a fire to broil our caribou ribs, and gathered some mildly acid berries of a variety neither of us had ever seen before, which we ate as a dessert. After luncheon George said he thought we had better go to the westward to look for the river.

"But how can it come through those mountains?" I asked.

"I don't know as it can," he replied. "But," pointing to one of the range, "I want to take a look at the country beyond from that high mountain."

So we returned to our canoe, and paddled to the westward a few miles through two lake expansions, which brought us to the foot of the mountains. We landed at a place where a small creek tumbled down through a rocky pass. George went up his mountain alone. During his absence, with my emergency kit, I caught ten six-inch trout to be divided between us for supper, as only two of our caribou ribs remained. Near dark George came back. After climbing halfway to the summit of his mountain, he had encountered perpendicular walls of rock that blocked his further progress.

We made a fire of old wigwam poles, and roasted our fish before it on a flat stone. A quart of hot tea between us washed down our meager supper, and then we made a bed of boughs. But when we tried to sleep the icy wind that blew through the pass caused us to draw closer to the fire, before which we alternately sat and lay shivering throughout the night. Having brought no axe with us, we could not build a fire of any size. I do not believe either of us slept more than half an hour.

"Which would you rather have, Wallace, a piece of bread or a blanket?" George would ask at frequent intervals.

"Bread," I always answered. At that he would chuckle. We had tasted nothing but venison and fish since the day we killed the caribou, and for bread we had an inexpressible craving.

"Anyway," George would say, "this cold will weaken the flies." And with this reflection he continued to comfort us as the nights became chillier.

In the morning we had to break the ice to get water for our tea, which with the two remaining caribou ribs constituted our breakfast. George then made another attempt at his mountain. Again he failed to reach the summit, and I failed to induce any more trout to rise. In a somewhat despondent mood we turned back, and paddled for some distance into the lake expansions to the eastward of the point where our river flowed out. Although we were compelled to start for "home" before obtaining any definite knowledge of the course of the river, we were of the opinion that it came from the east. For all we knew, however, the river might end in those lake expansions; we could not tell, as no current could be discerned, and having no food we could not continue the search.

It was five o'clock in the evening when we reached camp, tired out and as hungry as two wolves, and we astonished Hubbard with the amount of venison we put out of sight. While George was temporarily out of hearing, Hubbard said:

"It's bully good to see you back again, Wallace. I was disappointed when you didn't come back last night, and I've been dead lonesome. I got thinking of my wife and home, and the good things to eat there, and was on the verge of homesickness."

"We were mightily disappointed, too, at not getting back," said I between mouthfuls. "Up there on the lakes we put in the toughest night yet, and we were thinking of the venison and warm blankets down here at camp."

Hubbard was much discouraged and depressed at our report of the uncertain course of the river, although he was careful to conceal his feelings from George.

The next day (Sunday, August 16) we cut up our canvas guncases and used some of the material to rebottom our moccasins. What was left over we put away carefully for future use.

George cracked the caribou bones and boiled out the marrow grease. He stripped the fat from the entrails and tried out the tallow, preserving even the cracklings or scraps. "We'll be glad to eat 'em yet," said he. One of the hoofs he dressed and put with our store of meat. We preserved everything but the head, the entrails and three of the hoofs. The tallow we found an excellent substitute for lard.

In the afternoon Hubbard and I caught thirty trout in an hour at the rapid a mile and a half above our camp, and a few more in the river close by the camp. High living during the day raised all of our spirits. For breakfast we had the caribou heart, which George thought at first he would roast but changed his mind and served stewed. For dinner we had the tongue, the tidbit of the animal, boiled with pieces of other parts. Hubbard's second bullet had torn out the center of the tongue, but what there was of it was delicious. And at night we had the trout caught during the afternoon, to which, as a Sunday luxury, was added a cake of bread.

When we gathered around the fire in the evening, Hubbard had entirely recovered from his depression and took a more hopeful view of the river. We discussed the matter thoroughly, and decided that the river George and I had seen coming from the eastward must take a turn farther north and break through the Kipling Mountains, and that it might prove to be Low's Northwest River we all thought was possible.

At the same time we could not disguise the fact that it was extremely probable we should have to portage over the mountains, and the prospect was far from pleasing; but, ragged and almost barefooted though we were, not a man thought of turning back, and on Monday morning, August 17, we prepared to leave Camp Caribou and solve the problem as to where lay the trail of Michikamau.

# CHAPTER EIGHT

# "*Michikamau or Bust!*"

The temperature was 3 degrees below freezing when grey dawn at half past four o'clock that Monday morning bid us up and on. The crisp air and the surprising beauty of the morning stirred within us new hope and renewed ambition. And the bags of jerked venison and the grease gave us faith that we should succeed in reaching our goal. Though we had some food in stock, there was to be no cessation in our effort to get fish; our plan was for Hubbard to try his rod at the foot of every rapid while George and I did the portaging.

Before midday Hubbard had forty trout, one of them sixteen inches long—the biggest we had caught yet. We stopped for luncheon on the sandy shore of a pretty little lake expansion, and ate the whole morning's catch, fried in caribou tallow, with unsweetened coffee to wash it down. Then on we pushed towards the Kipling Mountains. At a narrow strait between two lakes we left Hubbard to fish, George and I going on two miles farther to the place where we had spent that chilly night while scouting, and where our camp for this night was to be pitched.

Our object in going there was to give George another chance to view the country on the other side of the mountain range. This time he was to try another peak. As he disappeared up the mountainside, I paddled back to get Hubbard, who was awaiting me with a good string of big trout. The two-mile stretch of lake from where Hubbard was fishing to our camping ground was as smooth as a sheet of glass. The sun hanging low over the mountains and reflecting their nude forms in the silvery water, and the dark green forest of fir trees on the shores moved Hubbard to exclamations of delight.

"Oh, if it could be painted just as it appears now!" he said. "Why, Wallace, this one scene is worth all the groaning we've done to get here. It's grand! grand!"

At dark George returned to camp with the report that from his peak he could see only higher mountains looming up to the westward. In the shadow of the grey rocks of the grim old mountains that so stubbornly held their secret of what lay beyond, we had a good supper of trout and were happy, though through the gulch the creek roared defiance at us, and off in the night somewhere a loon would break out at intervals in derisive laughter. At the base of the mountains the narrow lake reflected a million stars, and in their kindly light the snow and ice patches on the slopes above us gleamed white and brilliant.

With our day's work the listlessness from which we had recently suffered had entirely disappeared, and we felt ready to undertake any task, the more difficult the better. Hubbard suggested giving up route hunting if our river ended where we then were, and striking right across the mountains with our outfit on our backs, and we received the suggestion with enthusiasm. He talked, too, a great deal about snowshoeing in winter to St. Augustine on the St. Lawrence, cutting across country from the Kenemish River, which flows into Groswater Bay opposite Northwest River Post. This trip, which he held out as a possibility in the event of our missing the last steamer out from Rigolet, seemed to appeal to him immensely.

"I don't care if we are too late for the steamer," he said; "that snowshoeing trip would be a great stunt."

We found a great many wigwam poles near and in the pass hard by our camp, while by the creek we came across the remains of both summer and winter camps, probably those of hunters. "One of the beggars was high-toned," said George; "he had a stove." This was evidenced by the arrangement of stones within the circle of wigwam poles, and a few pieces of wood cut stove-size.

On Tuesday morning (August 18) we turned back and into the long, narrow lake expansions to the eastward, and soon satisfied ourselves that this was the right course. Our thermometer registered 28 degrees that morning. The day dawned clear and perfect; it was a morning when one draws in long breaths, and one's nerves tingle, and life is a joy. Early in the forenoon we reached rapids and quickly portaged around them; all were short, the largest being not more than half a mile. At ten o'clock we ate luncheon at the foot of one of the rapids where we caught, in a few minutes, fourteen large trout. Just above this rapid the river opened into long, narrow lakes, and the canoeing was superb. Suddenly the river took a sharp turn to the westward, and appeared to lead directly into the mountains. At that we sent up three rousing cheers—the river problem seemed to be solved; apparently the road to Michikamau lay straight before us.

A little above the bend in the river we came upon an old gander and goose and two unfeathered young. The gander with a great squawk and flapping wings took to the bush, but we killed the old goose with a rifle, and George "knocked over," as he expressed it, one of the young ones with a pistol. More luck (and food) came to us a little later. While George and I portaged around the last rapid that evening, Hubbard caught fifty trout averaging over a pound each. They jumped greedily to the fly, four or five rising at every cast.

Above this rapid the river again took the form of a long, narrow lake—a lake so beautiful that we were entranced. It was evening when we arrived, and the very spirit of peace seemed to brood over the place. Undoubtedly we were the first white men that had ever invaded its solitude, and the first human beings of any kind to disturb its repose for many years. On the north a barren, rocky bluff rose high above the water; at all other places the shores were low and wooded. A few miles to the westward could be seen the barren Kipling Mountains, and between them and us was a ridge of low hills covered with black-green spruce. The sun was setting in our faces as we paddled slowly along the lake, and as it went down behind the mountains a veil was gradually drawn over the lovely scene. Not a breath of air was stirring, and hardly a sound broke the stillness save the ripple at the bow of the canoe and the soft splash of the paddles. In the placid waters two otters were swimming and diving. One was timid and remained at a distance, but the other was bold and inquisitive and came close to the canoe. Here and there all over the lake, its mirror-like surface was broken by big jumping trout. Two loons laughed at us as we drew the canoe onto the sandy beach of a low jutting point, and they continued to laugh while we pitched our camp in the green woods near the shore and prepared our supper of roast goose. It was a feast day. With goose, plenty of trout and good water for paddling, it was a time to eat, drink, and be merry.

Our high spirits still remained when we broke camp in the morning (Wednesday, August 19), but they were destined soon to be dashed. Not long after we started we found ourselves in good-sized lakes, with arms extending in every direction. All day we hunted for the river, but found only small streams emptying into the lakes. The country now was much rougher, and much more rocky and barren, than any we had seen since we left the coast. The trees were more stunted and gnarled, and the streams usually had a bedrock bottom. In the course of the day Hubbard shot three rock ptarmigans—"rockers," George called them. They were the first we had seen, and were still wearing their mottled summer dress; later in the season they are a pure, spotless white. Towards evening we made our way to a point on the northwesterly part of the lakes where a small stream came through a mountain pass, and there went into camp.

We were much disappointed at our failure to find the river, but not disheartened. In order to make certain that we had not overlooked it, we decided to paddle back the next day as far as the last rapid and make one more careful search. Failing then to find the river, we should portage through the mountain pass at the entrance to which we had camped.

"Do you remember," asked Hubbard, "the slogan of the old Pike's Peakers?—'Pike's Peak or Bust?'"

"Yes," said I; "and very often they busted."

"Well," said Hubbard, "we'll adopt it and change it to our needs. '*Michikamau* or Bust,' will be *our* watchword now."

And sitting around the fire, we all took it up and repeated determinedly, "Michikamau or Bust!"

The morning of the next day (Thursday, August 20) we occupied in mending our moccasins with parts of the caribou skin. George also took the venison from the bags and hung it over the fire to give it a little more drying, as it had begun to mold. In the afternoon Hubbard and I, in accordance with the plan we had adopted, paddled back over our course and reexplored the lower lakes. We discovered nothing new. The fact was that these lakes were the source of the Beaver River.

While we were paddling about we came upon two old and two young loons. The old ones tried to lure us away from their young, by coming very near the canoe. The young loons made frequent dives, but we succeeded in catching one of them. Finally, however, we restored it to its parents, and when the loon family was reunited there was great rejoicing in the household. In the pool at the foot of the last rapid we spent an hour fishing, and caught eighty-one trout, averaging, perhaps, a half-pound each. Upon our return to camp in the evening we dressed our catch and hung the fish to dry over a slow, smoky fire.

The river having come to an end, our only course now was to cross the mountains, and on Friday (August 21), with "Michikamau or Bust!" for our slogan, we began our portage along the stream that flowed through the pass near our camp. A heavy rain was falling. During the first part of the day, in the course of which we crossed three small ponds, the travelling was fairly good; but during the latter part it was exceedingly rough and difficult. We pitched our tent that night on the divide; in other words, we had reached the place where small streams flowed both east and west.

The cold rain continued when we broke camp the next morning (Saturday, August 22). For a time we again encountered rough work, forcing a passage over rocks, and through thick brush and scrambling down high banks, and then, as we neared the end of the pass, the portage became less difficult. Before noon we came upon a lake of considerable size and unmistakable signs that in directing our course through the pass we had kept upon the old Indian trail. On the edge of the lake—we shall call it Lake Hope—trees had been blazed to make plain the exact point where the portage trail left the water, and near this place were sweat holes where the medicine men had given baths to the sick. Much drift wood showing axe cuttings was on the shore, and we picked up an old canoe paddle of Indian make. All this led us to believe we were on waters connected directly with Lake Michikamau (which was the fact), and we thought that possibly we had reached a deep bay said to extend from the main body of the lake some thirty miles in a southeasterly direction.

Where we launched our canoe the mountain pass was very narrow, and on the southerly side, rising almost perpendicularly from the water to a height of 800 or 900 feet, stood a hill of absolutely bare rock. The wind was blowing the rain in sheets over its face, and, despite the wet and chill, we paused to enjoy the grandeur of the scene. We had travelled about six miles through the pass, and this hill marked its end; the mountain barrier that at one time seemed so formidable had not proved so difficult to cross after all. And in accomplishing the pass we had reached the great interior plateau—the land that lay hidden behind the ranges.

After we had paddled along Lake Hope a hundred yards, we struck a sharp-pointed rock that tore a hole through the bottom of the canoe. This accident forced us to take refuge on a nearby island where George could repair the damage and procure gum from the spruce trees to cover the patch.

Sunshine came with Sunday morning (August 23), and we dried our blankets and camp outfit before starting forward, so that it was after ten o'clock when we quit the island. Lake Hope proved to be long and narrow, and we soon realized that it could not be Michikamau's southeast bay; but at the western end we hoped to find a strait connecting it with another lake, and as we approached the western end with a feeling of uncertainty as to what lay beyond, George remarked: "It's like goin' into a room where there's a Christmas tree."

Sure enough there was a strait, and as we turned into it, we saw beyond big water stretching away to the westward for miles. "There's a Christmas tree without a doubt," said Hubbard. We felt positive now that this second lake was Michikamau's southeast bay, and we broke the solemn stillness of the wilderness with three lusty cheers. It is violating no confidence to say here that the second lake was not Michikamau's southeast bay; it was simply the peculiarly-shaped body of water that appears on my map under the name, Lost Trail Lake.

Two and a half miles up Lost Trail Lake we climbed a barren ridge, where we found blueberries, mossberries and bake-apple berries. The latter berry is salmon-colored, and grows on a plant resembling that of the strawberry. The berry itself resembles in form the raspberry, and has a flavor like that of a baked apple, from which fact it derives its name. It ripens after the first frost. The mossberry is small and black, resembling in shape and size the blueberry, and is sweet and palatable after being touched with frost. It is usually found on the moss clinging to rocks. On the ridge it grew in abundance, and we ate a great many. The blueberry of Labrador is similar to the blueberry of the United States.

Some distance beyond where we got the berries we went into camp. Trolling on the way, we caught a namaycush (lake trout), the first we had seen on the trip. In our camp on Lost Trail Lake we were held all of Monday (August 24) by a gale that beat the water into a fury. We took advantage of the opportunity to try our gill net, sinking it on the lee shore; but it was so rotten it would not hold a fish large enough to get fast in it, and we finally threw it away as a useless incumbrance.

In the course of the day, Hubbard and George climbed a hill not far away, while I remained in camp to do some "chores." They found bake-apple berries in abundance—the only spot we came across where they grew in any great quantity—and had a good look at a lake we had previously sighted two miles to the north. This lake was larger than the one we were on, being about twenty-five miles long; it was, in fact, the largest body of water by far that we had seen since leaving Grand Lake. Its size impressed Hubbard with the fatal belief that it, rather than Lost Trail Lake, was connected with Michikamau, and to it he decided to go. Our experience there led us to call it Lake Disappointment.

We portaged into it on Tuesday morning (August 25). Our course was over a neck of land which was mostly soft marsh partially covered with spruce. We did not know then that in

73

abandoning Lost Trail Lake for Lake Disappointment we were wandering from the Indian trail to Michikamau. Some Indians I met during the winter at Northwest River Post told me that a river flowed out of the western end of Lost Trail Lake into the very southeast bay of Lake Michikamau we were longing so much to see. This was the trail. And we lost it.

We ate our luncheon on the southern shore of Lake Disappointment. That afternoon and the next two days (August 26 and 27) we spent in paddling about the lake in a vain search for a river. Thirty or more miles a day we paddled, and found nothing but comparatively small creeks. One of these we followed almost to its source, and then returned to the lake again. We were living pretty well. While we were on these lakes near the mountains we killed four geese and one spruce grouse, and caught about eighty half-pound trout, two two-pound namay-cush and a five-pound pike.

The pike we got in this unsportsmanlike manner: We were fishing for trout in a creek that emptied into Lake Disappointment in a succession of falls, and found that while there were some above the lower fall, none could be induced to rise where the creek at the foot of the lower fall made an ideal pool for them. We were lunching on a rock near this pool when Hubbard suddenly remarked:

"There's only one reason why trout don't rise here."

"What's that?" I asked.

"Pike," he answererd laconically, and left his luncheon to fasten a trolling hook on his trout line.

After he had fixed a piece of cork to the line for a "bobber," he baited the hook with a small live trout and dropped it into the pool. "Now we'll have a pike," said he.

Scarcely had he resumed his luncheon when the cork bobbed under, and he grabbed his rod to find a big fish on the other end. He played it around until it was near the shore, and as it arose to the surface I put a pistol bullet through its head. Then Hubbard hauled in the line, and he had our five-pound pike.

There were two occasions when we felt particularly like feasting. One was when we were progressing with a clear course ahead and were happy, and the other was when we were not sure of the way and were blue. That night we were blue; so we had a feast of goose and pike. Hubbard planked the pike, and it was excellent. All of our food was eaten now without salt, but we were getting used to its absence.

After our feast Hubbard astonished George and me by taking out a new pipe I had brought along to trade with the Indians, and filling it with the red willow bark George and I had been mixing with our tobacco. We watched him curiously as he lighted it; for, with the exception of a puff or two on a cigarette, he had never smoked before. He finished the pipe without flinching. I asked him how he liked it.

"Pretty good," he said. Then after a pause he added: "And I'll tell you what; if ever I start out again on another expedition of this sort, I am going to learn to smoke; watching you fellows makes me believe it must be a great comfort."

George and I had been mixing red willow bark with our tobacco, because our stock had become alarmingly low. In fact, it would have been entirely gone had not Hubbard presented us with some black plug chewing tobacco he had purchased at Rigolet to trade with the Indians. The plugs, having been wet, had run together in one mass; but we dried it out before the fire, and, mixed with the bark, it was not so bad. Later on George and I took to drying out the tea leaves and mixing them with the tobacco.

On Wednesday morning (August 26) when we left camp to continue the search for a river, we decided to leave the caribou skin behind us; its odor had become most offensive, and in spite of our efforts to keep out the flies they had filled it with blows and it was now fairly crawling with maggots. On Thursday when we were passing the same way, George gave a striking example of his prescience. He was at the stern paddle, and turned the canoe to the place where we had left the hide.

"What are you stopping for?" asked Hubbard.

"I thought I would get that caribou skin, wash it off, and take it along," said George.

"What in the world do you expect to do with it?"

"Well," answered George quietly, "we may want to eat it some day."

Hubbard and I both laughed. Nevertheless Hubbard jumped out of the canoe with George and helped him wash the skin, and we took it along. And, as George predicted, the day came when we were glad we did.

It was on Thursday night that, disgusted and weary, we gave up the search for a river. Our camp was on the north shore of Lake Disappointment, down near the western end. Hubbard now expressed the opinion that we should have to portage north or northwest across country. His idea was that by proceeding north we should eventually reach the river that Low had mapped as flowing from Michikamau, the so-called Northwest. If we reached the latitude in which the river was supposed to be and could not find it, Hubbard's plan then called for our turning directly west.

The situation that confronted us was serious. Hubbard had recently had another attack of diarrhea, and was weak. The patches we put on our moccasins would last only a day or two, and we were practically barefoot. Our rags were hanging in strips. Our venison was going rapidly, and our flour was practically gone. To portage across country meant that we should probably not have many opportunities for fishing, as we should not have any stream to follow. Getting game had proved uncertain. Even were we to face towards home, we had not sufficient provisions to carry us halfway to Northwest River Post.

That Thursday evening in camp we discussed the situation from all sides. We knew that if we pressed on winter in all probability would overtake us before we reached a post, but we decided that we should fight our way on to Lake Michikamau and the George River. There was no doubt about it, we were taking a long chance; nevertheless, we refused to entertain the thought of turning back. Daring starvation, we should on the morrow start overland and see what lay beyond the hills to the northward. "Michikamau or Bust!" was still our slogan.

CHAPTER NINE

# And There Was Michikamau!

From the northwesterly end of Lake Disappointment we portaged on Friday (August 28) across a neck of land to two small, shallow lakes that lay to the northward, and in the teeth of a gale paddled to the northern shore of the farther lake. There we went into camp for the day in order that Hubbard might rest, as he was still weak from the effects of his recent illness. We took advantage of the opportunity to patch up our moccasins and clothing as best we could, and held a long consultation, the outcome of which was, that it was decided that for the present, at least, we should leave behind us our canoe and the bulk of our camp equipment, including the tent, and push on with light packs, consisting of one blanket for each man, an axe, the two pistols, one rifle, and our stock of food.

Before us there apparently stretched miles of rough, rocky country. Our equipment and stock of food at this time made up into four packs of about one hundred pounds each. The canoe, water-soaked and its crevices filled with sand, must now have weighed nearly a hundred pounds. It was a most awkward thing to carry over one's head when the wind blew, and where there were rocks there was danger of the carrier falling and breaking, not only the canoe, but his own bones. This meant that if our entire outfit were taken along, practically every bit of land we travelled would have to be covered twice. In leaving the canoe behind, we, of course, should have to take chances on meeting intervening lakes; but, once in the region of northern Michikamau, there seemed a fair chance of our falling in with Indians that would take us down the George River, and the advantages of light travel were obvious with winter fast approaching.

The stock of food we had to carry would not weigh us down. The dried venison had been reduced to a few pounds, so that we had to eat of it sparingly and make our principal diet on boiled fish and the water in which it was cooked. We had just a bit of flour, enough to serve bread at rare intervals as a great dainty. Nothing remained of our caribou tallow and marrow grease. It is true we held in reserve the "emergency ration"; but this consisted only of eighteen pounds of pea meal, a pint of rice, and a small piece of bacon. This ration we had pledged ourselves to use only in case of the direst necessity, should we be compelled to make a forced retreat, and we felt we must not think of it at this time as food on hand.

In camp on Friday night I could see that Hubbard was worrying considerably. Nervously active by habit, he found delay doubly hard. The days we had spent on Lake Disappointment in a vain search for a river had been particularly trying on his nerves, and had left him a prey to many fears. The specter of an early winter in this sub-Arctic land began to haunt him constantly. The days were slipping away and were becoming visibly shorter with each sunset. If we could get to the Indians on the George, we should be safe; for they would give us warm skins for clothing and replenish our stock of food. But should we meet with more delays, and arrive on the George too late for the caribou migration, and fail to find the Indians, what then? Well, then, our fate would be sealed. Hubbard was the leader of the expedition, and he felt himself responsible, not only for his own life, but, to a large extent, for ours. It is little wonder, therefore, that he brooded over the possibilities of calamity, but with youth, ambition, and the ardent spirit that never will say die, he invariably fought off his fears, and bent himself more determinedly than ever to achieve the purpose for which he had set out. Frequently he confided his fears to me, but was careful to conceal all traces of them from George.

In light marching order we went out on Saturday morning (August 29), making rapid progress to the northward, through a thick growth of small spruce timber and over a low ridge; but scarcely had we gone a mile when we were compelled to halt. There in front of us was a small lake extending east and west. It was not more than an eighth of a mile across it, but a long distance around it. Back we went for the canoe, and at the same time brought forward the whole camp outfit. Again we tried light marching order, and again a lake compelled us to go back for the canoe and outfit. And thus it was all day: a stretch of a mile or so; then a long, narrow lake to cross, until finally we were forced to admit that our plan of proceeding with light packs and without the canoe was impracticable.

Hubbard was feeling stronger on Saturday evening, and we had a pleasant camp. George made a big fire of tamarack, and we lay before it on a couch of spruce boughs and ate tough boiled venison and drank the broth; and, feeling we had made some progress, we were happy, despite the fact that we were in the midst of a trackless wilderness with our way to Michikamau and the Indians as uncertain as ever.

Sunday morning (August 30) broke superbly beautiful, and the day continued clear and mild. We made an early start; for every hour had become precious. While we were doing this cross-country work without any streams to guide us, it was George's custom to go ahead all the way from half a mile to two miles and blaze a trail, so that when we were travelling back and forth bringing up the packs and the canoe we might not go astray. In the course of the morning we came to two small lakes, which we paddled over.

We had believed that our goose chases were over; for these birds now having grown their feathers, could fly, and were generally beyond the reach of our pistols and the uncertain aim of a rifle at anything on the wing. For two days we had heard them flying, and now and then would see them high in the air. But while we were crossing one of the small lakes this Sunday, five geese walked gravely down the bank and into the water ahead of the canoe. One of them we got with a pistol shot; the others flew away. In another lake we reached late in the day we came upon five or six ducks. They were not far away, but dived so frequently we were unable to shoot them with pistol or rifle. A shotgun might have enabled us to get nearly all the geese as well as the ducks and other game we saw on the wing and in the water on other occasions. We often expressed the regret that we had no shotgun with us. At one time Hubbard had intended that one should be taken, but later decided that the ammunition would be too bulky.

A low, semi-barren ridge running east and west lay just beyond the small blue-green lake in which we saw the ducks towards evening. About seven miles beyond the ridge to the north was a short range of high, barren mountains that were perhaps a trifle lower than the Kipling Mountains. Upon ascending the ridge we heard the rushing of water on the other side, which sound proved to come from a small fall on a stream expanding and stretching out to the eastward in long, narrow lakes. Apparently these lakes were the headquarters of a small river flowing to the southeast, and in all probability here was the source of the Red River, which, as I have described, flows into the Nascaupee some fifteen or eighteen miles above Grand Lake.

The whole character of the country had now changed. It was very rocky and steadily growing more barren. Ridges and hills extended to the mountains on the north. Great boulders were piled in confusion behind us and in front of us. Portaging over them had been most difficult and dangerous. A misstep might have meant a broken leg, and as it was, the skin had been pretty nearly all knocked off of our shins from the instep to the knee.

Below the fall we had discovered was a deep pool in which Hubbard caught, with his emergency kit and a tamarack pole, twenty trout averaging twelve inches in length. We camped near this pool. The hard work of the day had brought on Hubbard another attack of his old illness; apparently it was only by a great exertion of willpower that he kept moving at all during the afternoon, and at night he was very weak. Before supper he drank a cup of strong tea as a stimulant, and was taken immediately with severe vomiting.

Watching his suffering, the thought came to me whether, disregarding all other considerations, I should not at this point strongly insist on the party turning back. I was aware, however, of the grim determination of the man to get his work done, and was convinced of the uselessness of any attempt to sway him from his purpose. Moreover, I myself was hopeful of our ability to reach the caribou grounds; I felt sure that Hubbard's grit would carry him through. Looking back now, I can see I should have at least attempted to turn him back, but I am still convinced it would have been useless. I thoroughly believe only one thing would have turned the boy back at that time—force.

After this vomiting ceased, Hubbard said he felt better, but he ate sparingly of the boiled fish we had for supper. George and I also felt a bit weak, and our stomachs were continually crying out for bread or some other grain food. As we reclined before the fire, Hubbard had George tell us of various Indian dishes he had prepared. After he had entered into these gastronomic details with great gusto, George suddenly said:

"Wouldje believe it, fellus?—I once threw away a whole batch of cookies."

"*No!*" we both cried.

"Fact," said George.

"For Heaven's sake," said Hubbard, "why did you do it?"

"Well," said George, "it was when I first went cookin' in a surveyor's camp. The cookies wasn't as good as I thought they ought to be, and I was so ashamed of 'em that I took the whole lot out and buried 'em. Supposin'," added George, in an awed whisper, "supposin' we had 'em now!"

"Why what in the world would you do with them?" asked Hubbard.

"Um!" grunted George. "Well, I guess we'd find a way to use 'em, all right."

The story of the buried cookies started us all to talking of doughnuts, and cake, and pie, and Hubbard extolled the merits of the chocolate served at one of the New York hotels.

"Wallace," he at length asked, "do you like pig's knuckles?"

"I like," I replied, "anything that can be eaten."

"Well," confided Hubbard, "I know a place down on Park Row where they serve the best pigs' knuckles you ever ate. I used to go there for them when I was on the old *Daily News*. They cook them just right, and serve a big plate of nice greasy cabbage or sauerkraut with them, and a cup of pretty good coffee. We'll have to go there some time when we get back."

And until it was time to go to sleep Hubbard continued to talk of the good dinners he had eaten when a child and of those his wife had recently prepared at his Congers home.

As he had decided that before proceeding farther we should know something of the country that lay to the northward, Hubbard on Monday morning (August 31) sent George on a scouting trip to the short range of mountains just ahead. He and I planned to spend the day catching and drying fish. For some reason the fish refused to rise near the camp, and Hubbard, who was so weak he could hardly stand, returned to lie down, while I went farther down the stream. Towards luncheon-time I returned with only two or three small fish. Hubbard was still resting in the tent, but soon after I had begun to repair my fishing rod by the fire he came out and joined me.

"Oh, how glad I'll be, Wallace," he said, "to get to Michikamau and finish my work here and get home again! I've been wondering when that will be. I'm afraid," he added slowly, "I've been a bit homesick today."

"We'll surely get there soon, old man," I said encouragingly, "and when we do get there, we'll appreciate it more than ever. Just think how it will be to eat good bread, and all we want of it."

"Yes," he said, "and then we'll be glad we came here, and can laugh at the recollection of these terrible ridges, and the whole awful country, and the hard times we've been through. I'm dead glad I had just you two fellows come with me. If I'd had a single man that growled about the grub and work, or wanted to quit, it would have been hell. But we haven't had a growl or a word about quitting or turning back."

"There's no reason for quitting," said I. "And as for growling, there's no call for it. We've done the best we could, and that's enough to make any real man satisfied."

"That's so," said Hubbard. "Take things as they come and make the best of them—that's good philosophy. I was thinking that here it is the last of August, and we don't know where we are; and it bothered me some as I lay there in the tent. But we've done our best and ought to be satisfied."

In the afternoon I took my rod and went about three miles to the westward, where I came upon an isolated pond with no apparent outlet. Everywhere I could see the trout jumping, and by sundown had as long a string of them as I could conveniently carry. It was an hour after dark when I reached camp. George had returned, and they were beginning to fear that I was lost.

George had climbed the mountains, and he reported a fair line of travel to the northwest, with a "long lake that looked like a river," and, some distance northwest of that, "big water" and a tolerably good route for portages. What he told us led Hubbard to decide to continue on with the canoe and our entire outfit. George brought back with him two grouse he had shot.

The next morning (Tuesday, September 1) Hubbard was much better, and we began September with a renewed effort. It was rough and painful portaging over rocks and knolls. Every forty or fifty rods we came upon deep ponds with water so clear we could see the pebbles on the bottom. Between these ponds boulders were piled indiscriminately. In directing our course to the northwest we avoided the mountains that had lain just ahead. For two days we pushed on among the boulders, then over a wide marsh and through a heavy spruce growth, which brought us, on September 3, to George's "lake that looked like a river." Let us call it Lake Mary.

Along Lake Mary we paddled, in the pouring rain that began that day, some five miles to its western end; and there, near a creek that flowed into it, we found the remains of an old Indian camp. George looked the camp over critically and remarked:

"The beggars killed two caribou, and they broke every bone up and boiled out the last drop of grease."

"What was it—a summer or a winter camp?" asked Hubbard.

"A summer," said George. "And they'd been fishing, too. There's a good fishing place—just try it."

We did try it, and we had a fairly good catch of large trout. For supper we had a few of the trout boiled, together with the water, with one spoonful of flour for each man stirred in. We ate the fish entire, entrails, head, and all, and from that time on we let no part of the fish we caught be thrown away. Everything now in the way of food George divided carefully into three equal parts, even the fish broth. By this time we had not enough flour on hand to make more than half a dozen cakes of bread, and we continued to use only a spoonful or two a day for each man, mixing it with game or fish broth; in this way we hoped it would satisfy to some extent our craving for grain, and last longer.

As evening approached the sky cleared, and a big full moon tipped the fir trees with silver and set Lake Mary to gleaming. The air was filled with the perfume of the balsam and spruce, and it acted as a tonic on our spirits and drove away the depression of the day's work in the rain. Hubbard seemed to be as full of vim as ever, and all of us were quite contented.

Sitting on the couch of boughs, George looked up at the sky and said:

"There's a fine Indian story about that moon."

Of course Hubbard and I begged that he tell it to us.

"Well," said George, "it's a long story about a boy and girl that lived together in a wigwam by a great water. Their father and mother were dead, and the boy had learned to be a great hunter, because he had to hunt for them both, though he was young. One day he found a tree that was very high, and he climbed it, and told his sister to climb it with him; and they climbed higher and higher, and as they climbed, the tree grew taller and taller; and after a while they reached the moon. And then the boy lay down to sleep, and after a while he woke up with a bright light shinin' in his face—it was the sun passin' 'long that way. The boy said he would set a snare for the sun and catch it, and the next night he had his snare set when the sun came 'long, and he caught the sun, and then it was always bright on the moon.

"There's a lot more to that story," added George, after a pause, "and I'll tell it to you some time; but it's too long and too late to tell it tonight."

Unfortunately we never heard the continuation of the tale. George often hinted at interesting folklore stories about the Milky Way and different stars, and various other things in nature; but this was the nearest approach to a story we ever wrung from him.

From our last camp on Lake Disappointment to our camp at the western end of Lake Mary we had travelled about twenty-five miles. In leaving the latter camp on September 4 we inclined our course directly west, to reach the "big water" George had seen from his mountain. During the next four days we encountered bad weather. As evening came on the sky would clear and remain clear until morning, when the clouds and rain would reappear. On the fourth there was sleet with the rain, and on the sixth we had our first snow, which soon was washed away, however, by rain.

Our progress on the fourth was along the edge of a marsh between two low, wooded ridges, and then over the marsh and through several ponds, upon the shore of one of which we camped early in order that George might climb a hill, view the country and decide upon the shortest and best route to the "big water." He reported it about three miles ahead.

It had been our rule to defer our bathing until the evening's chill had quieted the flies, but now there was no need of that, as the colder weather had practically killed them for the season. About this time I noticed that Hubbard did not take his usual bath, and I remarked:

"The weather is getting pretty cold for bathing in the open, isn't it?"

"Yes," said Hubbard; "but I wouldn't let that stop me if I weren't ashamed of my bones. To tell you the truth, Wallace, I'm like a walking skeleton."

It was true. We were all very thin, but our lack of food told upon Hubbard's appearance the most, as he was naturally slender.

The "big water" George thought was only three miles away proved to be like the wisp of hay that is held before the donkey's nose to lead him on. Day after day we floundered through swamps and marshes, over rocky, barren hills, and through thick growths of willows and alders, and at the end of the day's journey it would apparently be as far off as ever. The explanation was that in the rarefied atmosphere of interior Labrador distances are very deceptive; when George reported that the "big water" was three miles ahead it must have been fully fifteen.

On the fifth, while crossing the barrens we came upon some blueberries and after eating our fill we were able to gather enough to supply each man with a big dish of them for supper. We were working our way over some bluffs on the afternoon of the sixth, when George, who was carrying the canoe, became separated from Hubbard and me. The wind was blowing hard, and he had difficulty in keeping the boat above his head. Suddenly I heard a call, and, looking back, saw George running after me, empty-handed. Hubbard did not hear the call, and went on. I dropped my pack, and waited for George to come up.

"You fellus better wait for me," he panted. "I can't manage the canoe alone in the wind, and if we get separated, I might strike the lake one place and you somewhere else. And," added George, sententiously, "you fellus have got the grub."

We shouted to Hubbard to wait, and when he answered, George and I returned for the canoe. Hubbard, however, kept on, and George and I carried the canoe ahead until we reached the thick woods into which he had disappeared; then George went back for my pack. Presently we heard Hubbard call from the depths of the woods, and a little later the sound of an axe.

As we learned later, he had dropped his pack, and was blazing a trail towards us in order that he might find it again. He was as nervous as George had been over his narrow escape from being permanently separated from the rest of the party, and at a time when such a happening would have had serious consequences for us all. Under the best of circumstances, the prospect of being left alone in the midst of that inhospitable wilderness was enough to appall.

On the seventh we reached a creek, and launched the canoe. Hubbard went ahead to fish below the rapids in the creek while George and I brought down the canoe and outfit, making several short portages. That night we camped two miles down the stream. Hubbard had caught, by hard work, thirty small trout, half of which we ate for supper.

We were still ravenously hungry after we finished the trout, but the bag contained only one more meal of venison and we did not dare draw on it. This, together with the difficulty we were having in reaching the "big water," set Hubbard to worrying again. He was especially anxious about the sufficiency of the material he had gathered for a story, fearing that if he failed to reach the caribou grounds there would not be enough to satisfy his publishers. I told him I thought he already had enough for a "bang-up" story.

"Anyway," I said, "we'll reach the caribou grounds, and see the Indians yet. George and I will go with you to the last ditch; you can count on us to the finish."

"All right," said Hubbard, evidently relieved. "If you boys aren't sick of it, it's on to the caribou grounds, late or not late. But I feel I've got you fellows in a tight place."

"We came with our eyes open," I replied, "and it's not your fault."

On the morning of September 8, following our stream out to a shoal, rocky bay, we reached the "big water" at last. It was the great body of water that I have mapped out as Windbound Lake. Forty miles we had portaged from Lake Disappointment. We were practically out of food of any kind. Looking over the great expanse of water stretching miles away to the westward, we wondered what our new lake had in store for us of hope and success, of failure and despair. Would it lead us to Michikamau? If not, what were we to do?

On its farther shore, about twenty miles to the northwest, rose in solemn majesty a great, grey mountain, holding its head high above all the surrounding world. It shall be known as Mount Hubbard. To this mountain we decided to paddle and view the country. Instinctively we felt that Michikamau lay on the other side. We launched our canoe after a light luncheon of trout and a small ptarmigan George had shot. Once in the course of the afternoon we stopped paddling to climb a low ridge near the shore and eat cranberries, which we found in abundance on its barren top. From the ridge we could see water among the hills in every direction. In the large lake at our feet were numerous wooded islands.

We camped at dusk on one of these islands, and on Wednesday, September 9, launched our canoe at daybreak, to resume our journey to Mount Hubbard. We reached its base before ten o'clock. Blueberries grew in abundance on the side of the mountain, which, together with the country near it, had been burned. One of us, it was decided, should remain behind to pick berries, while the others climbed to the summit. I volunteered for the berrypicking, but I shall always regret it was not possible for me to go along.

Before Hubbard and George returned, I had our mixing basin filled with berries, and the kettle half full. The day was clear, crisp and delightful—one of those perfect days when the atmosphere is so pure and transparent that minute objects can be distinguished for miles. On the earth and on the water, not a thing of life was to be seen. The lake, relieved here and there with green island-spots; the cold rocks of distant mountains to the northeast; the low, semi-barren ridges and hills that we had travelled over bounding the lake to the eastward, and a ridge of green hills west of the lake that extended southward from behind Mount Hubbard as far as the eye could reach—all combined to complete a scene of vast and solemn beauty; and I, alone on the mountainside picking blueberries, felt an inexpressible sense of loneliness—felt myself the only thing of life in all that boundless wilderness-world.

From the moment Hubbard and George had left me, I had not seen or heard them. But up the mountain they went through the burnt spruce forest, up for four miles over rocks, up and up to the top; and then to the westernmost side of the peak they went and looked—looked to the west; and there, only a few miles away, lay Michikamau with its ninety-mile expanse of water—the lake we so long had sought for and fought so desperately to reach. It was there, just beyond the ridge I had seen extending to the southward.

# CHAPTER TEN

# Prisoners of the Wind

I t was four o'clock in the afternoon, when the sun was getting low, that I, near the base of the mountain and still industriously picking berries, heard a shout from Hubbard and George at the canoe on the shore of the lake below. I was anxious to hear the result of their journey, and hurried down.

"It's there! it's there!" shouted Hubbard, as I came within talking distance. "Michikamau is there, just behind the ridge. We saw the big water; we saw it!"

In our great joy we fairly hugged each other, while George stood apart with something of Indian stoicism, but with a broad grin, nevertheless, expanding his good-natured features. We felt that Windbound Lake must be directly connected with Michikamau, and that we were now within easy reach of the caribou grounds and a land of plenty. It is true that from the mountaintop Hubbard and George had been unable to trace out the connection, as Windbound Lake was so studded with islands, and had so many narrow arms reaching out in the various directions between low, thickly-wooded ridges, that their view of the waters between them and Michikamau was more or less obscured; but they had no doubt that the connection was there.

"And," added Hubbard, after I had heard all about the great discovery, "good things never come singly. Look there!"

I looked where he pointed, and there on the rocks near George's feet lay a pile of ptarmigans and one small rabbit. I picked them up and counted them with nervous joy; there were nine—nine ptarmigans, and the rabbit.

"You see," said Hubbard reverently, "God always gives us food when we are really in great need, and He'll carry us through that way; in the wilderness He'll send us manna." On similar occasions in the past Hubbard had made like remarks to this, and he continued to make them on similar occasions in the future. Invariably they were made with a simplicity that robbed them of all cant; they came from the man's real nature.

While George dressed three of the birds, Hubbard and I built a fire on the rocks by the shore. Since early morning, when we had a breakfast of thin soup made with three thin slices of bacon and three spoonfuls of flour, we had had nothing to eat, and our hunger was such, that while dinner was cooking, we each took the entrails of a bird, wrapped them as George told us the Indians did, on the end of a stick, broiled them over the fire and ate them greedily. And when the ptarmigans were boiled what a glorious feast we had! In using a bit of bacon for soup in the morning we had drawn for the first time on our "emergency ration"—the situation seemed to warrant it; nevertheless, we were as bent as ever on hoarding this precious little stock of food.

At five o'clock we paddled up the lake to the northeast, to begin our search for the connection with Michikamau. Hubbard dropped a troll as we proceeded, and caught two two-pound namaycush, which, when we went into camp at dusk on a small island, George boiled entire, putting into the pot just enough flour to give the water a milky appearance. With this supper we had some of the blueberries stewed, and Hubbard said they would have been the "real thing if we only had a little sugar for them."

All day on September 10 we continued our search for the connection with Michikamau, finally directing our course to the southwest where a mountain seemed to offer a view of the waters in that direction. It was dark when we reached its base, and we went into camp preparatory to climbing to the summit in the morning. We had been somewhat delayed by wind squalls that made canoeing dangerous, and before we made camp rain began to fall. We caught no fish on the troll that day, but Hubbard shot a large spruce grouse. At our evening meal we ate the last of our ptarmigans and rabbit.

"George," said Hubbard, after we had eaten our supper, "you have a few more of mother's dried apples there. How would it be to stew them tonight, and stir in a little flour to thicken them? Wouldn't they thicken up better if you were to cook them tonight and let them stand until morning?"

"Guess they would," replied George. "There ain't many of 'em here. Shall I put them all to cook?"

"Yes," said Hubbard, "put them all to cook, and we'll eat them for breakfast with that small trout Wallace caught and the two ptarmigan entrails."

In the morning (September 11) we drew lots for the trout, and George won. So he took the fish, and Hubbard and I each an entrail, and, with the last of the apples before us that Hubbard's mother had dried, sat down to breakfast.

"How well," said Hubbard, "I remember the tree on the old Michigan farm from which these apples came! And now," he added, "I'm eating the last of the fruit from it that I shall probably ever eat."

"Why," said George, "don't you expect to get back to eat any more?"

"That isn't it," replied Hubbard. "Father signed a contract for the sale of the farm last spring, and they're to deliver the property over to its new owners on the fifteenth of this month. Father wanted me to come to the farm and run it, as he's too old to do the work any longer; but I had other ambitions. I feel half sorry now I didn't; for after all it's home to me, and always will be wherever I go in the world. How often I've watched mother gathering these apples to dry! And then, the apple butter! Did you ever eat apple butter, boys?"

George had not, but I had.

"Well," continued Hubbard, "there was an old woman lived near us who could make apple butter better than anybody else. Mother used to have her come over one day each fall and make a big lot for us. And, say, but wasn't it delicious!

"I've told you, Wallace, about the maple sugaring on the farm, and you had some of the syrup I brought from there when I visited father and mother before I came away on this trip. We used to bring to the house the very first syrup we made in the spring, while it was hot—the first, you know, is always the best— and mother would have a nice pan of red hot tea biscuits, and for tea she'd serve the biscuits with cream and the hot new syrup. And sometimes we'd mix honey with the syrup; for father was a great man with bees; he kept a great many of them and had quantities of honey. He had a special house where he kept his honey, and in which was a machine to separate it from the comb when the comb was not well filled. In the honey house on a table he always had a plate with a pound comb of white clover honey, and spoons to eat it with; and he invited every visitor to help himself.

"Once, I remember, a neighbor called on father, and was duly taken out to the honey house. He ate the whole pound. 'Will you have some more?' asked father. 'Don't care if I do,' said the neighbor. So father set out another pound comb, which the neighbor proceeded to put out of sight with a facility fully equal to that with which he demolished the first. 'Have some more,' said father. 'Thanks,' said the neighbor, 'but maybe I've had enough.' I used to wonder how the man ever did it, but I guess I myself could make two pounds of honey disappear if I had it now."

Hubbard poured some tea in the cup that had contained his share of the apple sauce, and after carefully stirring into the tea the bit of sauce that clung to the cup, he poured it all into the kettle in which the sauce had been cooked and stirred it again that he might get the last bit of the apples from the tree on that faraway Michigan farm. Then he poured it all back into his cup and drank it.

"I believe it sweetened the tea just a little," he said, "and that's the last of mother's sweet apples."

Breakfast eaten, we had no dinner to look forward to. Of course there was the "emergency ration," but we felt we *must not* draw on that to any extent as yet. Hubbard was much depressed, perhaps because of his reminiscences of home and perhaps because of our desperate situation. We still had to find the way to Michikamau, and the cold rain that fell this morning warned us that winter was near.

The look from the mountaintop near our camp revealed nothing, owing to the heavy mist and rain. Once more in the canoe, we started southward close to the shore, to hunt for a rapid we had heard roaring in the distance. Trolling by the way, we caught one two-pound namaycush. The rapid proved to be really a fall where a good-sized stream emptied into the lake. We had big hopes of trout, but found the stream too shoal and rapid, with almost no pools, and we caught only a dozen small ones.

Towards evening we took a northwesterly course in the canoe in search of the lake's outlet to Michikamau. While paddling we got a seven-pound namaycush, which enabled us to eat that night. Our camp was on a rock-bound island, partially covered with stunted, gnarled spruce and fir trees. The weather had cleared and the heavens were bright with stars when we drew our canoe high upon the boulder-strewn shore, clear of the breaking waves. The few small trout we had caught we stowed away in the bow of the canoe, as they were to be reserved for breakfast.

Early in the morning (September 12) we were awakened by a northeast gale that threatened every moment to carry our tent from its fastenings, and as we peered out through the flaps, rain and snow dashed in our faces. The wind also was playing high jinks with the lake; it was white with foam, and the waves, dashing against the rocks on the shore, threw the spray high in the air. Evidently there was no hope of launching the canoe that day, and assuming indifference to the driving storm that threatened to uncover us, we settled down for a much-needed morning sleep. At ten o'clock George crawled out to build a fire in the lee of some bushes and boil trout for a light breakfast. Soon he stuck his head in the tent, and his face told us something had happened even before he said:

"Well, that's too bad."

"What's too bad?" asked Hubbard anxiously.

"Somebody's stole the trout we left in the canoe."

"Who?" asked Hubbard and I together.

"Otter or somebody—maybe a marten." (George always referred to animals as persons.)

We all went again to look and make sure the fish were not

there somewhere; but they were really gone, and we looked at one another and laughed, and continued to make light of it as we ate a breakfast of soup made of three little slices of bacon, with two or three spoonfuls of flour and rice.

We occupied the day in talking—visiting, Hubbard called it—and mending. Hubbard made a handsome pair of moccasins, using an old flour sack for the uppers and a pair of skin mittens for the feet. George did some neat work on his moccasins and clothing, and I made my trousers look quite respectable again, and ripped up one pair of woolen socks to get yarn to darn the holes in another. Altogether it was rather a pleasant day, even though Hubbard's display of his beautiful new moccasins did savour of ostentation and thereby excite much heartburning on the part of George and me.

Our second day on the island was Sunday, September 13. We awoke to find that the wind, rain, and sleet were still with us. Our breakfast was the same as all our meals of the previous day—thin bacon soup. The morning we spent in reading from the Bible. Hubbard read Philemon aloud and told us the story. I read aloud from the Psalms. George, who received his religious training in a mission of the Anglican Church on James Bay, listened to our reading with reverent attention.

Towards noon the storm began to moderate, and in a short stroll about the island we found some blueberries and currants, which we fell upon and devoured. At one o'clock the wind abated to such an extent that we succeeded in leaving the island and reaching the mainland to the northeast. The wind continuing to abate, we paddled several miles in the afternoon looking in vain for the outlet. In the course of our search we caught a namaycush, and immediately put to shore to eat it. While it was being cooked we picked nearly a gallon of cranberries on a sandy knoll. We camped near this spot, and for supper had a pot of the cranberries stewed, leaving enough for two more meals.

For several days past now, when George and I were alone, he had repeated to me stories of Indians that had starved to death, or had barely escaped starvation, and a little later he spoke of these things in Hubbard's presence. To me he would tell how weak he was becoming, and how Indians would get weaker and weaker and then give up to it and die. He also spoke of how he had heard the big northern loons cry at night farther back on the trail, which cries, he said, the Indians regarded as sure signs of coming calamity. At the same time he was cheerful and courageous, never suggesting such a thing as turning back. His state of mind was to me very interesting. Apparently two natures were at war within him. One—the Indian—was haunted by superstitious fears: the other—the white man—rejected these fears and invariably conquered them. In other words, the Indian in him was panicky, but the white man held him fast. And in seeing him master his superstitious nature, I admired him the more.

Until this time it had been Hubbard's custom to retire to his blankets early, while George and I continued to toast our shins by the fire and enjoy our evening pipe. Then George would turn in, and I, while the embers died, would sit alone for an hour or so and let my fancy form pictures in the coals or carry me back to other days. In our Sunday night's camp on Wind-bound Lake, however, Hubbard sat with me long after George was lost in sleep, and together we talked of the home folks and exchanged confidences.

I observed now a great change in Hubbard. Heretofore the work he had to do had seemed almost wholly to occupy his thoughts. Now he craved companionship, and he loved to sit with me and dwell on his home and his wife, his mother and sister, and rehearse his early struggles in the university and in New York City. Undoubtedly the boy was beginning to suffer severely from homesickness—he was only a young fellow, you know, with a gentle, affectionate nature that gripped him tight to the persons and objects he loved. Our little confidential talks grew to be quite the order of things, and often as the days went by we confessed to each other that we looked forward to them during all the weary work hours; they were the bright spots in our dreary life.

A tremendous gale with dashes of rain ushered in Monday morning, September 14. Again we were windbound, with nothing to do but remain where we were and make the best of it. A little of our thin soup had to serve for breakfast. Then we all slept till ten o'clock, when Hubbard and I went out to the fire and George took a stroll through the bush on the shore, in the hope of seeing something to shoot. While I cleaned my rifle and pistol, Hubbard and I chatted about good things to eat and the days of yore.

"Well, Wallace," he said, "I suppose that father and mother are today leaving the old farm forever, and that I never can call it home again. I dreamed of it last night. Over fifty years ago father cleared that land when he was a young man and that part of Michigan was a wilderness. He made a great farm of it, and it has been his home ever since. How I hate to think of them going away and leaving it to strangers who don't love it or care more for it than any other plot of ground where good crops can be raised! Daisy [his sister] and I grew up together there, and I used to tell her my ambitions, and she was always interested. Daisy gave me more encouragement in my work than anyone else in the world. I'd never have done half so well with my work if it hadn't been for Daisy."

After a moment's silence, he continued:

"That hickory cleaning rod for the rifle we lost on a portage on the big river [the Beaver] father cut himself on the old farm and shaped it and gave it to me. That's the reason I hated so to lose it. If we go back that way, we must try to find it. Father wanted to come with me on this trip; he wanted to take care of me. He always thinks of me as a child; he's never quite realized I'm a grown man. As old as he is, I believe he could have stood this trip as well as I have. He was a forty-niner in California, you know, and has spent a lot of his life in the bush."

When George returned—empty-handed, alas!—we had our dinner. The menu was not very extensive—it began with stewed cranberries and ended there. The acid from the unsweetened berries made our mouths sore, but, as George remarked, "it was a heap better than not eatin' at all."

Perhaps I should say here that these were the hungriest days of our journey. What we suffered later on, the good Lord only knows; but we never felt the food-craving, the hunger-pangs as now. In our enforced idleness it was impossible for us to prevent our thoughts from dwelling on things to eat, and this naturally accentuated our craving. Then, again, as everyone that has had such an experience knows, the pangs of hunger are mitigated after a certain period has been passed.

In the afternoon George and I took the pistols and ascended a low ridge in the rear of the camp to look for ptarmigans. Soon George exclaimed under his breath:

"There's two! Get down low and don't let 'em see you; the wind blows so they'll be mighty wild. I'll belly round to that bush over there and take a shot."

He crawled or wriggled along to the bush, which was the nearest cover and about forty yards from the birds. With a dinner in prospect, I watched him with keen anxiety. I could see him lying low and carefully aiming his pistol. Suddenly, bang!—and one of the birds fluttered straight up high in the air, trying desperately to sustain itself; then fell into the brush on the hillside below. At that George raised his head and gave a peculiar laugh— a laugh of wild exultation—an Indian laugh. He was the Indian hunter then. I never heard him laugh so again, nor saw him look quite as he did at that moment. As the other bird flew away, he rose to his feet and shouted:

"I hit 'im!—did you see how he went? Now we'll find 'im."

But we didn't. We beat the bushes high and low for an hour, and finally in disappointment and disgust gave up the search. The bird lay there dead somewhere, but we never found it, and we returned to camp empty-handed and perhaps, through anticipation, hungrier than ever.

On Tuesday (September 15) the high west wind had not abated, and the occasional sleet-squalls continued. We were dreary and disconsolate when we came out of the tent and huddled close to the fire. For the first time Hubbard heard George tell his stories of Indians that starved. And there we were still windbound and helpless, with stomachs crying continually for food. And the caribou migration was soon to begin, if it had not already begun, and there seemed no prospect of the weather clearing.

97

We made an inventory of the food we were hoarding for an emergency, and found that in addition to about two pounds of flour, we had eighteen pounds of pea meal, a little less than a pint of rice, and a half a pound of bacon. George then told another story of Indians that starved. At length he stopped talking, and we sat silent for a long while, staring blankly at the blazing logs.

Slowly the minutes crawled. In great gusts the wind swept down, howling dismally among the trees and driving the sleet into our faces. Still we sat cowering in silence when Hubbard arose, pushed the loose ends of the partially burned sticks into the fire and stood with his back to the blaze, apparently deep in thought. Presently, turning slowly towards the lake, he walked down through the intervening brush and stood alone on the sandy shore contemplating the scene before him—the dull, lowering skies, the ridges in the distance, the lake in its angry mood protesting against his further advance, the low, wooded land that hid the gate to Michikamau.

Weather-beaten, haggard, gaunt and ragged, he stood there watching; then seemed to be lost completely in thought, forgetful of the wind and weather and dashing spray. Finally he turned about briskly, and, with quick, nervous steps, pushed through the brush to the fire, where George and I were still sitting in silence. Suddenly, and without a word of introduction, he said:

"Boys, what do you say to turning back?"

# CHAPTER ELEVEN

# We Give It Up

For a moment I was dazed at the thought—the thought of turning back without ever seeing the Indians or caribou hunt, and I could not speak. George, however, soon found his tongue. He was still willing to go on, if need be, and risk his life with us.

"I came to go with you fellus," he said, "and I want to do what you fellus do."

"But," I said to Hubbard, "don't you think it will be easier to reach the Indians on the George, or even the George River Post, than Northwest River Post? We must surely be near the Indians; we shall probably see the smoke of their wigwams when we reach Michikamau. It is likely we shall find them camping on the big lake—either Mountaineers or Nascaupee—and if we get to them they'll surely help us."

"Yes," answered Hubbard, "if we get to them they'll help us; but these miserable westerly and northwesterly gales may keep us on these waters indefinitely, or even on the shore of Michikamau at a spot where we may not be able to launch our canoe or reach the Indians for days, and that would be fatal. The caribou migration is surely begun, and perhaps is over already, and there's no use in going ahead."

I saw his point and acquiesced. "I suppose it's best to turn back as soon as the wind will let us," I said; "for it's likely to subside only for a few hours at a time at this season, and perhaps if we don't get out when we can, we may never get out at all. But what does George say?" I asked, turning to our plucky companion.

"Oh," said he, "I'd like to turn back, and I think it's safest; but I'm goin' to stick to you fellus, and I'm goin' where you go."

"Well," said Hubbard, "what's the vote?—shall we turn back or go on?"

"Turn back," said I.

"Very well, then," he replied quietly; "that's settled."

The decision reached, George's face brightened perceptibly, and I must confess we all felt better; a great burden seemed to have been lifted from our shoulders. It had required courage for Hubbard to acknowledge himself defeated in his purpose, but the acknowledgment once made, we thought of only one thing—how to reach home most quickly. Hubbard was now satisfied that the record of our adventures would make a "bully story," even without the material he had hoped to gather on the George, and his mind being easy on that point, he discussed with animation plans for the homeward trip.

"We'll have to catch some fish here," he said, "to take us over the long portage to Lake Disappointment. We ought to be able to dry a good bit of namaycush, and on the way we'll probably have a good catch of trout at the long lake [Lake Mary], and another good catch where I used the tamarack pole. And then when we get to Lake Disappointment we ought to get more namaycush."

"Yes," said I; "and the berries should help us some."

"What do you think the chances of getting caribou are?" Hubbard asked George.

"We saw some comin' up," replied George, "and there ought to be more now; I guess we'll find 'em."

"If we kill some caribou," continued Hubbard, "I think we'd better turn to and build a log shack, cure the meat, make toboggans and snowshoes, wait for things to freeze up, and then push on to the post over the snow and ice. We can get some dogs at the post, and we'll be in good shape to push right on without delay to the St. Lawrence. It'll make a bully trip, and we'll have lots of grub. What would we need to get at the post, George?"

"Well," said George, "we'd need plenty of flour, pork, lard, beans, sugar, tea, and bakin' powder; and we might take some condensed milk, raisins, currants, rice, and molasses, and I'd make somethin' good sometimes."

"That's a good idea," said Hubbard, whose mouth was evidently watering even as mine was. "And we might take some butter, too. And how would oatmeal go for porridge?—don't you think that would be bully on a cold morning?"

"Yes," assented George; "we could eat molasses on it, or thin up the condensed milk."

"We shall probably have caribou meat that we can take along frozen," Hubbard went on. "Frozen caribou meat is bully; it's better than when it's fresh killed. Did you ever eat any, Wallace?"

"No," said I; "the only caribou meat I've ever eaten was what we've had here."

"Then," said Hubbard, "there's a rare treat in store for you. The first I ever ate was on my Lake St. John trip. The Indian I had with me used to chop off pieces of frozen caribou with an axe, and fry it with lard, and we'd just drink down the grease. It was fine."

"It's great," said George.

"Well," said Hubbard, coming back to the present, "I'm dead glad we've decided to strike for the post. If this wind will ever let up, we must get at it and catch some fish. I lay awake most of last night thinking it all over and planning it all."

"I was awake most of the time, too," said George; "my feet were mighty cold."

There was no fishing on the day we decided to turn back, as the wind confined us to camp, and all we had to eat was rice and bacon soup; but our anticipations of home to some extent overcame the clamor of our stomachs, and we passed the time chatting about the things we intended to do when we regained "God's country."

"I'm going to take a vacation," said Hubbard. "I'll visit father and mother, if they're in the east, and sister Daisy, and maybe go to Canada with my wife and stay a little while with her people. What will you do, boys?"

I told of my plans to visit various relatives, and then George described a trip he was going to make to visit a sister whom he had not seen since he was a little boy, closing the description with a vivid account of the good things he would have to eat, and what he would cook himself. It was always so—no matter what our conversation was about, it sooner or later developed into a discussion of gastronomy.

In the evening Hubbard had me make out a list of the restaurants we intended to visit when we got back to New York and take George to. I have the list yet, but since my return I have never had the heart to go near any of the places it mentions. From the talk about restaurants Hubbard suddenly turned to lumber camps, asking George and me if we had ever visited one. We replied that we had not, and wondered what had brought lumber camps into his mind. We soon learned.

"You've missed something," he said. "We'll make it a point to call at Sandy Calder's camp when we go back, and make him give us a feed of pork and beans and molasses to sop our bread in. They're sure to have them."

"Do they have cake and pie?" asked George.

"Yes, in unlimited quantities; and doughnuts, too—at least they used to in the Michigan lumber camps I've visited."

"That sounds good," I remarked—"the pork and beans and molasses, best of all. When I was a boy I was fond of bread and molasses—good, black molasses—but I haven't eaten any since. I'd like to have a chance at some now."

"So should I," said Hubbard; "I'd just roll my bread in it lumberjack fashion."

"Do they have gingerbread in the camps?" asked George.

"Yes," said Hubbard; "gingerbread is always on the table."

"How do they make it?"

"Well, I don't just know; but I'll tell you what, George—if you want to know, I'll ask Mrs. Hubbard to show you when we get home, and I know she'll be delighted to do it. She's the best cook I ever knew."

"Do you think she would mind?"

"Oh, no; she'd be very glad to do it. You must stop at our house for a while before you go back to Missanabie, and she will teach you to cook a good many things."

And so our conversation continued until we turned to our blankets and sought the luxury of sleep, I to dream I was revelling in a stack of gingerbread as high as a house that my sisters had baked to welcome me home.

To our ever-increasing dismay, the northwest gale continued to blow almost unceasingly during the next few days. Sometimes towards evening the wind would moderate sufficiently to permit us to troll with difficulty along the lee shore of an island, but seldom were we rewarded with more than a single namaycush, and so far from our getting enough fish to carry us over our long portage to Lake Disappointment, we did not catch enough for our daily needs, and were compelled to draw on our little store of emergency provisions. On Wednesday (September 16) we ate the last bit of bacon and the last handful of rice we had so carefully hoarded. We succeeded that day in reaching the rapid where we caught the few trout that some animal stole from us, and there we camped. From this point we believed we could more readily gain the bay where we had entered the lake, and begin our retreat when the wind subsided.

The Canada jay, a carrion bird about the size of a robin that is generally known through the North as the "whiskey jack," had always hovered about our camps and been very tame when, in the earlier days of our trip, we had refuse to throw away; but now these birds called at us from a greater distance, seeming to know we were looking at them with greedy eyes. George told us that their flesh had saved many an Indian from starvation, and that the Indians looked upon them with a certain veneration and would kill them only in case of the direst need. Our compunctions against eating carrion birds had entirely disappeared, and the course of the whiskey jacks in holding aloof from camp when they were most needed used to make George furious.

"See the blamed beggars!" he would ejaculate. "Just look at 'em! We've been feedin' 'em right along, and now when it's their turn to feed us, look at 'em go!"

On Thursday (September 17) George got his revenge. Stealthily he crept up on a whiskey jack in the bush and shot it with a pistol. "They're pretty tough," he said, upon returning with his prize to camp, "and will take a long time to cook." We did not care for that; we ate that bird, bones and all, stewed in a big pot of water with two or three spoonfuls of flour and an equal amount of pea meal.

That was our breakfast. We had no luncheon; for although we spent the entire day trolling up and down the lee shore, it was not until evening that we caught any fish. The wind was icy and set us all a-shiver, our hands were benumbed by the cold water, and we were just beginning to despair when we landed a two-pound namaycush, and a little later a five-pounder. Then, wet to the skin and chilled to the bone, we paddled back to camp, to cheer ourselves up with a good fire and a supper of one-third of the larger fish, a dish of stewed sour cranberries and plenty of hot tea.

"I feel more satisfied every time I think of our decision to turn back," said Hubbard, as, with supper eaten, we reclined comfortably before the fire. "I had a pretty hard night of it though, on Monday; for I hated to turn back without seeing the Indians."

"I was awake thinkin' about it, too," said George. "I told you about havin' cold feet, and that they kept me awake." He paused, and we felt that something was coming. At length out it came: "Well, they did, but that wind out in the lake kept me awake more than the cold feet. I knew that wind was makin' the huntin' good down the bay, the game was comin' down there now, and the young fellus I used to hunt with had been wishin' for this very wind that was keepin' us here, and they were glad to see it, and were out shootin' waveys [a species of wild goose]; and here we boys was, up against it for sure."

Hubbard and I had to laugh at George's confession, and we joked him a little about being homesick.

"Well," said Hubbard, "we'll soon get away now; this wind must let up some time. Talking about the bay reminds me that I want to arrange for a trip to Hudson's Bay next summer. I want a nice, easy trip that I can take Mrs. Hubbard on. I'd like to go up early and return in the fall, and maybe get some wavey shooting. Could you get one or two good men besides yourself to go with us, George?"

George said he thought he could, and after Hubbard had invited me to make one of the party, they went into minute details as to the food they would take with them, planning an elaborate culinary outfit.

Just before George went to bed, Hubbard and I, using the trees that stood close to the fire for a support, stretched a tarpaulin over our heads, to shelter us from the rain and sleet. Beyond the circle of our bright-blazing fire the darkness was profound. As the wind in great blasts swept over the tops of the trees, its voice was raised to piercing shrieks that gradually died away into low moans. We thought of the vast wilderness lying all about us under the pall of a moonless and starless night. Where had all the people in the world gone to, anyway?

But, sitting there on our couch of boughs beneath the tarpaulin, in the grateful warmth of the high-leaping flames, we found it very cozy. And we talked of the places and persons that were somewhere beyond the solitudes.

"You don't mind sitting here for a while and chatting, do you, b'y?" said Hubbard. "It's very cold and shivery in the tent." "B'y" was a word we had picked up from the Newfoundland fishermen, who habitually use it in addressing one another, be the person addressed old or young. At first Hubbard and I called each other "b'y" in jest, but gradually it became with us a term almost of endearment.

"No, b'y," I answered; "I would much rather be out here with you than in the tent."

"I was thinking," said Hubbard, "of how I loved, in the evening after dinner last winter, to sit before the wood fire in our grate at Congers, and watch the blaze with Mina [Mrs. Hubbard] near me. What a feeling of quiet, and peace, and contentment, would come to me then!—I'd forget all about the grind at the office and the worries of the day. That's real happiness, Wallace—a good wife and a cheerful fireside. What does glory and all that amount to, after all? I've let my work and my ambition bother me too much. I've hardly taken time for my meals. In the morning I'd hurry through breakfast and run for my train. I haven't given my wife and my home the attention they deserve. That wife of mine, Wallace, deserves a great deal of attention. She's always thinking of my comfort, and doing things to please me, and cooking things I like. But I must be boring you with all this talk about my own affairs."

"No, b'y," I said; "I like to hear about them. I've always been interested in witnessing how happy you and your wife have been together."

"She's been a good wife to me, Wallace; and as time has gone on since our marriage we've grown closer and closer together."

"I see you're like every other man that gets a good wife —you've found the real key to the house of a man's happiness."

"That's so. A single man, or a man with an uncongenial wife whom he doesn't love and who doesn't love him, may be as rich as Croesus, and gain all the honors in the world, and he won't possess an atom of the happiness of a poor man congenially married. Did I ever tell you about the day I was married?—the trouble I had?"

"I don't remember that you did. Although I suspected something unusual on foot, I didn't hear of your marriage until after the deed was done. You didn't take me into your confidence, you know."

"That was because we had never camped together then, b'y. If we had camped together, I'd have told you all about it. Mina and I had not intended to get married so soon. We were to have been married in the spring, but that January I received an assignment for a trip through the South, and I knew it would keep me away until after our wedding date. I didn't want to postpone the wedding, so I decided, if I could get Mina's consent, to make my trip our honeymoon. She was at her parents' home in Canada, and there was no time to lose, and I telegraphed asking her to come on at once and get married. She was a brick and consented, and then I was in such a nervous state of anticipation I was afraid the folks where I was stopping would discover something was up, so the day before I expected Mina to arrive I ran over to Jersey to spend the night with my old friend Dr. Shepard, the minister.

"Well, Mina's train was due at the Grand Central Station early in the morning, and I had to catch a train from Jersey a little after five o'clock to meet her. I was afraid I'd oversleep, and I kept awake nearly all night. Long before the train was due I was down at the station and took a seat in the waiting room. And what do you suppose I did?"

"What?" said I.

"Why," said Hubbard, with a cheerful grin, "I fell to thinking so hard about what was going to happen that I sat there in the station and let the train I was so afraid to lose come and go without ever hearing it."

Under the sleet-covered tarpaulin, there in the interior of Labrador, Hubbard and I laughed heartily.

"And was the bride-elect kept waiting?" I asked.

"No," said Hubbard; "I hustled over a couple of miles to another line and got a train there, and as Mina fortunately didn't arrive as early as expected, I was in time."

The fire had died down and the darkness was beginning to close in upon us. I arose to renew the fire, and when the logs had begun to blaze again, and I had resumed my seat, I saw that the drawn and haggard look had returned to Hubbard's face, and that he was staring wistfully out over the fire into the impenetrable gloom.

"What is it, b'y?" I said.

"That was a great trip, Wallace—that southern trip. I want to visit some of the places again with Mina and live over our honeymoon. And," he went on—"yes, I want some more of the good southern cooking. You ought to eat their cornbread, Wallace!—there's nothing like it anywhere else in the world. They cook corn meal in a dozen ways, from corn pone to really delicate dishes. And they know how to cook chickens, too. Their chickens and yams and cornbread are great. It makes my mouth water to think of even the meals I've eaten in the mountaineers' cabins—wild hog, good and greasy; wild honey, hoecake, and strong black coffee. When I get home I'm going to experiment in camp with cooking corn meal, and I've got an idea that a young sucking pig roasted before the fire like George roasted the goose would be great."

There we were, plunged once more into a discussion about food, and it was after midnight when the talk about roasting pigs, and stuffing pigs, and baking this, and baking that, came to an end. Even then Hubbard was loath to seek the tent, it was so "cold and shivery"; but he expressed himself as being fairly comfortable when he had followed my example and toasted himself thoroughly before the fire immediately before turning in with a pair of socks on his feet that had been hung up to warm.

On Friday (September 18) a fierce northwest gale again kept us on the lee shore, and all we got on the troll was a three-quarter-pound namaycush. Hubbard and I also fished conscientiously at the rapid near which we were still camping, and our combined efforts yielded us only two eight-inch trout and a twenty-inch trout. Trying as we were to get fish ahead for our long portage, it was most depressing.

Despite the steady gnaw, gnaw at the pit of our stomachs, we had cut down our meals to the minimum amount of food that would keep us alive; we were so weak we no longer were sure where our feet were going to when we put them down. But all the fish we had to smoke was two or three. And on Friday night we ate the last bit of our flour; it was used to thicken the water in which we boiled for supper some entrails, a namaycush head and the two little trout we had caught during the day.

All that night the northwest gale was accompanied by gusts of rain and snow. On Saturday (September 19) the mercury dropped to 32 degrees, and the air was raw. Not a single fish were we able to catch. George and I smoked a pipe for breakfast, while Hubbard imbibed the atmosphere. A bit of the smoked fish we had hoped to keep, boiled with a dash of pea meal in the water, did us for luncheon and supper.

Heretofore we had slept each rolled in his own blanket, but it was so cold in the tent that night we had to make a common bed by spreading one blanket beneath us on a tarpaulin and lying spoon-fashion with the other two blankets drawn over us. The blankets were decidedly narrow for three men to get under, and it was necessary for us to lie very close together indeed; but our new method enabled us to keep fairly warm and we continued its use.

On Sunday (September 20) the temperature dropped to 29

and the squalls continued. In desperation we broke camp in the morning and tried to cross the lake with our outfit, but the wind soon drove us back to shelter. While we were out on the lake we caught a namaycush on the troll, and this fish we had for luncheon, together with some cranberries we found on a ridge near where we had taken refuge on the shore. A little later I was attacked with vomiting and faintness. When I tried to swing an axe, I reeled and all but lost consciousness.

Late in the afternoon the squalls subsided, and we made another attempt to escape from the prison in which we were slowly starving. Fortunately the wind continued fair and there were no cross-seas; and on and on we paddled in the direction of—home! Oh, the great relief of it! For nearly two weeks we had been held on that dreadful lake. Day after day the relentless storm had raged, while hunger leered at us and tormented us with its insistent clamor as we, with soaked rags and shivering bodies, strove vainly to prevent the little stock of food from diminishing that we felt was our only hold on life. And now we were going home!

Darkness had long since fallen when we reached an island near the point where we had entered the lake. In a driving rain we pitched our camp. For supper we had the last of the little stock of fish that we had been able to dry. This meant that, in addition to our stock of tea, the only food we had left on hand was sixteen pounds of pea meal. But we did not worry. We were going home. And on Monday morning, September 21, though the wind was again blowing a gale, and the passage among the spray-covered rocks was filled with risk, we paddled over to the mainland, ready to begin our race for life down the trail we had fought so hard to ascend.

# CHAPTER TWELVE

# The Beginning of the Retreat

U pon reaching the mainland we stopped to assort and dry our baggage. All of us felt we had entered upon a race against starvation, and everything that was not strictly necessary to aid our progress to Northwest River Post we threw away. In addition to many odds and ends of clothing we abandoned about three pounds of tea. Tea was the one thing of which we had carried an abundance, and though we had used it freely, we had more than we deemed necessary to carry us through.

While we were nearing the shore, we sighted three little ducklings bobbing up and down in the tumbling waves and repeatedly diving. They were too far off to reach with a pistol, and Hubbard took his rifle. It seemed almost like attacking a fly with a cannon, but with our thoughts on grub, none of us was impressed with its incongruity then. After Hubbard had fired two or three shots, one of the ducklings suddenly turned over. We paddled to it with feverish haste, and found that it had been stunned by a ball that had barely grazed its bill. It was a lucky shot; for if the bullet had gone through the duckling's body there would have been little left of it to eat.

While George and I were drying the camp equipment, Hubbard caught five small trout in the stream that emptied into the lake at this point—the stream we had followed down. These fish we ate for luncheon. Once more ready to start, we pushed up the stream to the place where we had last camped before reaching the lake, and there we again pitched our tent. For supper we made soup of the duckling. It was almost like coming home to reach this old camping ground, and it cheered us considerably. The first day of the forty-mile portage we had to make before reaching fairly continuous water had been, as a whole, depressing.

Rain, accompanied by a cold wind, began to fall early in the afternoon. The weather was so cold, in fact, that the trout would not rise after we caught the five near the lake, and this made us uneasy as to how the fishing would prove farther down the trail. The day's journey, moreover, had made it clear, in spite of our efforts to hide the fact from one another, that we were much weaker than when we last had made portages. We had reached the stage where none of us could carry the canoe alone. Decidedly we were not the same men that had set out so blithely from the post eight weeks before. As for myself, I had shortened my belt thirteen inches since July 15.

It became the custom now for George and me to go ahead with the canoe for a mile or so while Hubbard brought forward in turn each of the three packs for about an eighth of a mile. Then George and I would return to him, and, each taking a pack, we would advance to the place where the canoe had been left. Sometimes, however, this routine was varied, Hubbard now and then helping George with the canoe while I juggled with the packs until they returned to me. Despite the fact that we had fewer as well as lighter packs to carry than on the up trail, our progress was slower because of our increasing weakness. Whereas it had taken us three days on the up trail to portage the fifteen miles between Lake Mary and Windbound Lake, it now took us five days to cover the same ground.

On Tuesday, September 22, the second day of our portage, it rained all the time, and for the greater part of the day we floundered through marshes and swamps. We caught no fish and killed no game. Hubbard tried to stalk a goose in a swamp, wading above his knees in mud and water to get a shot; but he finally had to fire at such long range that he missed, and the bird flew away, to our great disappointment. Our day's food consisted of half a pound of pea meal for each man. During the day Hubbard had an attack of vomiting, and at night, when we reached our second camping ground above the lake, we were all miserable and thoroughly soaked, though still buoyed up by the knowledge that we were going home.

The cold rain continued on the twenty-third until late in the day, when the sky cleared and evening set in cold and crisp. That day I was attacked with vomiting. Our food was the same as on the day previous, with the addition of some mossberries and cranberries we found on the barren ridge over which we crossed. It was another day of hard portaging on stomachs crying for food, and when we pitched our camp we were so exhausted that we staggered like drunken men. Silent and depressed, we took our places on the seat of boughs that George had prepared by the roaring fire; but after we had eaten our meager supper and drunk our tea, and our clothes had begun to dry in the genial glow, we found our tongues again; and, half forgetting that, starving and desperate, we were still in the midst of the wilderness, far from human help, we once more talked of the homes that were calling to us over the dreary wastes; talked of the dear people that would welcome us back and of the good things they would give us to eat; talked until far into the night, dreading to go to the cold tent and the wet blankets.

We awoke on the morning of the twenty-fourth to find six inches of snow on the ground and the storm still raging, with the temperature down to 28. Soon after we began plodding through the snow on a pea-soup breakfast, George left us to hunt geese. The night before he had told Hubbard he would kill a goose in the morning, if he were permitted to go on with a rifle. He had heard the geese flying, and believed they had alighted for the night in a small lake some distance ahead. The knowledge that he was a famous goose hunter "down the bay" made his confidence impressive; still we were doubtful about his succeeding in his quest; for the geese had been so hard to approach of late we were beginning to fear we should never shoot any more. For half an hour after George had taken his pack and a rifle and gone on, Hubbard and I slowly followed his trail through the snow. Then in the distance we heard a "Bang!" and after a short interval, "Bang!—Bang!"—three shots in all.

"He's seen them," said Hubbard.

"And shot one," said I.

"I'm not so sure of that," returned Hubbard; "I'm afraid they flew and he tried to wing them, and if that's the case the chances are against him."

Presently we came upon George's pack near the western end of the little lake, and we stopped and anxiously waited for him to appear. In a few moments he came.

"You can kick me," he began with apparent disgust; then, observing the look of keen disappointment upon Hubbard's haggard face, he quickly changed his tone. "That's all right, fellus," he said; "I got a goose. I saw 'em out there fifty yards from shore, and I bellied along through the brush as close as I dared, and fired and knocked one over. Then the others flew out about two hundred yards farther, and I thought I'd chance another shot; for if I didn't try I wouldn't get another, and if I did I *might* knock one over. So I shot again and *did* get another. Then the resk of the flock rose up, and I tried to wing one, but missed, and they've gone now. But there's two dead ones out in the lake."

Joy?—the word fails to express our feeling. George and I hurried back for the canoe, and when we paddled out, there, sure enough, were the two geese, one dead and the other helpless with a broken wing. George ended the life of the wounded goose with a pistol, and we paddled back to our packs and built a big fire in the lee of a thick clump of trees. The snow had turned into a fierce, driving rain, but that did not bother us. To dress the geese did not take long. We put the giblets and entrails to boil immediately, and, to quiet our impatience while waiting for them to cook, George cut from the necks a piece of skin and fat for each of us. These we warmed on the end of a stick, taking great care not to heat them enough to permit a single drop of the oil to escape from the fat; then, half raw as they were, we ate them down greedily and found them delicious. It was really wonderful how much happiness that bit of game brought us. As we were eating the giblets and entrails and drinking the broth, we freely admitted that never before had we sat down to such a banquet.

"And," remarked Hubbard, "just think how original is our menu. I'll bet there isn't a menu in New York that contains boiled goose entrails."

On the twenty-fifth the fierce northwest gale still blew, and the air was again filled with snow. But still we pushed onward. Let the wind blow, and the snow and rain come as they liked, they could not stop us—we were going home. We portaged this day to another of our old camps by a small lake. On the evening before we had eaten the wings and feet of the geese boiled. For breakfast we had half a goose, for luncheon we had pea soup, and at night we had the other half of the goose left over from the morning. We scorched the bones in the fire and ate even them. These meals did not begin to satisfy our appetites, but they were sufficient to give us a little new life.

While we were sitting around the fire Hubbard wished me to promise to spend Thanksgiving Day with him that year—if we reached home in time. For two years I had spent the day at his home, and Thanksgiving, he said, must be our reunion day always. No matter what happened, we must always make a special effort to spend that day together in the years to come. We must never drift apart. We were brothers, comrades—more than brothers. We had endured the greatest hardships together, had fought our way through that awful country together, had starved together; and never had there been a misunderstanding, never a word of dissension.

From this time on we talked less about what we should eat when we reached civilization. True, we would sometimes lapse into restaurant and home-dinner talks, but we fought against it as much as possible, realizing that to permit our thoughts to dwell on good things to eat accentuated our distress. Gradually we talked more and more of childhood's days, and incidents, long forgotten, came vividly before us. It was a psychological phenomenon I cannot account for; but it was the case with all of us —Hubbard, George, and myself.

During these trying times we had one never-failing source of amusement, which, because it was the only one, was all the more valued and taken advantage of. I refer to our appearance. George had shaved once since we had gone into the country, but neither Hubbard nor I had known the caress of a razor since we left the post on July 15. None of us had felt the loving touch of the scissors upon his hair since leaving New York in June, and our heads were shaggy masses of more or less dishevelled and tangled locks. Long-continued exposure to sun and storm and the smoke of campfires had covered our faces with a deep coat of brown. Our eyes were sunken deep into their sockets. Our lips were drawn to thin lines over our teeth. The skin of our faces and hands was stretched tight over the bones. We were almost as thin, and almost the color of the mummies one sees in museums.

As for our clothing, it was still hanging upon us, and that is about all that can be said of it. Our trousers, full of rents, were tied together with pieces of fish line. The bottoms of our moccasins were so hopelessly gone that we had our feet wrapped in rags, with pieces of fishline tied around what remained of the uppers. Our flannel shirts were full of rents. Around our necks we wore red bandanna handkerchiefs. Our soft felt hats had become shapeless things so full of rents that if it were not for the bandanna handkerchiefs we wore in them our hair would have protruded at every point.

Frequently we would picture ourselves walking into our homes or through the streets of New York as we then were, and laugh at the thought. "Wallace," Hubbard would say, "the cops wouldn't let you walk a block; they'd run you in sure. You're the most disreputable-looking individual I ever saw, by long odds." And I would retort: "I'd make a good second to you; for you're the worst that ever happened."

It was on Saturday morning, the twenty-sixth, that we reached the western end of Lake Mary and completed fifteen miles of our forty-mile portage. We pitched our tent, as we had done before, on the site of the old Indian camp, near the brook George had pointed out as a good fishing place. The rain and wind continued in the morning, but at midday the sun came out and we were able to dry our blankets. Always we waited for the sun to dry the blankets; for we had so many articles of clothing burned while hanging before the fire we did not dare to trust the blankets near it.

While we were following our old trail to the lake, Hubbard

115

decapitated a duck with a rifle bullet, and we went into camp with high hopes of more food in the way of fish. Hubbard's rod was hopelessly broken, so he took mine, now much wound with linen thread, but still usable if not very pliable, and while I made camp and George prepared the duck for luncheon, he caught twenty trout of fair size, which caused our spirits to run high.

Luncheon over, Hubbard resumed his fishing, and I stole away with my rifle along the marshes in the hope of seeing a caribou. When I returned towards dusk without having sighted any game, I found a stage over the fire and George hanging up trout to dry. Hubbard, it appeared, had caught ninety-five more. Our exultation knew no bounds. We had not dreamed of any such catch as that. By remaining in camp and fishing another day, we should, at this rate, be able to dry nearly enough trout to see us through to Lake Disappointment.

We were as happy and as free from care as children. Our great success here made us feel sure that down below, where we had caught so many fish on our inbound journey, we should again get plenty—all we should need, in fact—and our safety seemed assured. We admitted we had felt doubts as to the outcome, which we had not expressed out of consideration for one another. But now we felt we could look forward to reaching home as a certainty. And, feeling freer to indulge our fancies, our talk at once returned to the good things we were going to eat.

Sunday, the twenty-seventh, was warm and clear, with a southwest wind, and everything seemed favorable for more fish. For breakfast we ate the last of our goose, and for luncheon trout entrails and roe. While George and I were drying fish during the forenoon, Hubbard caught fifty more. One big fellow had sores all over his body, and we threw it aside. Towards noon the fish ceased to rise, the pool probably being fished out. After luncheon I again left camp with my rifle in the vain hope of sighting a caribou.

The gloom of night was beginning to gather when I returned. As I approached, stepping noiselessly on the mossy carpet of the forest, I saw Hubbard sitting alone by the bright-burning fire, mending his moccasins. Something in his attitude made me pause. He was bareheaded, and his long, unkempt hair hung halfway down to his shoulders. As he sat there in the red glow of the fire, with the somber woods beyond and the lonely stretch of lake below, and I took note of his emaciated form and his features so haggard and drawn, I seemed for the first time to realize fully the condition to which the boy had been brought by his sufferings. And while I stood there, still unobserved, I heard him softly humming to himself:

> Rock of Ages, cleft for me,
> Let me hide myself in Thee.

How strangely the old hymn sounded among those solitudes! After a little I again started to advance, and as I stepped upon a dry branch Hubbard stopped his singing and looked up quickly.

"Wallace," he exclaimed, "I'm glad to see you! George and I have been having a long Sunday talk and we missed you. We were wishing you'd come. No luck?"

"No," said I; "nothing but old trails; not a fresh track anywhere. What were you talking about?"

"We had a chapter from the Bible and a little talk about it. I've been thinking about my class of boys in the Sunday school at Congers, and how glad I'll be to get back to them again; I've a lot I want to tell them. It's restful just to think of that little church, and this Sunday afternoon I've been thinking about it a good deal."

George was lying in the tent, and Hubbard and I joined him and continued our conversation there. Hubbard spoke of the luck we had had in catching trout, saying: "It's God's way of taking care of us so long as we do our best." It was wonderful to see how, as his body became weaker, his spirit grew brighter. Steadily he became more gentle and affectionate; the more he suffered the more his faith in the God of his youth seemed to increase.

Early the next morning (September 28) George, who was the first to be stirring, poked his head into the tent, and with an air of mystery asked me for my pistol. A moment later we heard a shot. Hubbard and I both looked out, to see George returning with empty hands and an expression of deep chagrin.

"What are you shooting at now?" asked Hubbard.

"The blackest marten I ever saw," said George. "I knocked him over, but he got on his feet again and was into the lake and away before I could reach him. The beggar was right here in camp tryin' to make off with that fish with sores we threw away. He might have made good eatin' if we'd got him."

As the day was squally with snow, and a heavy wind was kicking up a sea on the lake, we decided to remain in camp another day and smoke the fish a little more. While we kept the smoke going under the stage, we sat by the fire and chatted. The day's rations consisted of three fish for each man at each of the three meals. By way of a little variety we roasted some of the fish on sticks. We were all very weak, but George explained that away.

"The Indians," he said, "always go to pieces after they've been hard up for a while and finally get grub. Then they feed up and get strong again. It's the grub comin' all of a sudden that makes you weak. Your mind feelin' easier, you feel you can't do anything."

Hubbard and I agreed that George was right. Our minds certainly had relaxed; homeward bound with enough fish on hand to last us for several days, we had no doubts as to the future. We decided, however, that whatever the weather conditions in the morning might be, we should break camp and push on with the greatest possible speed, as it was the part of wisdom to make our supply of fish carry us down the back trail as far as possible. So we went to our blankets more than eager for the morning's start, and more confident we should get out safely than at any time since we began the retreat.

CHAPTER THIRTEEN

# *Hubbard's Grit*

Two things soon became plain after our struggle back to the post was resumed. One was that winter was fast closing in upon us; the other was that Hubbard's condition was such as might well cause the gravest concern. The morning that we broke camp on Lake Mary (Tuesday, September 29), was ushered in by a gale from the west and driving snow. The mercury had dropped to 24, and all of us were a-shiver when we issued from the tent. While George and I were preparing the outfit for travel Hubbard caught twelve trout in the pool. On the lake we encountered as heavy a sea as our little canoe could weather, and we had to struggle hard for an hour to reach the farther shore. Upon landing, Hubbard was again attacked with diarrhea. George and I carried the packs up the high bank to a sheltered spot in the woods, but when I returned to Hubbard he insisted on helping me to carry the canoe. Up the steep ascent we labored, and then, as we put the canoe down, Hubbard said:

"I'm dead tired and weak, boys; I think I'll have to take a little rest."

After building him a roaring log fire, George and I carried the canoe a mile and a half ahead through the driving snow, which was of the wet kind that clings to every bush and tree, robing the woods in a pure and spotless white that inevitably suggests fairyland. But I was not in a mood to admire the beauty of it all. Upon our return to Hubbard he announced that we should have to camp where we were for the day, that he might have time to recuperate. The delay affected him keenly. We should eat nearly as much food in our idleness as we should in moving onward, and the thought of drawing on our thirty-five pounds of dried fish without making progress was anything but pleasant.

119

The wintry weather did not worry us; for we knew the snow then falling would disappear before the ground became covered for good, and we felt sure we should reach the Susan Valley before freezing-up time, in which event ice would assist rather than retard our progress, as even with the Susan River open it would be impossible to use the canoe in its shoal, rapid waters. As for Hubbard's condition, I suppose it worried me more than anyone else. George had failed to note the signs of increasing weakness in our leader that I had, and Hubbard himself was so under the influence of his indomitable spirit that for a long time he apparently did not realize the possibility of an utter collapse.

By the campfire that night he was confident we should be able to make up the next day for the delay caused by his weakness. For a long time he sat silently gazing into the fire, but as he had just been expressing a longing to see his wife, if only for a moment, I knew he did not see the blaze before him. He was looking into another fire—a big, wood fire in an old-fashioned fireplace in the cheerful sitting room of a faraway Congers home, and his wife was by his side. He put out his arm to draw her closer to him. I could see it all and understand—understand the look of perfect happiness that his fancy's picture brought to his face. But when George arose to throw some more logs on the fire, the shower of sparks that flew heavenward brought him suddenly back to reality—to the snow-covered woods of Labrador.

"I hope we shall be able to find another house in Congers with a fireplace such as our old one had," he said, turning to me as if he knew I had been reading his thoughts. "In the evening we sit long before the fire without lighting the lamp. Sometimes we make believe we're camping, and make our tea and broil some bacon or melt some cheese for our crackers over the coals, and have a jolly time. I want you, b'y, to visit us often and join us in those teas, and see if you don't find them as delightful as we do."

The next morning (September 30) Hubbard said he was much better, and gave the order to advance. We made a short march, camping just beyond the long swamp on the edge of the boulder-strewn country we had found so hard to traverse on the upward trail. On the way we stopped for a pot of tea at a place in the swamp where we had previously camped, and there discovered a treasure; namely, the bones of a caribou hoof we had used in making soup. We seized upon the bones eagerly, put them in the fire and licked the grease off them as it was drawn out by the heat. Then we cracked them and devoured the bit of grease we found inside.

It was agreed that from this point George and I should carry the canoe about two miles ahead, while Hubbard carried the packs to a convenient place beyond the swamps and there pitched camp. It was about dusk when George and I, after a laborious struggle among the boulders and brush, put the canoe down and turned back. As we approached the place that had been selected for a camp, we looked expectantly for the glow of the fire, but none was to be seen. At length we heard axe strokes, and came upon Hubbard cutting wood. He greeted us with rather a wan smile.

"I've been slow, boys," he said. "I haven't got the firewood cut yet, nor the boughs for the bed. I've only just pitched the tent."

"I'll get the other axe," I said quickly, "and help you while George builds the fire."

"No, no," he protested; "you get the boughs while I'm getting the wood."

"I can get the boughs after we have the wood chopped; it won't take me long and you must let me help you."

At that Hubbard said, "Thank you, b'y," in a tone of great relief. Then he added slowly, "I'm still a bit weak, and it's hard to work fast tonight."

It was the first time since we left the post that he consented to anyone doing any part of his share of the work. It is true that since we had turned back I had been relieving him of his share of carrying the canoe, but I was able to do so only by telling him I much preferred toting the boat to juggling with the packs. From this time on, however, he consented, with less resistance, to George or myself doing this or that while he rested by the fire. The fact was he had reached the stage where he was kept going only by his grit.

October began with tremendous gales, and a driving rain mixed with sleet that removed all traces of the snow. The sleet stung our faces, and we frequently had to take refuge from the blasts in the lee of bushes and trees so as to recover our breath; but we managed to advance our camp three miles on the first, pitching the tent on the shore of one of the limpid ponds among the boulders. For supper we ate the last of the dried fish, which again left us with only the diminishing stock of pea meal, and none of us did much talking when we crouched about the fire.

On Friday (October 2), with high hopes of getting fish, we hurried ahead with our packs to the pool where Hubbard had caught the big trout with his emergency kit and the tamarack pole, and near which we had camped for a day while he rested and George made a trip to the mountains from which he discovered Lake Mary and Windbound Lake. The sight of the old camping place brought back to me the remembrance of how sick Hubbard had been there a month before, and how the thought had come to me to try to make him give up the struggle.

The weather was very unfavorable for trouting—a cold west wind was blowing accompanied by snow squalls—but Hubbard caught two within a few minutes, and George boiled them with a bit of pea meal for luncheon. Then, leaving Hubbard to try for more fish, George and I went back to the canoe. While we were returning to camp, George shot a duck with my rifle. It was a very fat black duck, and we gloated long over its fine condition. Only three more trout rewarded Hubbard's afternoon's work. However, we had duck for supper, and were nearer home, and that comforted us.

I remember that while we sat by the fire that evening George produced from somewhere in the recesses of his pockets a New York Central Railroad timetable on which was printed a buffet lunch menu, and handed it to us with the suggestion that we give our orders for breakfast. Hubbard examined it and quickly said:

"Give me a glass of cream, some graham gems, marmalade,

oatmeal and cream, a jelly omelette, a sirloin steak, lyonnaise potatoes, rolls, and a pot of chocolate. And you might bring me also," he added, "a plate of griddle cakes and maple syrup."

Every dish on that menu card from end to end we thoroughly discussed, our ultimate conclusion being that each of us would take a full portion of everything on the list and might repeat the order.

It was on this evening also that, while calculating the length of time it would take us to travel from point to point on our back trail, we began the discussion as to whether it would be better to stick to the canoe on the "big river" (the Beaver) and follow it down to its mouth, wherever that might be, or abandon the canoe at the place where we had portaged into the river from Lake Elson, and make a dash overland with light packs to the Susan Valley and down that valley to the hunters' cabins we had seen at the head of Grand Lake, where we hoped we might find a cache of provisions. Hubbard was strongly in favor of the latter plan, while George and I favored the former. As the reader knows, I had a great dread of the Susan Valley, and I expressed my feelings freely. But we all had the idea that the "big river" emptied into Goose Bay (the extreme western end of Hamilton Inlet), and Hubbard reasoned that we might reach the broad waters of the bay far from a house, be windbound indefinitely and die of starvation on the shore. On the other hand, we were sure of the route through the Susan Valley, and, in his opinion, it would be better to bear the ills we had borne before than fly to others we know not of. I cannot deny that his argument had weight, but we decided that for the present we should hold the matter in abeyance. One thing we felt reasonably sure of, and that was we should get fish in the big river, and we eagerly counted the days it would take us to reach it.

Bright and cold and crisp was Saturday morning (October 3), with black wind-driven clouds and occasional snow squalls later in the day. About noon, when Hubbard had gone ahead with a pack, George and I sighted two small black ducks while we were canoeing across a pond. They were quietly swimming about fifty yards in front of us. I passed my rifle ahead to George.

He carefully knelt in the canoe, and took a deliberate aim while I held my breath. Then, Crack! went the rifle, and but one duck rose on the wing. Quick as a flash, without removing the rifle from his shoulder, George threw the lever forward and back. Instantly the rifle again spoke, and the bird in the air tumbled over and over into the water. The first duck had been decapitated; the other received a bullet through its body.

The moment was intense; for we had only a little fish for breakfast, and the outlook for other meals had seemed dismal indeed; but George was stoicism itself; not a word did he utter, nor did a feature of his face change. When, after picking up the ducks, we touched the shore, I jumped out, took his hand and said: "George, you're a wonder." But he only grinned in his good-natured way and remarked: "We needed 'em." Tying the birds' legs together, he slung them over his shoulder, and proudly we marched to the place where Hubbard was awaiting us, to make his heart glad with our good fortune. One of the ducks we ate on the spot, and the other we had for supper at our camp by a little pond among the moonlit hills.

The thermometer registered only 10 degrees above zero on Sunday morning (October 4), but there was not a cloud in the sky, and we should have enjoyed the crisp, clear air had it not been for the ever-present specter of starvation. All the food we had besides the pea meal was two of the fish Hubbard had caught two days before. One of these we ate for breakfast, boiled with a little pea meal. Our old trail led us up during the forenoon to the shore of one of the larger of the small lakes with which the country abounded. This lake we crossed with difficulty, being compelled to break the ice ahead of the canoe with our paddles.

On the opposite shore we stopped to make a fire for tea— that was all we thought we should have for luncheon; just tea. George stepped into the timber to get wood, and in a moment returned and asked me for my pistol.

"I saw a partridge in there," he said quietly.

Presently Hubbard and I heard the pistol crack, and we counted, at short intervals, four shots.

"There's something up," said Hubbard, and we started to

our feet just as George came in view with a grin on his face and *four* spruce grouse in his hand. He always did those things in that quiet, matter-of-fact way.

Two of the birds George cooked immediately, and as he served to each an equal share, Hubbard said:

"Boys, we should thank the Lord for this food. It has seemed sometimes, I know, as if He had forgotten us; but He has not. Just now when we needed food so much He gave us these partridges. Let us thank Him."

So we bowed our heads for a moment, we three gaunt, ragged men, sitting there by our fire in the open, with the icy lake at our backs and the dark wilderness of fir trees before us.

During the afternoon we bagged two more grouse. Hubbard shot them as they fluttered up before him on the trail, and a meal on the morrow was assured. The day's work practically completed our forty-mile portage; for we camped at night on the first little lake north of Lake Disappointment. It was well that we had about reached fairly continuous water. None of us would have been able to stand much longer the strain of those rough portages day after day. Fortunate as we had been in getting game at critical moments since leaving Windbound Lake, the quantity of food we had eaten was far below that which was necessary to sustain the strength of men who had to do hard physical work.

It had become so that when we tried to sit down our legs would give way and we would tumble down. Hubbard was failing daily. He habitually staggered when he walked, and on this last day of our long portage he came near going all to pieces nervously. When he started to tell me something about his wife's sister, he could not recall her name, although it had been perfectly familiar, and this and other lapses of memory appeared to frighten him. For a long time he sat very still with his face buried in his hands, doubtless striving to rally his forces. And the most pitiable part of it was his fear that George and I should notice his weakness and lose courage.

But he rallied—rallied so as again to become the inspirer of George and me, he who was the weakest physically of the three.

# CHAPTER FOURTEEN

# Back through the Ranges

In our camp on the first little lake north of Lake Disappointment we ate on Monday morning (October 5) the last of the grouse we had killed on the previous day, and when we started forward we again were down to the precious little stock of pea meal. In a storm of snow and rain we floundered with the packs and canoe through a deep marsh, until once more we stood on the shore of the big lake where we had spent the weary days searching for a river—Lake Disappointment. We built a fire on the shore to dry our rags and warm ourselves; for we were soaked through and shivering with the cold. Then we launched the canoe and paddled eastward.

Late in the afternoon we landed on an island that contained a semi-barren knoll, but which otherwise was wooded with small spruce. On the knoll we found an abundance of mossberries, and soon after we had devoured them we happened upon a supper in the form of two spruce grouse. George and Hubbard each shot one. The sun's journey across the sky was becoming noticeably shorter and shorter, and before we had realized that the day was spent, night began to close in upon us, and we pitched camp on the island.

In the morning (October 6) our breakfast flew right into camp. George crawled out early to build a fire, and a moment later stuck his head in the tent with the words, "Your pistol, Wallace." I handed it out to him, and almost immediately we heard a shot. Then George reappeared, holding up another spruce grouse.

"This grub came right to us," he said; "I knocked the beggar over close by the fire."

While we were eating the bird, Hubbard told us he had been dreaming during the night of home. Nearly every day now we heard that he had been dreaming the night before of his wife or his mother; they were always giving him good things to eat, or he was going to good dinners with them.

It had rained hard during the night, but with early morning there came again the mixture of rain and snow we had endured on the day before. When we put off in the canoe, we headed for the point where we expected to make the portage across the two-mile neck of land that separated Lake Disappointment from Lost Trail Lake; but soon we were caught by a terrific gale, and for half an hour we sat low in the canoe doing our best with the paddles to keep it headed to the wind and no one speaking a word. The foam dashed over the sides of our little craft, soaking us from head to foot. Tossed violently about by the big seas, we for a time expected that every moment would be our last. Had George been less expert with the stern paddle, we surely should have been swamped. As it was, we managed, after a desperate struggle, to gain the lee side of a small, rocky island, upon which we took refuge.

At length the wind abated and the lake became calmer, and, venturing out once more, we made for the mainland some distance to the west of where we had intended to make our portage. There we stumbled upon a river of considerable size flowing in a southwesterly direction from Lake Disappointment into Lost Trail Lake. This river we had missed on the up trail and here had lost the old Indian trail to Michikamau. I volunteered to take my rifle and hunt across the neck of land separating the two lakes while Hubbard and George ran the rapids; but presently I heard them calling to me, and, returning to the river, found them waiting on the bank.

"We'll camp just below here for the night," said Hubbard, "and finish the river in the morning. I couldn't manage my end of the canoe in a rapid we were shooting and we got on a rock. You'd better shoot the rapids with George after this."

I suppose Hubbard's weakness prevented him from turning the canoe quickly enough when occasion required, and he realized it.

All we had to eat that night was a little thin soup made from the pea meal, and an even smaller quantity had to serve us for breakfast. In the morning (October 7) we shot the rapids without incident down into Lost Trail Lake, and, turning to the eastward, were treated to a delightful view of the Kipling Mountains, now snow-capped and cold-looking, but appearing to us so much like old friends that it did our hearts good to see them. It was an ideal Indian summer day, the sun shining warmly down from a cloudless sky. Looking at the snow-capped peaks that bounded the horizon in front of me, I thought of the time when I had stood gazing at them from the other side, and of the eagerness I had felt to discover what lay hidden beyond.

> Something hidden. Go and find it. Go and look behind
>    the Ranges—
> Something lost behind the Ranges. Lost and waiting for
>    you. Go!

Well, we had gone. And we had found what lay hidden behind the ranges. But were we ever to get out to tell about it?

We stopped on the shore of Lost Trail Lake to eat some badly needed cranberries and mossberries. The mossberries, having been frozen, were fairly sweet, and they modified, to some extent, the acid of the cranberries, so that taken together they made a luncheon for which we, in our great need, were duly grateful. After eating as many of the berries as our stomachs would hold, we were able to pick a pan of them to take with us.

Paddling on, we passed through the strait connecting Lost Trail Lake with Lake Hope, and, recalling with grim smiles the enthusiastic cheers we had sent up there a few weeks before, sped rapidly across Lake Hope to the entrance of our old mountain pass, camping for the night on a ridge near the old sweat holes of the medicine men. Our supper consisted of a little more pea soup and half of the panful of berries.

While we were lying spoon-fashion under the blankets at night, it was the custom for a man who got tired of lying on one side to say "turn," which word would cause the others to flop over immediately, usually without waking. On this night, however, I said "turn over," and as we all flopped, Hubbard, who had been awake, remarked: "That makes me think of the turnovers and the spicerolls mother used to make for me." And then he and I lay for an hour and talked of the baking days at the homes of our childhood. Under-the-blanket talks like this were not infrequent. "Are you awake, b'y?" Hubbard would ask. "Yes, b'y," I would reply, and so we would begin. If we happened to arouse George, which was not usual, Hubbard would insist on his describing over and over again the various Indian dishes he had prepared.

Weak as we were upon leaving Lake Hope (October 8), we did a heroic day's work. We portaged the entire six miles through the mountain pass, camping at night on the westernmost of the lakes that constitute the headwaters of the Beaver River, once more on the other side of the ranges. We did this on a breakfast of pea soup and the rest of our berries, and a luncheon of four little trout that Hubbard caught in the stream that flows through the pass. I shot a spruce grouse in the pass, and this bird we divided between us for supper. It was a terrible day. The struggle through the brush and up the steep inclines with the packs and the canoe so exhausted me that several times I seemed to be on the verge of a collapse, and I found it hard to conceal my condition. Once Hubbard said to me:

"Speak stronger, b'y. Put more force in your voice. It's so faint George'll surely notice it, and it may scare him."

That was always the way with Hubbard. Despite his own pitiable condition, he was always trying to help us on and give us new courage. As a matter of fact, his own voice was getting so weak and low that we frequently had to ask him to repeat.

And the day ended in a bitter disappointment. On our up-trail we had had a good catch of trout at the place where the stream flowing out of the pass fell into the lake near our camp, and it was the hope of another good catch there that kept us struggling on to reach the end of the pass before night. But Hubbard whipped the pool at the foot of the fall in vain. Not a single fish rose. The day had been bright and sunshiny, but the temperature was low and the fish had gone to deeper waters.

It was a dismal camp. The single grouse we had for supper

served only to increase our craving for food. And there we were, with less than two pounds of pea meal on hand and the fish deserting us, more than one hundred and fifty miles from the post at Northwest River. By the fire Hubbard again talked of home.

"I dreamed last night," he said, "that you and I, Wallace, were very weak and very hungry, and we came all at once upon the old farm in Michigan, and mother was there, and she made us a good supper of hot tea biscuits with maple syrup and honey to eat on them. And how we ate and ate!"

But George's customary grin was missing. In silence he took the tea leaves from the kettle and placed them on a flat stone close by the fire, and in silence he occasionally stirred them with a twig that he broke from a bush at his back. At length, the tea leaves having dried sufficiently, he filled his pipe from them, and I filled my pipe. We had not had any tobacco to smoke for many days.

The silence continued. On my right sat George, his cheeks sunken, his eyes deep down in their sockets, his long black hair falling over his ears—there he sat stiffly erect, puffing his tea leaves with little apparent satisfaction and gazing stoically into the fire. I could guess what was passing through his mind—the stories of the Indians that starved.

On my left was Hubbard. He had assumed the attitude that of late had become characteristic when he was dreaming of his wife and his mother and his faraway home. His elbows were resting on his knees, and his hands were supporting his head. His long hair hid his bony fingers and framed his poor, wan face. His sunken eyes, with their look of wistful longing, were fixed on the blazing logs.

The silence became so oppressive that I had to break it:

"George," I said, "were you never hungry before?"

"Never in my life was short of grub till now," he answered shortly.

At that Hubbard, aroused from his reverie, looked up.

"Well, I can tell you, George," he said, "there are worse places than Labrador to starve in."

"How's that?" grunted George.

"If you had been as hungry as I have been in New York City, you'd know what I mean," said Hubbard. "It's a heap worse to be hungry where there's lots of grub around you than in the bush where there's none. I remember that when I first went to New York, and was looking for work, I found myself one rainy night with only five cents in my pocket. It was all the money I had in the world, and I hadn't any friends in the city, and I didn't want to write home, because nearly all the people there had no faith in my venture. I was soaking wet and good and hungry; I hadn't been eating much for several days. Well, I went to a bakery and blew in my last nickel on stale rolls and crullers and took them to my room. Then I took off my wet clothes and got into bed to get warm and snug, and there I ate my rolls and crullers, and they were bully. Yes, I remember that although my room rent was overdue, and I didn't know where my breakfast was coming from, I was supremely happy; I sort of felt I was doing the best I could."

We went to bed that night feeling that our lives now depended on whether fish could be caught below.

More than anxious were we for the morrow, because then we should go to the first rapid on the Beaver River below the lakes, and there in the pool, where two fishings had yielded us more than 130 trout on the up trail, test our fortunes.

The morning (October 9) dawned crisp and wintry. The sun rose in a cloudless sky and set all the lake a-glinting. On the peaks of the Kipling Mountains the sunbeams kissed the snow, causing it to gleam and scintillate in brilliant contrast to the deep blue of the heavens above and the dark green of the forests below. Under normal circumstances we should have paused to drink in the beauty of it all; but as we in our faithful old canoe paddled quickly down over the lake I am afraid that none of us thought of anything save the outcome of the test we were to make of our fortunes at the rapid for which we were bound. It is difficult to be receptive to beauty when one has had only a little watered pea meal for breakfast after a long train of lean and hungry days. We were glad only that the sun was modifying the chill air of the dawn, thus increasing our chance of getting fish.

How friendly the narrow lake looked where we had seen the otter at play at sunset and where the loons had laughed at us so derisively. And the point where we had camped that August night and roasted our goose seemed very homelike. We stopped there for a moment to look for bones. There were a few charred ones where the fire had been. They crumbled without much pressure, and we ate them. No trout were jumping in the lake now—its mirror-like surface was unbroken. All was still, very still. To our somewhat feverish imagination it seemed as if all nature were bating its breath as if tensely waiting for the outcome at the fishing pool.

I can hardly say what we expected. I fear my own faith was weak, but I believe Hubbard's was strong—his was the optimistic temperament. How glad we were to feel the river current as it caught the canoe and hurried it on to the rapid! Suddenly, as we turned a point in the stream, the sound of the rushing waters came to us. A few moments more and we were there. Just above the rapid we ran the canoe ashore, and Hubbard with his rod hurried down to the pool and cast a fly upon the water.

# CHAPTER FIFTEEN

# George's Dream

Since the weather had become colder we always fished with bait, if any were available, and so, when after a few minutes a small trout took Hubbard's fly, he made his next cast with a fin cut from his first catch. Before he cast the fly, George and I ran the canoe through the rapid to a point just below the pool where we had decided to camp. Then, leaving George to finish the work of making camp, I took my rod and joined Hubbard. All day long, and until after dusk, we fished. We got sixty. But they were all tiny, not averaging more than six inches long.

The test of our fortunes was not encouraging. Hubbard especially was disappointed, as he had been cherishing the hope that we might catch enough to carry us well down the trail. And what were sixty little fish divided among three ravenous men! We ate fifteen of them for luncheon and eighteen for supper, and began to fear the worst. The pea meal now was down to one and a half pounds.

It was late when we gave up trying to get more fish, but we sat long by the fire considering the possibility of finding scraps at the camp down the Beaver where we had killed the caribou on August 12, The head, we remembered, had been left practically untouched, and besides the bones there were three hoofs lying about somewhere, if they had not been carried off by animals. We knew that these scraps had been rotting for two months, but we looked forward hopefully to reaching them on the morrow.

No lovelier morning ever dawned than that of Saturday (October 10), and until midday the weather was balmy and warm; but in the afternoon clouds began to gather attended by a raw west wind. While George and I shot the rapids, Hubbard fished them, catching in all seventeen little trout. Some of the rapids George and I went through in the canoe we should never, under ordinary conditions, have dreamed of shooting. But George expressed the sentiments of all of us when he said: "We may as well drown as starve, and it's a blamed sight quicker." Only when the river made actual falls did George and I resort to portaging. However, we did not make the progress we had hoped, and much disappointed that we could not reach Camp Caribou that night, we camped at the foot of the last fall above the lake expansion on the shore of which George and I had ascended a hill to be rewarded with a splendid view of the country and the Kipling Mountains. Our day's food consisted of three trout each at each of our three meals.

Sunday (October 11) was another perfect day. It was wintry, but we had become inured to the cold. We each had a pair of skin mittens, which although practically gone as to the palms, served to protect our hands from the winds. Before we started forward I read aloud John 17. Again in the morning we divided nine little trout among us, and the remaining eight we had for luncheon. The weather was now so cold that do what we would we never again could induce a trout, large or small, to take the bait or rise to the fly.

In the course of the day George took two long shots at ducks, and missed both times; it would have been phenomenal if he hadn't. There was one little fall that we could not shoot, and we landed on the bank to unload the canoe. All three of us tried to lift the canoe so as to carry it about thirty yards down to where we could again launch it, but we were unable to get it to our heads and it fell to the ground with a crash. Then we looked at one another and understood. No one spoke, but we all understood. Up to this time Hubbard and I had kept up the fiction that we were "not so weak," but now all of us knew that concealment no longer was possible, and the clear perception came to us that if we ever got out of the wilderness it would be only by the grace of God.

With difficulty we dragged the canoe to the launching place, and on the way found the cleaning rod Hubbard's father had made for him, which had been lost while we were portaging around the fall on our upward journey. Hubbard picked the rod up tenderly and put it into the canoe.

An hour before sunset we reached Camp Caribou, the place were we had broiled those luscious steaks that twelfth of August and had merrily talked and feasted far into the night. Having dragged the canoe up on the sandy shore, we did not wait to unload it, but at once staggered up the bank to begin our eager search for scraps. The head of the caribou, dried and worm-eaten, was where we had left it. The bones we had cut the meat from were there. The remnants of the stomach, partially washed away, were there. But we found only two hoofs. We had left three. Up and down and all around the camp we searched for that other hoof; but it was gone.

"Somebody's taken it," said George. "Somebody's taken it, sure—a marten or somebody."

When all the refuse we could find had been collected, and the tent had been pitched on the spot where it stood before, George got a fire going and prepared our banquet of bones and hoofs. The bit of hair that clung to the skin on the upper part of the hoofs he singed off by holding them a moment in the fire. Then, taking an axe, he chopped the hoofs and bones up together, and placed some of the mess in the kettle to boil. A really greasy, though very rancid, broth resulted. Some of the bones and particularly the hoofs were maggoty, but, as Hubbard said, the maggots seemed to make the broth the richer, and we drank it all. It tasted good. For some time we sat gnawing the gristle and scraps of decayed flesh that clung to the bones, and we were honestly thankful for our meal.

The bones from which we made our broth were not thrown away. On the contrary we carefully took them from the kettle and placed them with the other bones, to boil and reboil them until the last particle of grease had been extracted. There was little left on the head save the hide, but that also was placed with the pile of bones, as well as the antlers, which were in velvet, and what remained of the stomach and its contents.

After we had finished gnawing our bones, George sat very

quiet as if brooding over some great problem. Finally he arose, brought his camp bag to the fire, and, resuming his seat, went low into the recesses of the bag. Still holding his hand in the bag, he looked at me and grinned.

"Well?" said I.

"Sh-h-h," he replied, and slowly withdrawing his hand held up—an ounce package of cut plug tobacco!

I stared at the tobacco, and then again caught George's eye. Our smiles became beatific.

"I've been savin' this for when we needed it most," said George. "And I guess the time's come."

He handed me the package, and I filled my pipe, long unused to anything save leaves from the teapot and red willow bark. Then George filled his pipe.

From the fire we took brands and applied them to the tobacco. Deep, deep were our inhalations of the fragrant smoke.

"George," said I, "however in the world could you keep it so long?"

"Well," said George—puff, puff—"well, when we were gettin' so short of grub"—puff—"thinks I"—puff—"the time's comin'"—puff, puff—"when we'll need cheerin' up"—puff—"and, says I,"—puff—"I'll just sneak this away until that time comes."

"George," said I, lying back and watching the smoke curl upward in the light of the fire, "you are not a half bad sort of a fellow."

"Wallace," said he, "we'll have a pipeful of this every night until it is gone."

"I'd try it, too," said Hubbard wistfully, "but I know it would make me sick, so I'll drink a little tea."

After he had had his tea, he read to us the First Psalm. These readings from the Bible brought with them a feeling of indescribable comfort, and I fancy we all went to our blankets that night content to know that whatever was, was for the best.

With the first signs of dawn we were up and had another pot of bone broth. Again the morning (October 12) was crisp and beautiful, and the continuance of the good weather gave us new courage. While the others broke camp, I went on down the river bank in the hope of finding game, but when, after I had walked a mile, they overtook me with the canoe I had seen nothing. While boiling bones at noon, we industriously employed ourselves in removing the velvet skin from the antlers and singeing the hair off. In the forenoon we encountered more rapids. Once Hubbard relieved me at the stern paddle, but he was too weak to act quickly, and we had a narrow escape from being overturned.

While making camp at night, George heard a whiskey jack calling, and he sneaked off into the brush and shot it. We reserved it as a dainty for breakfast. As we sat by the fire gnawing bones and chewing up scorched pieces of antlers, we again discussed the question as to whether we should stick to the canoe and run the river out to its mouth or abandon the canoe where we had entered the river. As usual George and I urged the former course.

"When you're in the bush stick to your canoe as long as you can," said George; "that's always a good plan."

But Hubbard was firm in the belief that we should take the route we knew, and renewed his argument about the possibility of getting windbound on Goose Bay, into which we thought the river flowed. Being windbound had for him especial terrors, due, I suppose, to his normally active nature. Another thing that inclined him towards taking the old trail was his strong faith that we should get trout in the outlet to Lake Elson, where we had such a successful fishing on the inbound journey. He argued, furthermore, that along what we then thought was the Nascaupee River we should be able to recover the provisions we had abandoned soon after plunging into the wild.

"However," he said in closing, "we'll see how we feel about it tomorrow. I'll sleep on it."

I remember I dreaded so much a return to the Susan Valley that I told Hubbard it seemed like suicide to leave the river we were on and abandon the canoe. I felt strongly on the subject and expressed my opinion freely. But it was a question of judgment about which one man's opinion was as likely to be right as another's and, recognizing this, we never permitted our discussions as to the best course to follow to create any ill-feeling.

On Tuesday (October 13) the weather continued to favor us. We shot the rapids without a mishap, and camped at night within three miles of where we had entered the river. But still the question about leaving it was undecided. The whiskey jack and a bit of pea meal helped our pot of bone broth at breakfast, and in addition to more broth we had in the evening some of the caribou stomach and its contents and a part of a moccasin that Hubbard had made from the caribou skin and had worn full of holes. Boiled in the kettle the skin swelled thick and was fairly palatable.

Clouds and a sprinkle of rain introduced the morning of Wednesday (October 14). While the bones were boiling for breakfast, George brought out the caribou skin that he had picked up on the shore of Lake Disappointment after we had abandoned it. Now as he put a piece of it in the kettle, we recalled his prophesy that some day we might want to eat it, and laughed. Into the pot also went one-sixth of a pound of pea meal together with a few lumps of flour that we carefully scraped from a bag we had thrown away in the summer and found near the camp. While we were eating this breakfast (and really enjoying it) we again considered the problem as to whether or not we should leave the river. In the course of the discussion George said quietly:

"I had a strange dream about that last night, fellus."

We urged him to tell us what it was.

"It was a strange dream," he repeated, and hesitated. Then: "Well, I dreamed the Lord stood before me, very beautiful and bright, and He had a mighty kind look on His face, and He said to me: 'George, don't leave this river—just stick to it and it will take you out to Grand Lake where you'll find Blake's cache with lots of grub, and then you'll be all right and safe. I can't spare you any more fish, George, and if you leave this river you won't get any more. Just stick to this river, and I'll take you out safe.'

"The Lord was all smilin' and bright," continued George, "and He looked at me very pleasant. Then He went away, and I dreamed we went right down the river and came out in Grand

Lake near where we had left it comin' up, and we found Blake there, and he fed us and gave us all the grub we wanted, and we had a fine time."

It was quite evident that George was greatly impressed by his dream. I give it here simply for what it is worth. At the same time I cannot help characterizing it as remarkable, not to say extraordinary; for none of us had had even a suspicion that the river we were on emptied into Grand Lake at all, much less that its mouth was near the point where we left the lake. But I myself attached no importance to the dream at the time, whatever I may think now; I was chiefly influenced, I suppose, in my opposition to the abandonment of the river by the unspeakable dread I had felt all along of returning to the Susan Valley—was it a premonition?—and no doubt it was only natural that Hubbard should disregard the dream.

"It surely was an unusual dream," he said to George; "but it isn't possible, as you know, for this river to empty into Grand Lake. We were talking about leaving the river until late last night, and you had it on your mind—that's what made you dream about it."

"Maybe it was," said George calmly; "but it was a mighty strange dream, and we'd better think about it before we leave the river. Stick to the canoe, Hubbard, that's what I say. Wallace and I'll shoot the rapids all right. They're sure to be not so bad as we've had, and I think they'll be a lot better. We can run 'em, can't we, Wallace?"

I added my opinion to George's that there would be more water to cover the rocks farther down, and said that however bad the rapids might be I should venture to take the stern paddle in every one that George dared to tackle. But Hubbard only said:

"I still think, boys, we should take the trail we know."

"That means suicide," I said for the second time, rather bitterly, I fear. "We'll surely leave our bones in that awful valley over there. We're too weak to accomplish that march."

Once more Hubbard marshalled his arguments in favor of the overland route, and George and I said no more that morning.

Soon after we relaunched the canoe something occurred to

change the current of our thoughts. A little way ahead of us, swimming slowly down the river, George espied a duck. No one spoke while we landed him, rifle in hand, on the bank. Cautiously he stole down among the alders and willows that lined the shore, and then crawled on hands and knees through the marsh until the duck was opposite to him. It seemed a very small thing for a rifle target while it was moving, and as George put the rifle to his shoulder and carefully aimed, Hubbard and I watched him with nerves drawn to a tension. Once he lowered the rifle, changed his position slightly, then again raised the weapon to his shoulder. He was deliberation personified. Would he never fire? But suddenly the stillness of the wilderness was broken by a loud, clear report. And Hubbard and I breathed again, breathed a prayer of gratitude, as we saw the duck turn over on its back. With his long black hair falling loosely over his ears, ragged, and dripping wet with the marsh water, George arose and returned to us. Stopping for a moment before entering the canoe, he looked heavenward and reverently said:

"The Lord surely guided that bullet."

It was still early in the morning when we arrived at the point where we had portaged into the river. George prepared the duck—small it was but very fat—for a delicious, glorious luncheon, and while it was cooking we had our last discussion as to whether or not we should leave the river.

"Well," I at length said to Hubbard, "a final decision can be deferred no longer. It's up to you, b'y—which route are we to take?"

"I firmly believe," said Hubbard, "that we should stick to our old trail."

George and I said no more. The question was settled. Hubbard was the leader. Immediately after luncheon we set to work preparing for the march overland. In addition to several minor articles of equipment, we decided to leave behind us the artificial horizon, the sextant box, and one of the axes. When our light packs had been prepared, we turned the canoe bottom up on the river bank. I hated to leave it. I turned once to pat and stroke the little craft that had carried us so far in safety. To me it was one of our party—a dear friend and comrade. It seemed cruel to abandon it there in the midst of the wilderness. In my abnormal state of mind I could scarcely restrain the tears.

But the best of friends must part, and so, shouldering our light packs, we bid the canoe a last farewell, and staggered forward to the horrors in store for us on the trail below.

# CHAPTER SIXTEEN

# At the Last Camp

We began our march back to the Susan Valley with a definite plan. Some twenty-five miles below, on the Susan River, we had abandoned about four pounds of wet flour; twelve or fifteen miles below the flour there was a pound of powdered milk, and four or five miles still further down the trail a pail with perhaps four pounds of lard. Hubbard considered the distances and mapped out each day's march as he hoped to accomplish it. We had in our possession, besides the caribou bones and hide, one and one-sixth pounds of pea meal. Could we reach the flour? If so, that perhaps would take us on to the milk powder, and that to the lard; and then we should be within easy distance of Grand Lake and Blake's winter hunting cache.

Hubbard was hopeful; George and I were fearful. Hubbard's belief that we should be able to reach the flour was largely based on his expectation that we should get fish in the outlet to Lake Elson. His idea was that the water of the lake would be much warmer than that of the river. He had, poor chap! the fatal faculty, common to persons of the optimistic temperament, of making himself believe what he wanted to believe. Neither George nor I remarked on the possibilities or probabilities of our getting fish in Lake Elson's outlet, and just before we said good-bye to the canoe Hubbard turned to me and said:

"Wallace, don't you think we'll get them there? Aren't you hopeful we shall?"

"Yes, I hope," I answered. "But I fear. The fish, you know, b'y, haven't been rising at all for several days, and perhaps it's better not to let our hopes run too high; for then, if they fail us, the disappointment won't be so hard to bear."

"Yes, that's so," he replied; "but it makes me feel good to look forward to good fishing there. We *will* get fish there, we *will!*

Just say we will, b'y; for that makes me feel happy."

"We *will*—we'll say we will," I repeated to comfort him.

Under ordinary conditions we should have found our packs, in their depleted state, very easy to carry; but, as it was, they weighed us down grievously as we trudged laboriously up the hill from the river and over the ridge to the marsh on the farther side of which lay Lake Elson. On the top of the ridge and on the slope where it descended to the marsh we found a few mossberries, which we ate while we rested. Crossing the marsh, we stepped from bog to bog when we could, but a large part of the time were knee-deep in the icy water and mud. Our feet at this time were wrapped in pieces of a camp blanket, tied to what remained of the moccasin uppers with pieces of our old trolling line. George and I were all but spent when we reached our old camping ground on the outlet to Lake Elson, and what it cost Hubbard to get across that marsh I can only imagine.

As soon as we arrived Hubbard tried the fish. It did not take him long to become convinced that there was no hope of inducing any to rise. It was a severe blow to him, but he rallied his courage and soon apparently was as full of confidence as ever that we should be able to reach the flour. While Hubbard was trying the fish, George looked the old camp over carefully for refuse, and found two goose heads, some goose bones, and the lard pail we had emptied there.

"I'll heat the pail," he said, "and maybe there'll be a little grease sticking to it that we can stir in our broth." Then, after looking at us for a moment, he put his hand into the pail and added: "I've got a little surprise here. I thought I'd keep it until the bones were boiled, but I guess you might as well have it now."

From out of the pail he brought three little pieces of bacon—just a mouthful for each. I cannot remember what we said, but as I write I can almost feel again the thrill of joy that came to me upon beholding those little pieces of bacon. They seemed like a bit of food from home, and they were to us as the rarest dainty.

George reboiled the bones with a piece of the hide and the remainder of the deer's stomach, and with this and the goose bones and heads we finished our supper. We were fairly comfortable when we went to rest. The hunger pangs were passing now. I have said that at this time I was in an abnormal state of mind. I suppose that was true of us all. The love of life had ceased to be strong upon us. For myself I know that I was conscious only of a feeling that I must do all I could to preserve my life and to help the others. Probably it was the beginning of the feeling of indifference, or reconciliation with the inevitable, that mercifully comes at the approach of death.

In the morning (Thursday, October 15) we again went over our belongings, and decided to abandon numerous articles we had hitherto hoped to carry through with us—my rifle and cartridges, some pistol ammunition, the sextant, the tarpaulin, fifteen rolls of photograph films, my fishing rod, maps, and notebook, and various other odds and ends, including the cleaning rod Hubbard's father had made for him.

"I wonder where father and mother are now," said Hubbard, as he took a last look at the cleaning rod. For a few moments he clung to it lovingly; then handed it to me with the words, "Put it with your rifle and fishing rod, b'y." And as I removed the cartridge from the magazine, and held the rifle up for a last look before wrapping it in the tarpaulin, he said: "It almost makes me cry to see you leave the fishing rod. If it is at all possible, we must see that the things are recovered. If they are, I want you to promise me that when you die you'll will the rod to me. It has got us more grub than anything else in the outfit, and it's carried us over some bad times. I'd like to have it, and I'd keep and cherish it always."

I promised him that he certainly should have it. Well, the rod *was* recovered. And now when I look at the old weather-beaten piece of wood as it reposes comfortably in my den at home, I recall this incident, and my imagination carries me back to those last fishing days when Hubbard used it; and I can see again his gaunt form arrayed in rags as he anxiously whipped the waters on our terrible struggle homeward. It is the only thing I have with which he was closely associated during those awful days, and it is my most precious possession.

As we were chewing on a piece of hide and drinking the water from the reboiled bones at breakfast, Hubbard told us he had had a realistic dream of rejoining his wife. The boy was again piteously homesick, and when we shouldered with difficulty our lightened packs and began the weary struggle on, my heart was heavy with a great dread. Dark clouds hung low in the sky, but the day was mild. Once or twice while skirting Lake Elson we halted to pick the few scattering mossberries that were to be found, once we halted to make tea to stimulate us, and at our old camp on Mountaineer Lake we again boiled the bones and used the water to wash down another piece of the caribou hide.

In the afternoon George took the lead, I followed, and Hubbard brought up the rear. Suddenly George stopped, dropped his pack, and drew Hubbard's pistol, which he carried because he was heading the procession. Hubbard and I also halted and dropped our packs. Into the brush George disappeared, and we heard, at short intervals, the pistol crack three times. Then George reappeared with three spruce grouse. How our hearts bounded! How we took George's hand and pressed it, while his face lighted up with the old familiar grin! We fingered the birds to make sure they were good and fat. We turned them over and over and gloated over them. George plucked them at once that we might see their plump bodies. It is true we were not so very hungry, but those birds meant that we could travel just so much the farther.

We pushed on that we might make our night camp at the place where we had held the goose banquet on the third of August—that glorious night when we were so eager to proceed, when the northern lights illuminated the heavens and the lichens gleamed on the barren hill. Hubbard, I noticed, was lagging, and I told George quietly to set a slower pace. Then, to give Hubbard encouragement, I fell to the rear. The boy was staggering fearfully, and I watched him with increasing consternation. "We must get him out of here! We must! We *must!*" I kept saying to myself. The camping place was only two hundred yards away when he sank on the trail. I was at his side in a moment. He looked

145

up at me with a pitiful smile, and spoke so low I could scarcely hear him.

"B'y, I've got to rest here—a little—just a little while . . . you understand. . . . My legs—have given out."

"That's right, b'y, take a little rest," I said. "You'll be all right soon. But rest a little. I'll rest a bit with you; and then we'll leave your pack here, and you walk to camp light, and I'll come back for your pack."

In a few minutes he got bravely up. We left his pack and together walked slowly on to join George at the old goose camp on Goose Creek. Then I returned for the pack that had been left behind.

George boiled one of the grouse for supper. Hubbard told us he was not discouraged. His weakness, he said, was only momentary, and he was sure he would be quite himself in the morning, ready to continue the march homeward. After supper, as he was lying before the fire, he asked me, if I was not too tired, to read him the latter part of the sixth chapter of Matthew. I took the Book and read as he requested, closing with the words:

"Wherefore, if God so clothe the grass of the field, which today is, and tomorrow is cast into the oven, shall he not much more clothe you, O ye of little faith? Therefore take no thought, saying, What shall we eat? or, What shall we drink? or, Wherewithal shall we be clothed? (For after all these things do the Gentiles seek:) for your heavenly Father knoweth that ye have need of all these things. But seek ye first the kingdom of God and His righteousness; and all these things shall be added unto you. Take therefore no thought for the morrow; for the morrow shall take thought for the things of itself. Sufficient unto the day is the evil thereof."

"How beautiful, how encouraging that is!" said Hubbard, as I put away the Book. He crawled into the tent to go to sleep. Then: "I'm so happy, b'y, so very, very happy tonight . . . for we're going home . . . we're going home." And he slept.

Before I lay down I wrote in my diary:

"Hubbard is in very bad shape—completely worn out physically and mentally—but withal a great hero, never complaining

146

and always trying to cheer us up."

George said he was sick when he went to rest, and that added to my concern.

Friday morning (October 16) came clear, mild, and beautiful. I was up at break of day to start the fire, and soon was followed by George and a little later by Hubbard. We all said we were feeling better. George shot a foolhardy whiskey jack that ventured too near the camp, and it went into the pot with a grouse for breakfast. The meal eaten, we all felt very much stronger, but decided that more outfit must be abandoned. I gave George my extra undershirt and a blue flannel shirt, both of which he donned. Every scrap we thought at the time we could do without, including many photograph films and George's blanket, was cached.

After Hubbard read aloud John 15, we resumed the struggle. Naturally George and I relieved Hubbard of everything he would permit us to. The fact was, we could not have taken much more and moved. When Hubbard broke down on the trail, it was strictly necessary for me to make two trips with the packs; although his weighed something less than ten pounds, I could not have carried it in addition to my own if my life had depended upon it.

Just below the place where Hubbard caught so many fish that day in August that we killed the geese, we stopped for a moment to rest. Hardly had we halted when George grabbed Hubbard's rifle, exclaiming, "Deer!" About four hundred yards below us, a magnificent caribou, his head held high, dashed across the stream and into the bush. He was on our lee and had winded us. No shot was fired. One fleeting glance, and he was gone. Our feelings can be imagined. His capture would have secured our safety.

We struggled on. At midday we ate our last grouse. At this stopping place George abandoned his waterproof camp bag and his personal effects that he might be able to carry Hubbard's rifle. This relieved Hubbard of seven pounds, but he again failed before we reached our night camp. It was like the previous evening. With jaws set he tottered grimly on until his legs refused to carry him farther, and he sank to the ground. Again I helped him into camp, and returned for his pack.

We pitched the tent facing a big rock so that the heat from the fire, blazing between, might be reflected into the tent, the front of which was thrown wide open. Of course George and I did all the camp work. Fortunately there was not much to do; our camps being pitched on the sites of previous ones, we had stakes ready to hand for the tent, and in this part of the country we were able to find branches and logs that we could burn without cutting. We still had one axe with us, but neither George nor I had the strength to swing it.

The night was cold and damp. For supper we had another piece of the caribou hide, and water from the much-boiled bones with what I believed was the last of the pea meal—about two spoonfuls that Hubbard shook into the pot from the package, which he then threw away. As we reclined in the open front of the tent before the fire, I again read from the Bible, and again a feeling of religious exaltation came to Hubbard. "I'm so happy, and oh! so sleepy," he murmured, and was quiet. He did not make his usual entry in his diary. In my own diary for this date I find:

"Hubbard's condition is pitiable, but he bears himself like the hero that he is—trying always to cheer and encourage us. He is visibly failing. His voice is very weak and low. I fear he will break down at every step. O God, what can we do! How can we save him!"

On Saturday (October 17) threatening clouds overcast the sky, and a raw wind was blowing. It penetrated our rags and set us a-shiver. At dawn we had more water from the bones and more of the hide. Cold and utterly miserable, we forced our way along. Our progress was becoming slower and slower. But every step was taking us nearer home, we said, and with that thought we encouraged ourselves. At noon we came upon our first camp above the Susan River. There George picked up one of our old flour bags. A few lumps of moldy flour were clinging to it, and he scraped them carefully into the pot to give a little substance to the bone water. We also found a box with a bit of baking powder still in it. The powder was streaked with rust from the tin, but we ate it all.

Then Hubbard made a find—a box nearly half full of pasty mustard. After we had each eaten a mouthful, George put the remainder in the pot. He was about to throw the box away when Hubbard asked that it be returned to him. Hubbard took the box and sat holding it in his hand.

"That box came from Congers," he said, as if in a reverie. "It came from my home in Congers. Mina has had this very box in her hands. It came from the little grocery store where I've been so often. Mina handed it to me before I left home. She said the mustard might be useful for plasters. We've eaten it instead. I wonder where my girl is now. I wonder when I'll see her again. Yes, she had that very box in her hands—in *her* hands! She's been such a good wife to me."

Slowly he bent his head, and the tears trickled down his cheeks.

George and I turned away.

It was near night when we reached the point near the junction of the Susan River and Goose Creek where we were to cross the river to what had been our last camping ground in the awful valley, and which was to prove our last camp in Labrador. Hubbard staggered along during the afternoon with the greatest difficulty, and finally again sank to the ground, completely exhausted. George took his pack across the river. While he crouched there on the trail, Hubbard's face bore an expression of absolute despair. At length I helped him to his feet, and in silence we forded the shallow stream.

Our camp was made a short distance below the junction of the streams, among the fir trees a little way from the river bank. Here and there through the forest were numerous large rocks. Before one of these we pitched the tent, with the front of it open to receive the heat from the fire as it was reflected from the rock. More bone water and hide served us for supper, with the addition of a yeast cake from a package George had carried throughout the trip and never used. Huddling in the front of the tent, we counselled.

"Well, boys," said Hubbard, "I'm busted. I can't go any farther—that's plain. I can't go any farther. We've got to do something."

In the silence the crackling of the logs became pronounced.

"George," Hubbard continued, "maybe you had better try to reach Blake's camp, and send in help if you're strong enough to get there. If you find a cache, and don't find Blake, try to get back with some of the grub. There's that old bag with a little flour in it—you might find that. And then the milk powder and the lard farther down. Maybe Wallace could go with you as far as the flour and bring back a little of it here. What do you say, b'y?"

"I say it's well," I answered. "We've got to do something at once."

"It's the only thing to do," said George. "I'm willin', and I'll do the best I can to find Blake and get help."

"Then," said Hubbard, "you'd better start in the morning, boys. If you don't find the bag, you'd better go on with George, Wallace; for then there would be no use of your trying to get back here. Yes, boys, you'd better start in the morning. I'll be quite comfortable here alone until help comes."

"I'll come back, flour or no flour," I said, dreading the thought of his staying there alone in the wilderness.

We planned it all before Hubbard went to sleep. George and I, when we started in the morning, were to carry as little as possible. I thought I should be able to reach the flour bag and be back within three days. We were to prepare for Hubbard a supply of wood, and leave him everything on hand that might be called food—the bones and the remainder of the hide, a sack with some lumps of flour sticking to it that I had recovered at this camp, and the rest of the yeast cakes. George and I were to depend solely on the chance of finding game.

"I'm much relieved now," said Hubbard, when it had all been settled. "I feel happy and contented. I feel that our troubles are about ended. I am very, very happy and contented."

He lay down in his blanket. After a little he said:

"B'y, I'm rather chilly; won't you make the fire a little bigger."

I threw on more wood, and when I sat down I told him I should keep the fire going all night; for the air was damp and chill.

"Oh, thank you, b'y," he murmured, "thank you. You're so good." After another silence, the words came faintly: "B'y, won't you read to me those two chapters we've had before?—the fourteenth of John and the thirteenth of First Corinthians . . . I'd like to hear them again, b'y . . . I'm very . . . sleepy . . . but I want to hear you read before . . . I go . . . to sleep."

Leaning over so that the light of the fire might shine on the Book, I turned to the fourteenth of John and began: " 'Let not your heart be troubled.' " I paused to glance at Hubbard. He was asleep. Like a weary child, he had fallen asleep with the first words. The dancing flames lit up his poor, haggard, brown face; but upon it now there was no look of suffering; it was radiant with peace.

George lay on his side, also asleep. Thus I began a night of weary vigil and foreboding. My heart was heavy with a presentiment of something dreadful. In the forest beyond the fire the darkness was intense. There was a restless stir among the fir tops; then a weary, weary sighing. The wind had arisen. I dozed. But what was that! I sat suddenly erect.

On the canvas above me sounded a patter, patter, patter. Rain!

Gradually the real and the seeming became blended. Beyond the fire-glow, on the edge of the black pall of night, horrid shapes began to gather. They leered at me, and mocked me, and oh! they were telling me something dreadful was going to happen. A sudden jerk, and I sat up and stared wildly about me. Nothing but the sighing treetops, and the patter, patter, patter of the rain. The fire had died down. I struggled to my feet, and threw on more wood.

Again the horrid shapes leered at me from out the gloom. Then I heard myself exclaiming, "No, no, no!" The nameless dread was strong upon me. I listened intently for Hubbard's breathing. *Had it ceased?* I crawled over and peered long and anxiously at his face—his face which was so spectral and wan in the uncertain firelight. Twice I did this. A confused sense of things evil and malicious, a confused sense of sighing wind and pattering rain, a confused sense of starts and jerks and struggles with wood, and the night wore on.

The black slowly faded into drab. The trees, dripping with moisture, gradually took shape. The day of our parting had come.

CHAPTER SEVENTEEN

# *The Parting*

I t was a drizzling rain, and the somber clouds hung low in the sky. The wind appeared to be steadily increasing. The day was Sunday, October 18. Presently George sat up, rubbed his eyes and gazed about him for a moment in bewilderment.

"Mornin', Wallace," he said, when he had collected his senses, "that blamed rain will make the travellin' hard, won't it?"

He tied the pieces of blanket to his feet, and started for the river to get a kettle of water with which to reboil the bones. The movement aroused Hubbard, and he, too, sat up.

"How's the weather, b'y?" he asked.

"It makes me think of Longfellow's 'Rainy Day,'" I replied. "'The day is cold, and dark, and dreary.'"

"Yes," he quickly returned: "but

> Be still, sad heart, and cease repining;
> Behind the clouds is the sun still shining."

I looked at him with admiration.

"Hubbard," I exclaimed, "you're a wonder! You've a way of making our worst troubles seem light. I've been sitting here imagining all sorts of things."

"There's no call to worry, b'y," he smilingly said, "we'll soon have grub now, and then we can rest and sleep—and get strong."

He arose from his blanket, and walked out of the tent to look at the sky. Slowly he returned, and sank wearily down.

"I'm feeling stronger and better than I did last night," he said; "but I'm too weak to walk or stand up long."

When our breakfast of bones and hide boiled with a yeast cake was ready, he sat up in the tent to receive his share. While drinking the water and chewing the hide, we again carefully considered how long it should take George to reach Grand Lake,

153

and how long it would be before help could arrive, if he were able to obtain any, and how long it would require me to reach the flour and return. It was, roughly speaking, forty miles to Grand Lake, and fifteen miles to the flour.

That there was room for doubt as to whether my strength would carry me to the flour and back again, we all recognized; and we fully realized, that if George failed to reach Grand Lake, or, reaching there, failed to find Blake or Blake's cache, our doom would be sealed; but so long had death been staring us in the face that it had ceased to have for us any terror. It was agreed, however, that each man should do his best to live as long as possible. I told Hubbard I should do my utmost to be back in three days, even if I did not find the flour.

Hubbard remained seated in the front of the tent while George and I went about gathering a supply of wood that we thought should last him until someone returned. George also brought a kettle of water from the river, and thoughtfully placed it near the fire for Hubbard's use in boiling the bones and hide, all of which we left with him together with the yeast and some tea. I also turned over to him the pair of blankets he had delivered to me at Halifax—the birthday gift from my sisters.

These preparations for Hubbard's comfort completed, George and I returned to the tent to arrange the kits we were to take with us. Hubbard sat in the middle of the tent towards the rear; George and I on either side of him in the front. Hubbard gave George his pistol and compass, and I had my own pistol and compass. The pistols we fastened to our belts along with a sheath knife and tin cup. Having a case for my compass, I wore it also on my belt; George placed his in his pocket. Each of us had half a blanket, this to be our only covering at night. George placed his half, together with a tea pail and some tea, in the waterproof bag he had been using to carry food. This bag he bound with a pack strap, leaving a loop to sling over his shoulder. I also bound my half a blanket with a pack strap, thinking as I did so that I soon might want to eat the strap. And then, when George and I had filled our waterproof boxes with wax taper matches, and placed a handful of pistol cartridges in our pockets, we were ready to start.

At this point I suggested it might be well for each man to make a note of such disposition as he desired made of his effects. George made an entry in his notebook, and asked Hubbard to write when we were gone a letter to Mr. King, the Hudson's Bay Company's agent at Missanabie, in reference to his (George's) affairs at that post. I then made the last entry in my diary, and with it wrote what I believed might be a last message to my sisters and my friend and associate in business, Mr. Alonzo G. McLaughlin. I put the diary with my other papers in my camp bag, and placed the bag in the rear of the tent, where the note Hubbard was to write for George was also to be placed; we believed that if worst came to worst the tent was more likely to be found than our bodies down on the trail. Hubbard had been watching us silently while we did these things, and now he said:

"Wallace, if you get out of this, and I don't, you'll have to write the story of the trip."

I expressed some doubt as to my ability, but he made me promise I would do the best I could. I also promised, at his request, that if I survived him I should place his diary in his wife's hands.

"Thank you, b'y," he said. "And now before you leave me won't you read to me again?—I want to hear that fourteenth chapter of John and the thirteenth of First Corinthians. I fell asleep last night while you were reading, I was so tired. I'm sleepy now, very sleepy; but I'll keep awake this time while you read."

I got my testament from my camp bag and read both chapters through, noting as I read that the look of happiness and peace was returning to Hubbard's poor, wan face. When I had finished, he said quietly:

"Thank you, b'y, thank you very much. Isn't that comforting?—'Let not your heart be troubled.' It makes me feel good. I've faith that we'll all be saved. I'm not worried. McLean was caught just as we are. He sent a man for help and got out all right. God will send us help, too."

"Yes," said I, "and we shall soon be safe home."

"We'll soon be safe home," repeated Hubbard—"safe home. How happy that makes me feel!"

It was time for George and me to go. But I could not say good-bye just yet. I turned my back to Hubbard and faced the fire. The tears were welling up into my eyes, and I struggled for self-control. George sat silent, too, and his face was strangely drawn. For a full ten minutes we sat silently gazing into the fire. Finally George arose.

"Well, Wallace, we'd better start now."

"Yes," I said; "we'd better start."

I collected myself as best I could, and, turning to Hubbard, held out my hand.

"Good-bye, b'y; I'll be back soon." And then, as I looked into his poor, wistful eyes, I broke down and sobbed.

I crawled over to him, and put my arm about him. I kissed his cheek, and he kissed my cheek. We embraced each other, and for a moment held our faces close together. Then I drew away.

George was crying, too. The dear fellow went over to Hubbard, stooped and kissed his cheek.

"With God's help, I'll save you, Hubbard!"

Hubbard kissed his cheek, and they embraced.

George slung his bundle on his shoulder, and I took up mine. We turned to go. But I had to return. I stooped and again kissed Hubbard's cheek, and he again kissed mine. He was quite calm—had been calm throughout. Only his eyes shone with that look of wistful longing.

"Good-bye, boys, and God be with you!"

"Good-bye!"

"Good-bye!"

And George and I left him. About twenty yards away I turned for a last look at the tent. Hubbard evidently had immediately lain down; for he was not to be seen. All I saw was the little peak of balloon silk that had been our home for so many weeks, the fire blazing between it and the big rock, the kettle of water by the fire, and the white moss and the dripping wet fir trees all about.

\* \* \*

Some 150 yards farther on George and I forded a brook, after which our course was through closely-grown, diminutive fir trees until we came to a series of low, barren knolls. On these knolls we found some mossberries. Then we pushed on. It was dreadfully slow travelling. The wind was in the east, and was rising. The drizzling rain had become a downpour, and it was dashed into our faces in sheets. The cold was increasing. Our hands were stiff and numb. Somewhat after midday George threw down his pack. "We'll have a spell [rest] and a cup of tea to warm us up," he said.

I did not protest. The previous night had been a trying one, and I was very tired. We drew together some wood. With his sheath knife George whittled some shavings, and a fire was soon blazing. When the kettle had been placed over the fire to boil, George drew out of his bag a package—yes, it was a half-pound package of pea meal! At first I could not believe my eyes, and I stood stupidly staring as George prepared to stir some of it into the kettle. At length I found my tongue.

"George," I cried indignantly, "where did you get that pea meal?"

"Hubbard gave it to me this morning while you were getting' wood," he answered promptly.

"But why did you take it?"

"He made me take it. I didn't want to, but he said I must. He said we'd be workin' hard, and we'd need it, and if we didn't have somethin' to eat, we couldn't travel far and couldn't get help to him. We ought to have it as much for his sake as for ours, he said, and I had to take it from him to make him feel right."

Hubbard had evidently reserved that last half-pound of pea meal to be used in a last extremity, and as the argument he had used to force it on George had been at least specious, I could say nothing. George put one-third of the package (one-sixth of a pound) into the kettle, and we each drank a pint of the soup. It was very thin, but it did us good.

After a half-hour's rest, we pressed on as rapidly as possible, but when night overtook us we could not have travelled more than six miles from camp. To the storm, as well as our weakness, was due our slow progress. As the afternoon wore on, the storm became furious. The rain descended in drenching sheets, and staggering blasts of wind drove it into our faces. Even if darkness had not stopped us, further progress in the face of the tempest would have been impossible.

We selected for our bivouac as sheltered a spot as possible in a spruce growth, hauled together a good supply of small dead trees and made a fire. For supper we had one-half of what remained of the pea meal, reserving the other half (one-sixth of a pound) for breakfast. There was a little comfort to be gained from the fire. The rain still descended upon us in sheets. The blast of wind drove the smoke into our eyes and blinded us. Despite our weariness we could not sleep. George lay down, but I sat crouching before the fire. We tried to keep our pieces of blanket over our heads, but when we did so we nearly suffocated. Now and again one or the other would rise to throw on more wood. Towards midnight the wind shifted, and snow began to fall. It fell as I never saw snow fall before. And the wind never ceased, and the smoke was more blinding than ever, and the night grew colder.

There were fully six inches of snow on the ground when the clouds broke just before dawn, and before the first rays of the sun greeted us the wind died away. It was Monday, October 19. With the return of daylight we ate the rest of the pea meal, and resumed our march down the valley. The daylight proved that my eyes had been greatly affected by the smoke of our night's fire. Everything had a hazy appearance. George complained of the same trouble. Soon after we started, George came upon a grouse track in the fresh snow, and followed it to a clump of bushes a short distance off. He aimed his pistol with great care, but the bullet only knocked a few feathers out of the bird, and it flew away, to George's keen chagrin and my bitter disappointment.

The flour bag we were to look for was on the opposite or south side of the river, and it was necessary to cross. Before noon we reached a place at which George said it would be as easy to ford the stream as at any other. The icy water came almost up to our armpits, but we made the other shore without mishap. There we halted to build a fire and thaw ourselves out; for immediately upon emerging from the river our clothing froze hard and stiff. While waiting we had some hot tea, and as quickly as possible pushed on. We *must* reach the flour bag that night.

I found it hard to keep the pace George was setting, and began to lag woefully. Several times he had to wait for me to overtake him. We came upon a caribou trail in the snow, and followed it so long as it kept our direction. To some extent the broken path aided our progress. In the afternoon we came upon another grouse track. George followed it to a clump of trees, where the bird was discovered sitting on a limb. This time his aim was accurate, and the bird fell at his feet. Quickly he plucked the wings, cut them off and handed me one with the remark: "They say raw partridge is good when a fellu's weak." It was delicious. I ate the wing, warm with the bird's life blood, bones and all, and George ate the other wing.

I soon found it utterly impossible to keep George's pace, and became so exhausted that I was forced to take short rests. At length I told George he had better go ahead and look for the flour; that I should rest, follow his trail and overtake him later. He went on, but just over the bare knoll we were crossing I found him sitting in the snow waiting for me.

"I don't feel right to go ahead and leave you," he said. "Do you see that second knoll?" He pointed to one of a series of round barren knolls about half a mile down the river.

"Yes," I answered.

"Well, don't you remember it? No? Why, that's where we camped when we threw the flour away, and that's where we'll stop tonight. We'd better eat a mouthful to help us on."

He had plucked the head and neck of the grouse, and now proceeded to cut them off near the body. To me he gave the neck, and ate the head himself—raw, of course.

It was just dusk when we reached the knoll George had designated. Straightway he went to a bush, ran his hand under it and pulled out—the bag we were looking for. We opened it eagerly. As has been said, we left about four pounds of flour in it. Now there was a lump of green and black mold. However, we rejoiced at finding it; for it was something and it might sustain our lives. It might send George to the lard, and keep Hubbard and me until help could arrive.

On this side of the Susan the country for some distance had been burned; but, while there were no standing trees, and the place was entirely unsheltered, fallen spruce trees covered the ground in every direction, so we found no difficulty in getting together a good pile of dry wood for our night's fire, and we soon had a rousing big one going. For supper we ate all of the grouse boiled with some of the flour mold stirred in. It was a splendid supper.

I had not sat long before the fire when I felt a strange sensation in my eyes. It was as if they had been filled with sharp splinters, and I found it impossible to open them. I was afflicted with smoke-blindness, which is almost identical in its effect to snow-blindness. George filled my pipe with dried tea leaves and just a bit of his precious tobacco; then lit it for me, as I could not see to do it myself. After our smoke we lay down, and I slept heavily; it was practically the first sleep I had had in three days. Some time in the night George awoke me to make me eat a little of a concoction of the moldy flour and water, cooked thick and a trifle burned after the style of *nekapooshet*, an Indian dish of which George was very fond. At the first signs of dawn he again roused me, saying:

"It's time to be up, Wallace. We're goin' to have more snow to travel in."

He was right. The clouds were hanging low and heavy, and the first scattering flakes were falling of a storm that was to last for ten days. I was able to open my eyes in the morning, but everything still looked hazy. We boiled some of the wretched moldy flour for breakfast, and then divided what remained, George taking the larger share, as he had the most work to do. Looking critically at my share, he asked:

"How long can you keep alive on that?"

"It will take me two days to reach Hubbard," I replied, "and the two of us might live three days more on it—on a pinch."

"Do you think you can live as long as that?" said George, looking me hard in the eye.

"I'll try," I said.

"Then in five days I'll have help to you, if there's help to be had at Grand Lake. Day after tomorrow I'll be at Grand Lake. These fellus'll be strong and can reach camp in two days, so expect 'em."

It was time for us to separate.

"George," I asked, "have you your Testament with you?"

"It's the Book of Common Prayer," he said, drawing it from his pocket; "but it's got the Psalms in it."

He handed me the tiny leather-covered book, but I could not see the print; the haze before my eyes was too thick. I returned the book to him, and asked him to read one of the Psalms. Quite at haphazard, I am sure, he turned to the ninety-first, and this is what he read:

> Whoso dwelleth under the defense of the Most High; shall abide under the shadow of the Almighty.
>
> I will say unto the Lord, Thou art my hope, and my stronghold: my God, in Him will I trust.
>
> For He shall deliver thee from the snare of the hunter: and from the noisome pestilence.
>
> He shall defend thee under His wings, and thou shalt be safe under His feathers: His faithfulness and truth shall be thy shield and buckler.
>
> Thou shalt not be afraid for any terror by night: nor for the arrow that flieth by day;
>
> For the pestilence that walketh in darkness: nor for the sickness that destroyeth in the noon-day.
>
> A thousand shall fall beside thee, and ten thousand at thy right hand: but it shall not come nigh thee.
>
> Yea, with thine eyes shalt thou behold: and see the reward of the ungodly.
>
> For Thou, Lord, art my hope: Thou hast set Thine house of defense very high.
>
> There shall be no evil happen unto thee: neither shall any

plague come nigh thy dwelling.

For He shall give His angels charge over thee: to keep thee in all thy ways.

They shall bear thee in their hands: that thou hurt not thy foot against a stone.

Thou shalt go upon the lion and adder: the young lion and the dragon shalt thou tread under thy feet.

Because He hath set His love upon me, therefore will I deliver Him: I will set Him up, because He hath known my name.

He shall call upon me, and I will hear Him: yea, I am with Him in trouble; I will deliver Him and bring Him to honor.

With long life will I satisfy Him: and show Him my salvation.

The Psalm made a deep impression upon me. "For He shall give His angels charge over thee: to keep thee in all thy ways." How strange it seems, in view of what happened to me, that George should have read that sentence.

We arose to go on our separate ways, George twenty-five miles down the valley to Grand Lake, and I fifteen miles up the valley to Hubbard. The snow was falling thick and fast.

"You'd better make a cape of your blanket," suggested George. "Let me fix it for you."

He placed the blanket around my shoulders, and on either side of the cloth where it came together under my chin made a small hole with his knife. Through these holes he ran a piece of our old trolling line, and tied the ends. Then he similarly arranged his own blanket.

I held out my hand to him.

"Good-bye, George. Take care of yourself."

He clasped my hand warmly.

"Good-bye, Wallace. Expect help in five days."

Near the top of a knoll I stopped and looked back. With my afflicted eyes I could barely make out George ascending another knoll. He also stopped and looked back. I waved my hand to him, and he waved his hand to me and shouted something unintelligible. Then he disappeared in the snow, and as he disappeared a silence came on the world, to remain unbroken for ten days.

# CHAPTER EIGHTEEN

# Wandering Alone

With every hour the storm gathered new force, and over the barren knolls, along which my course for some distance lay, the snow whirled furiously. The track George and I had made on our downward journey soon was obliterated. Once in the forenoon, as I pushed blindly on against the storm, I heard a snort, and, looking up, beheld, only a few yards away, a big caribou. He was standing directly in my path. For a second he regarded me, with his head thrown back in fear and wonder; and then, giving another snort, he dashed away into the maze of whirling snow.

My eyes troubled me greatly, and the pain at length grew so intense that I was forced to sit down in the snow for perhaps half an hour with both eyes tightly closed. I was keeping some distance from the river, as the obstructions here were fewer than near the bank. In the afternoon it occurred to me that I might have turned in my course, and I took my compass from its case, to satisfy myself that I was going in the right direction; but my sight was so impaired that I could not read the dial, nor be certain which way the needle pointed. And I wondered vaguely whether I was becoming totally blind.

My day's progress was not satisfactory. I had hoped to reach the place where George and I had forded the river, and cross to the north shore before bivouacking, but in the deepening snow it was impossible. With the first indications of night, I halted in a thick spruce grove near the river and drew together a fairly good supply of dead wood. On the under side of the branches of the fir trees was generally to be found a thick growth of hairy moss, and with a handful of this as tinder it did not take me long to get a good fire blazing. Close to the fire, I threw a pile of spruce boughs that I broke from low branches and the smaller trees. I melted snow in my cup for water, and in this put a few lumps of mold from the flour bag, eating the mixture after it had cooked a while. On the couch of boughs by the fire I spent a fairly comfortable night, waking only at intervals to throw on more wood and shake the snow from my back.

The storm was still raging in the morning (Wednesday, October 21). With the first grey streaks of dawn, I boiled another cup of snow water and mold, and then, slinging the flour bag over my shoulder, began my day's struggle. The snow was now knee-deep. Soon I reached the fording place. The river was beginning to freeze over. For two or three yards from shore the ice bore my weight; then I sank up to my waist in the cold current. Approaching the other shore, I broke the outer ice with my arms until it became thick enough to permit me to climb out upon it.

The ice that immediately formed on my clothing made walking impossible, and reluctantly I halted to build a fire and dry myself. This took fully an hour and a half, to my extreme vexation. I realized now that my hope of reaching Hubbard that night was vain. While I dried my clothing, I made a cup of tea. I had just enough left for two brewings, so after drinking the tea I preserved the leaves for further use, wrapping them carefully in a bit of rag. Once more on my way up the valley, I found, to my consternation and almost despair, that my eyes would again compel me to stop, and for nearly an hour I sat with them closed. That night, with the snow still falling, though very lightly, I made my couch of boughs by a fairly comfortable fire, and rested well.

On Thursday morning (October 22) a light snow was falling, and the weather was very cold. The cup of thin gruel that I made from the green lumps of mold nauseated me, and I had to brew some tea to settle my stomach and stimulate me. With my piece of blanket drawn over my head to protect my ears from the biting wind, and with my hands wrapped in the folds, I continued my struggle towards camp. I had to force my way, blindly and desperately, through thick clumps of fir trees, and as the branches were hanging low under their weight of feathery snow, I continually received a deluge of snow in my face.

My stock of matches was small and time was precious, and I did not stop at noon to build a fire. Even when night began to close in upon me I still plodded on, believing that I now must be near Hubbard. The snow was falling gently, and as there was a moon behind the clouds the night was sufficiently light for me to make my way tediously through the trees, with the roar of the rapids to guide me. It must have been near midnight when, utterly exhausted, I was forced to abandon the hope of finding Hubbard before morning. Fearing that the mold would again sicken me, I ate nothing when I halted; I simply collected a few dry sticks and huddled for the remainder of the night by a miserable fire, dozing and awaking with a shudder from awful dreams.

The storm continued during the night, and with the morning of Friday (October 23) broke upon the world and me with renewed fury. I prepared myself another dose of the mold, and forced it down. I was nervously anxious to get on and find Hubbard. I knew I must be near him now, although the snow had changed the whole face of the country and obliterated all the landmarks. Soon I crossed a brook, frozen and covered with snow, that I felt must be the one near our camp. Eagerly I looked about me for the tent. Because of the falling snow and the snow-bent branches, I could scarcely see twenty yards in any direction. From snow-covered rock to snow-covered rock I went, believing each in turn to be the tent, but always to meet disappointment. Repeatedly I stopped to peer into the maze of snow for smoke. But there was none. Again and again I shouted. But there was no answer. The tent was really near me, but it kept its secret well.

I travelled on and on. I became desperate. Over and over I repeated to myself, "I must find Hubbard before night comes— I *must* find him—I must—I must." At length the first signs of night warned me that I must collect my wood, that I might be as comfortable as possible through the dreary hours of darkness. As night came on the storm moderated. The wind ceased. An unwonted, solemn, awful stillness came upon the world. It seemed to choke me. I was filled with an unutterable, a sickening dread. Hubbard's face as I had last seen it was constantly before me. Was he looking and waiting for me? Why could I not find him? I must find him in the morning. I must, I *must*. Before going to sleep I made some more gruel and tea, drinking them both as a duty.

The snow was falling gently on Saturday (October 24), the wind had mercifully abated, and the temperature was somewhat milder. After more gruel and the last cup of tea I was to have in my lonely wanderings, I renewed my search for Hubbard. I decided that possibly I was below the camp, and pushed on to the westward. Finally I became convinced I was in a part of the country I had never seen before. I began to feel that possibly I was far above the camp; that a rescuing party had found Hubbard, and that, as my tracks in the snow had been covered, they had abandoned the hope of finding me and had returned. They might even have passed me in the valley below; it was quite possible. But perhaps George's strength had failed him, and help never would come to any of us.

I turned about, and again started down the valley. After a time I attempted to cross the ice on the river, to try and discover some familiar landmark on the south shore. In midstream, where the current had not permitted thick ice to form, I broke through. The water was nearly up to my armpits. Standing there with the icy current swirling about me, I said, "What's the use?" It seemed to me I had reached the limit of human endurance. Instead of trying to struggle on, how much pleasanter to permit myself to sink beneath the water and thus end it all! It would be such a relief to die.

Then there came to me the remembrance that it was my duty to live as long as I could. I must do my best. As long as I had any strength left, I must exert myself to live. With a great effort I climbed out on the hard ice, and made my way back to the north shore. Night was approaching. I staggered into the spruce growth, and there came upon the same brook I have previously mentioned as crossing. Near its bank I made my night fire. That fire was within two hundred yards of the tent. Perhaps it is just as well that I did not know it.

The snow, which had fallen rather mildly all day, thickened with the coming of night. All the loose wood was now buried under the snow, and it was with difficulty that I gathered a scant supply for the night. My wet rags were freezing hard and stiff. I moved about, half-dazed. I broke only a few branches for my bed, and sat down. Scarcely had I done so when a woman's voice came to me, kindly and low and encouraging.

"Hadn't you better break a few more boughs?" it said. "You will rest better then."

There was no mistaking the voice. It was clear and distinct. It was the voice of my wife, who had been dead for more than three years. I remember it did not impress me as being at all strange that my wife, who was dead, should be speaking to me up there in the Labrador wilderness. It seemed to me perfectly natural that she should be looking after my comfort, even as she had done in life. I arose and broke the boughs.

I am not a spiritist. I have never taken any stock in the theory that the spirits of the dead are able to communicate with the living. So far as I have thought about them at all, it has been my opinion that spiritists are either fools or frauds. But I am endeavoring to give a faithful account of my feelings and sensations at the time of which I am writing, and the incident of the voice cannot be ignored. Perhaps it was all a delusion—a hallucination, if you will, due to the gradual breaking down of my body and mind. As to that, the reader can form his own conclusions. Certain it is, that from this time on, when I needed help and encouragement the most, I felt a vague assurance that my wife was by my side; and I verily believe, that if it had not been for this—hallucination, delusion, actuality, reality, or whatever it may have been—I should now be in a land where the truth about these things is probably known for certain.

At times I even thought I saw my wife. And often, often throughout those terrible days her voice came to me, kindly and low and encouraging. When I felt I really could plod no farther through the snow, her voice would tell me not to lose heart, but to do my best, and all would be right in the end. And when, wearied beyond measure at night, I would fall into a heavy sleep,

and my fire would burn low, a hand on my shoulder would
arouse me, and her voice would tell me to get up and throw on
more wood. Now and again I fancied I heard the voice of my
mother, who died when I was a boy, also encouraging and reassuring me. Indescribably comforting were those voices, whatever
their origin may have been. They soothed me, and brought balm
for my loneliness. In the wilderness, and amid the falling snow,
those that loved me were ministering unto me and keeping me
from harm. At least, so it seemed to me. And now, as I think of
those dear voices, and feel once more that loving touch on my
shoulder, there comes back to me that verse from the Psalm
George read at our parting—"For He shall give His angels charge
over thee, to keep thee in all thy ways."

It is all like a half-dream to me now. I know that after
Saturday night (October 24), when I bivouacked within a stone's
throw of Hubbard's tent, I lost all count of the days, and soon
could not recall even the month. I travelled on and on, always
down the valley. Sometimes I fancied I heard men shouting,
and I would reply. But the men did not come; and I would say
to myself over and over again, "Man proposes, God disposes; it
is His will and best for all."

The flour mold nauseated me to such an extent that for a
day at a time I could not force myself to eat it. The snow clogged
in all that was left of my cowhide moccasins (larigans), and I
took them off and fastened them to my belt, walking thereafter
in my stocking feet. I wore two pairs of woolen socks, but holes
already were beginning to appear in the toes and heels. The
bushes tore away the legs of my trousers completely, and my
drawers, which thus became the sole protection of my legs from
the middle of my thighs down, had big holes in them. Each night
I cut a piece of leather from my moccasin uppers, and boiled it
in my cup until morning, when I would eat it and drink the
water. I found afterward, carefully preserved in my match box,
one of the brass eyelets from the moccasins. Probably I put it
away thinking I might have to eat even that.

I knew there was something the matter with my feet; they
complained to me every night. They seemed to me like individu-

als that were dependent upon me, and they told me it was my duty to care for them. But I gave no heed to their complaints. I had enough to do to care for myself. My feet must look out for themselves. Why should *I* worry about them?

And still it snowed, night and day—sometimes gently, sometimes blindingly; but always it snowed. Once while plodding along the side of a rocky hill, I staggered over the edge of a shelving rock and fell several feet into a snowdrift. I was uninjured, but extricating myself was desperately hard work, and it was very pleasant and soft in the snow, and I was so tired and sleepy. Why not give it up and go to sleep? But she was with me, and she whispered, "Struggle on, and all will be well," and reluctantly I dragged my poor old body out.

There were times when the feeling was strong upon me that I had been alone and wandering on forever, and that, like the Wandering Jew, I must go on forever. At other times I fancied I was dead, and that the snow-covered wilderness was another world. Instinctively I built my fire at night under the stump of a fallen tree, if I could find one; for the rotten wood would smolder until morning, and a supply of other wood was very hard to get.

One evening I remember crossing the river, which had now gone into its long winter sleep tucked away under a blanket of ice and snow, and building a fire under a rotten stump on the south side behind a bank near the shore. I felt that I must be well down the valley. My supply of wood was miserably small, but I had worked hard all day and could not gather any more. I fell down by the fire and struggled against sleep. She told me I must not sleep. When I dozed, her hand on my shoulder would arouse me. Thus the night passed.

At dawn I realized in a vague sort of way that the clouds had at last broken away; that the weather was clear and biting cold. Before me was the river. It had been a raging torrent when I first saw it; now it lay quiet and still under its heavy winter blanket. At my back the low bank with its stunted spruce trees hid the ridge of barren, rocky hills and knolls that lay beyond.

A few embers of the rotten stump were smoldering, sending

skyward, with each fitful gust of the east wind, a fugitive curl of smoke. A few yards away lay a dead tree, with its branches close to the snow. If I could break some of those branches off, and get them back to my smoldering stump, I might fan the embers into a blaze, get some heat and melt snow in my cup for a hot drink. Not that I craved the drink or anything else, but it perhaps would give me strength to go just a littler farther.

I pulled my piece of ragged blanket over my shoulders and struggled to my feet. It was no use. I swayed dizzily about, took a few steps forward and fell. I crawled slowly back to the smoldering stump and tried to think. I felt no pain; I was just weary to the last degree. Should I not now be justified in surrendering to the overpowering desire to sleep? Perhaps, I argued, it would strengthen me. I could no longer walk; why not sleep? But still I was told that I must not. . . .

Was Hubbard still waiting and watching for me to come back?—somewhere in that still wilderness of snow was he waiting and watching and hoping? Perhaps he was dead, and at rest. Poor Hubbard! . . .

Why did not the men come to look for us—the trappers that George was to send? Had they come and missed me, and gone away again? Or was George, brave fellow, lying dead on the trail somewhere below? How long had I been wandering, anyway? . . .

My sisters in faraway New York, were they hoping and praying to hear from me? Perhaps they never would. There was a certain grave in a little cemetery on the banks of the dear old Hudson. It had been arranged that I should lie beside that grave when I went to sleep forever. Would they find my bones and take them back? . . .

How enthusiastic Hubbard had been for this expedition! It was going to make his reputation, he thought. Well, well, man proposes, God disposes; it was His will and best for all. . . .

I found myself dozing, and with an effort to recover myself sat up straight. The sun was making its way above the horizon. I looked at it and hoped that its warming rays would give me strength to do my duty—my duty to live as long as I could. Any-

171

way, the storms had passed! the storms had passed!

I dozed again. It may have been that I was entering upon my final sleep. But gradually I became hazily conscious of an unusual sound. Was it a shout? I was aroused. I made a great effort and got on my feet. I listened. There it was again! It *was* a shout, I felt sure it was a shout! With every bit of energy at my command, I sent up an answering "Hello!" All was silent. I began to fear that again I had been deceived. Then over the bank above me came four swarthy men on snowshoes, with big packs on their backs.

# CHAPTER NINETEEN

# The Kindness of the Breeds

The unintelligible words that George shouted to me from the knoll after we parted on Tuesday (October 20) were an injunction to keep near the river, as the men he would send to rescue Hubbard and me would look for us there. As he proceeded down the valley his progress was slow and tedious, owing to his weakness, the rough country, and the deepening snow. Towards noon he came upon the newly made track of a porcupine, followed it a short distance into a clump of trees, where he soon saw the round quill-covered animal in the snow and shot it. Immediately he built a fire, and singed off quills and hair. Then, as he related to me afterwards, he considered, talking aloud to himself, what was best to do with his prize.

"There's them fellus up there without grub," he said. "Maybe I'd better turn about and take 'em this porcupine. But if I do, it won't last long, and then we'll be worse off than ever. This snow's gettin' deeper all the time, and if it gets so deep I can't walk without snowshoes, we'll all die for sure. No, I'd better go on with this porcupine to help me."

So after boiling a piece of the porcupine in his tea kettle and eating it, he continued down the valley. By his fires he always talked to himself to keep himself company, and that night he said:

"This's been a tough day, and I ain't where I ought to be. But I'll eat a good snack of this porcupine now with some of the flour, and in the mornin' I'll have another good snack, and that'll make me stronger and I can travel farther tomorrow. I ought to get most to Grand Lake tomorrow night."

But so far from getting anywhere near Grand Lake the next day, he did not complete his twenty-five-mile journey for several days to come. The snow became so deep he could hardly push through it. He carefully hoarded the bones of his porcupine, thinking he might have to eat them; but Providence sent him more food. When the first porcupine was eaten, he came upon and killed another, and when that was gone, he shot a third. He also succeeded in shooting several grouse. If it had not been for this game, he would not have lived to do the hard work that was before him.

The pieces of blanket in which his feet were wrapped were continually coming off, and frequent halts were necessary to readjust them. He must not let his feet freeze; for then he would not be able to walk, and not only would he perish himself, but "there'd be no hope for them fellus up there." One day he came upon a man's track. He was exultant. That it was a trapper's trail he had no doubt. Staggering along it with all the speed he could command, he shouted wildly at every step. Presently he discovered that he was following his own trail; he had been travelling in a circle. The discovery made him almost frantic. He stopped to reason with and calm himself. Said he, so that all the listening wilderness might hear:

"Them fellus up there in the snow have got to be saved. I said to Hubbard, 'With God's help I'll save you,' and I'm a-goin' to if my legs hold out and there's anybody at Grand Lake." And then he went on.

His progress down the valley that day was only a mile and a half. It was most discouraging. He must do better. The powdered milk we had abandoned he did not find, but on October 26 he recovered our old lard pail. Some of the lard he ate, some he used in cooking a grouse, and the rest he took along with him.

Below the place where he bivouacked that night the snow was not so deep, and early the next morning George once more beheld the broad waters of Grand Lake. The journey he had expected to make in three days had actually taken him seven. He arrived at Grand Lake three days after I, wandering in the valley above, lost all track of time.

A few miles above its mouth the Susan River bends to the southward, and from that direction reaches the little lake that lies just north of the extreme western end of Grand Lake, so that George, proceeding down the river on the south bank, even-

tually came to the little lake's western shore. Along this shore
he made his way until he reached the point of land formed by
the little lake and the branch of the Beaver River that flows a
little south of east to merge its waters in the little lake with those
of the Susan. The water here had not been frozen, and George
found his further progress arrested. He was in a quandary. The
trapper's tilt for which he was bound was on the south shore of
Grand Lake about seven or eight miles from its western end,
and in order to reach the tilt he would have to continue on south
around the end of the lake.

The land on the other side of the swirling stream to which
George had come was the island at the mouth of the Beaver that
separates it into two branches, and which forms the western
shore of the swift stream or strait that, flowing to the southward,
discharges the waters of the little lake into Grand Lake. George
thought, however, that this island was a part of the western
boundary of Grand Lake, and he determined to reach it. But
how? To swim across was impossible. Well, then, he would build
a raft. And, although he had no implements, he did. He hauled
together several fallen trees, laid them in a row and bound them
at one end with his pack strap and at the other with a piece of
our old trolling line. When this was done, he hacked himself a
pole with his sheath knife, threw his bag containing a piece of
a porcupine and some grouse on the raft, launched it, jumped
on it himself and pushed out into the stream.

One or two good shoves George gave with his pole, and
then found he no longer could touch bottom. He was at the
mercy of the swift current. Down into the little lake he was swept,
and thence through the strait right out into Grand Lake. A high
sea was running, and the frail raft promptly began to fall to
pieces. "Have I escaped starvin' only to drown?" thought George.
It certainly looked like it. "But," said he to himself, "if I drown
them fellus up there will be up against it for sure." So he determined not to drown. He got down on his hands and knees, and,
although the icy seas broke relentlessly over him, he held the
floating sticks in place, at the same time clinging tenaciously to
his food bag; for, as he confided to me later, "it would have been

just as bad to escape drownin' only to starve as it would have been to escape starvin' only to drown."

Farther out on the broad bosom of the lake George was carried. "Now," said he, "if I jump, I'll drown; and if I don't, I'll drown anyway. So I guess I'll hang on a little longer." And hang on he did for something like two hours, when the wind caught his raft and drove it back to the southern end of the island at the mouth of the Beaver. "You can't lose me," said George, as he landed. He and his game bag were saved, but his difficulties were not ended by any means.

While the wind was driving him back, George caught sight of the branch of the Beaver that flows almost due south directly into Grand Lake, forming the island's western shore. Standing on this shore, he made a shrewd guess. "I'll bet," he said, "my dream was right, and here we have the same river we were on when we said good-bye to the canoe." What interested him the most, however, was a rowboat he espied a little south of the island on the opposite shore. Apparently it had been abandoned. "If I can reach that boat," said George, "and it'll float, and I don't find Blake or any grub at his tilt, I'll put right off for the post, and send help from there to them fellus up there."

There was no doubt about it, he would have to take chances with another raft. Although his rags were beginning to freeze to his body, he did not stop to build a fire, neither did he wait to eat anything. At first it seemed hopeless to try to launch a raft; for the bank on the western side of the island was very steep. Farther north, however, ice had formed in the river for some distance from the shore, and to this ice George dragged fallen trees and bound them as he had done before. It was the labor of hours, the trees having to be dragged for considerable distances. Once more afloat, George found no difficulty in touching bottom with his pole, and in the gathering dusk he reached the other shore.

Supposing that he was still many miles from a place where there was any possibility of finding a human being, he decided to bivouac for the night; but first he must examine the rowboat he had sighted from the island. This made necessary the fording of a small stream. Hardly had he emerged from the water, when, from among the spruce trees farther back from the shore, there came a sound that brought him to a sudden standstill and set his heart to thumping wildly against his ribs. It was a most extraordinary sound to hear when one supposed one was alone in a wilderness, and when all had been solemnly still save for the dashing of waves upon a shore. On the night air there came floating to George the cry of a little child.

"When I heard that youngster scream," said George, in telling me about the incident, "I knew folks was there, and I dropped my bag, and I tore my piece of blanket from my shoulders, and I runned and I runned."

In the course of the summer Donald Blake had built himself a log house on the spot to which George was so wildly fleeing. The rowboat George had spied belonged to him, but the house, standing back in a thick clump of trees, had not been visible from the water. On the evening of George's arrival, Donald and his brother Gilbert were away, and Donald's wife and another young woman who stayed with her to keep her company were alone. The latter young woman, with Mrs. Blake's baby in her arms, was standing at the door of the house, when suddenly she heard a crashing noise in the bush in front of her, and the next moment there loomed up before her affrighted vision in the gloaming the apparition of a gaunt and ragged man, dripping wet, and running towards her with long, black hair and straggling beard streaming in the wind. She turned and fled into the house.

"O Mrs. Blake! O Mrs. Blake!" she cried, "'tis somethin' dreadful comin'! 'tis sure a wild man!"

Greatly alarmed, Mrs. Blake went to the door. George, panting and still dripping, stood before her.

"Lord ha' mercy!" she piously exclaimed, throwing up her arms.

"Don't be scared, ladies," panted George; "I couldn't hurt a rabbit. Ain't there any men here?"

His ingratiating manner reassured the frightened women, and explanations followed. All the natives of the vicinity of Hamilton Inlet had been wondering what had become of us, and

177

Mrs. Blake quickly grasped the situation. Kindness itself, she took George in. Donald and Gilbert, she said, would be back directly. She made him hot tea, and put on the table for him some grouse stew, molasses, and bread and butter, all the time imploring him to sit down and warm himself. But George was too excited to sit down. Up and down he paced, the melting ice on his rags making tiny rivulets on his hostess' spotless floor. Most of the breeds who live near the western end of Hamilton Inlet are remarkably cleanly, this probably being due to their Scotch blood.

George at length calmed himself sufficiently to turn his attention to the meal that had been prepared for him. He had salt for his meat, molasses to sweeten his tea and a bountiful supply of good bread. He ate greedily, which fact he soon had cause to regret; for later in the evening he began to bloat, and for several days thereafter he writhed with the colic. But for the present he thought of nothing save the satisfaction of the appetite that had been regenerated by the food he had been able to obtain after leaving me. It was especially difficult for him to tear himself away from the bread. As there must be an end to all things, however, George eventually stopped eating, and then he started to go for his bag. But Mrs. Blake said:

"No, Donald'll get he. Sit down, sir, and rest."

A little later Donald and Gilbert appeared. We had made Donald's acquaintance, it will be remembered, at Rigolet; it was he who had sailed his boat up the Nascaupee and had given us the most information about that river. When he had heard George's story, there was no need to urge him to make haste. Lithe, ambitious, and in the habit of doing a dozen things at a time, Donald was activity itself. His brother Gilbert, a young fellow of seventeen, commonly called Bert, was also eager to start to the rescue of Hubbard and me. They told George it was fortunate he had arrived when he did, as in a day or so they would have been away on their trapping paths.

"But didn't you see Allen Goudie's tilt, sir?" asked Donald, when George had finished telling about his trip down what he supposed to be the Nascaupee River. "She's on th' Nascaupee right handy to th' bank, and in fair sight from th' river, sir."

"If there's a tilt on the Nascaupee," said George, "you can kick me."

Donald asked him to tell more about the river we were on, and George drew a rough map of its leading features. Then it was that George learned that the river of our distress was really the Susan.

"And we passed right by the mouth of the Nascaupee?" he asked.

He was informed that such was the case.

"Well," said George, "I'll be blamed!" "Blamed" was George's most violent expletive: I never heard him use profanity.

Donald told George he must not think of going back with the rescuing party, as his weakness would retard its progress. So George marked on the map he had made of the Susan's course the general situation of our last camp. He warned Donald that the deep snow up the valley might have prevented me from reaching the tent, but that in any event they would find me near the river.

Hearing that, Donald quickly decided that more men were needed for the rescuing party; for if either Hubbard or I was found alone the party would have to separate in order to continue the search for the other man. The packs, besides, would be too heavy for two men to carry and make the rapid progress that was necessary. Fortunately Allen Goudie and a young fellow named Duncan McLean were at the former's winter tilt on the Nascaupee, seven miles across the lake from Donald's. The hour was late and the lake was rough, but Donald and Gilbert started for them in their rowboat immediately after making ready their packs of provisions and camp equipment, prepared for an early start up the Susan the next day.

At noon (October 28) they were back with both Allen and Duncan, and at once loaded the packs into the boat. Then the four men rowed up through the little lake to the first rapid on the Susan, hauled the boat up on the shore, donned their snow-shoes, shouldered their packs, and started up the valley. Running when they could, which the rough country would not permit of their doing often, they camped at night ten miles above their boat.

The next morning (October 29) they cached some provisions to lighten their packs, and as they proceeded fired a rifle at intervals, thinking there was now a chance of coming upon either Hubbard or me. As a matter of fact they must have passed me towards evening. They were on the north side of the river, and it was the evening when I staggered down the north shore, to cross the ice at dusk and make my last bivouac in the lee of a bank on the south shore. Whether I had crossed the river before they came along, or whether, hidden by the trees and the falling snow, I passed them unobserved on the same shore, I do not know; the fact is, they camped that night about a mile and a half above me, and about twelve miles below Hubbard's tent.

There was only one thing that saved me from being left alone to die—these trappers' keen sense of smell. In the morning (October 30) while they were breaking camp preparatory to continuing on up the valley, Donald Blake fancied that he smelled smoke. He spoke to Allen Goudie about it, and both men stood and sniffed the air. Yes, Allen smelled smoke, too. It was unmistakable. The wind was blowing up the valley; therefore someone must have a fire below them. Hastily finishing the work of breaking camp, the four men shouldered their packs and turned back.

Close down to the shore of the river they scrambled, and hurried on, shouting and discharging a rifle. At length they paused, to give exclamations of satisfaction. They had found my track leading across the ice to the other shore. Only a moment they paused, and then, following the trail, they broke into a run, redoubling their shouts and repeatedly discharging the rifle. They had smelled my smoldering rotten stump, but if a whiff of smoke was now rising it was too small for them to see. My trail, however, led them to the bank over which they heard my feeble answering shout. So down the bank they scrambled, to come to a sudden halt, transfixed with amazement, as they told me afterwards, that such a wreck as I could stand and live.

The spectacle I presented certainly must have been an unusual one—a man all skin and bones, standing in drawers and stocking feet, with the remnants of a pair of trousers about his hips, there in the midst of the snow-covered forest. They were heavily clad and had their caps pulled far down over their ears to protect them from the biting wind, while I did not even have my hat on.

It was some time before I could realize that living men were before me. As if in a half-dream, I stood stupidly gazing at them. But with the return of sensibility I recollected that George had gone to find Donald Blake, and gradually it dawned upon me that he was there. I spoke his name—"Donald Blake." At that Donald stepped forward and grasped my hand warmly and firmly like an old friend.

"Did George get out and send you?" I asked.

"Yes, sir; it was he that sent us, sir. He's safe at my house."

"Have you found Hubbard?"

"Not yet, sir. We smelled smoke a mile and a half above, where our camp was last night, an' came down to find you, sir."

I remember telling Donald that he had better leave me something to eat, and go on to Hubbard as fast as he could. He replied that Duncan and Bert, the two young fellows, would stay with me, while he and Allen would continue on up the valley. During this talk, the kind-hearted trappers had not been idle. While two of them cut wood for a rousing fire and put the kettle on for tea, the others made a cozy couch close to the blaze and sat me on it. They gave me a very small piece of bread and butter.

"You'd better eat just a small bit at first, sir," said Allen. "You're fair starved, and much grub at th' beginnin' might be th' worse for you."

Before I had my tea, Donald and Allen were ready to start. Allen hesitated for a moment; then asked:

"If the other man be dead, sir?"

"Dead?" I said. "Oh, no, he won't be dead. You'll find him in the tent waiting for you."

"But if he be dead?" persisted Allen. "He may be, and we sure can't bring th' body out now, sir."

Although still struggling against the fear that my reason told me was only too well founded, I requested, that in the event of what they thought possible proving to be the case, they wrap the body in the blankets they would find in the tent, and build for it a stage high enough from the ground to protect it from animals. I also asked that they bring back with them all the things they should find in the tent, including the rifle and camera, and especially the books and papers of all descriptions.

Promising that all should be done as I wished, and again cautioning me against eating too much, Allen and Donald departed, leaving me a prey to anxiety and fear as to the news they should bring back.

CHAPTER TWENTY

# *How Hubbard Went To Sleep*

A pot of hot tea soon was ready, and I drank some of it. "I hopes you feels better, sir," then spoke young Duncan McLean. "A smoke'll taste good now. Got a pipe, sir?"

I produced my pipe, and he held out to me a plug of tobacco. "Take he an' fill th' pipe, sir."

With the plug in my possession, I drew my sheath knife to cut it. But Gilbert Blake objected.

"He's a big un, sir, to cut tobacca with. Let me fill he, sir."

Obediently I handed him my pipe to be filled, and when it had been returned to me one of the boys struck a match and held it to the bowl while I puffed. Then Duncan took the plug from the log where Gilbert had left it, and, holding it out to me, said:

"He's yours, sir; I brought he for you. An'," added Duncan impressively, "there's more when he's gone, sir."

The tea and the great leaping blaze warmed me, the tobacco stimulated me, and my tongue was loosed. I talked and I talked. It was good to have human society and human sympathy again. The boys told me how George had finally reached them after his struggles, and what news of the world they had heard. After a little they gave me a bit more bread, and told me I had better sleep while they built a break to keep the wind, which had shifted to the west, from my couch. And, while watching them fell trees for the windbreak and vaguely wondering whether I should ever be strong and able to move about like that again, I did go to sleep.

When, after an hour had passed, I awoke, the boys made me drink more tea and eat another piece of bread. Then Duncan took his rifle, and remarking, "The's deer signs right handy, an' a bit o' deer's meat might do you good, sir," strode off into the bush. Late in the afternoon he returned without having been rewarded in his hunt, and took a seat with Gilbert near my feet as I reclined on the boughs. Twilight came and then darkness, and I, lying before the crackling flames, wondered, as they burned ever brighter, whether Donald and Allen had yet found Hubbard, and hoped against hope that they had found him alive. Instinctively I felt that I should prepare for the worst, but I cudgelled my brain for specious arguments to make myself believe he had survived, and went on hoping.

My feet had been paining me all day. I tried to take off my socks, but blood clots held them fast to the raw flesh. The fact was, they had been frozen. It was hardly to be wondered at—the wonder was, how I, wandering for ten days in a bitter snowstorm almost naked as to my lower extremities, escaped with my life. Under ordinary circumstances, a physician has told me, the exposure would have killed me in short order; but, having been living in the open for months, I had become gradually inured to the cold, and the effect of the exposure was thus greatly mitigated. There were only two or three nights on the entire trip when any of us went to bed with dry feet, and that none of us ever had the slightest symptom of a cold certainly speaks volumes for an out-of-door life.

Although I ate very sparingly on the day the trappers found me, I soon began to suffer greatly from bloating and nausea. In the night I was very ill. The boys did everything they could for me. They were excellent nurses, those rough, brown fellows of the forest, anticipating my every wish. When once or twice in the night I tried to walk a few steps from the fire to relieve my nausea, their faces and actions showed plainly their concern. That I might not stagger into the fire, they would rise to stand between it and me. One of them remained awake all night, to keep the fire going and to help me should I need anything.

The sun was again showing itself above the horizon, setting the expanse of fir trees and snow aglow, and the boys, having placed the kettle over the fire for breakfast, were cutting more wood, when Donald and Allen suddenly came over the bank, as they had done on the morning before. Their packs were as large as ever, and they had Hubbard's rifle. I knew at once that the worst had happened. "His wife and mother!"—like lightning the thought flashed through my mind. A dizziness came over me, and for a moment I could not breathe. Donald spoke:

"Yesterday evenin' we found th' tent, sir. He were fastened up tight with pins on th' inside, an' hadn't been opened since th' snow began. Says I to Allen, sir, 'Th' poor man's dead, 'tis sure he's dead.' An' Allen he opened th' tent; for I had no heart to do it, sir, and there th' poor man was, wrapped all up in th' blankets as if sleepin', sir. But he were dead, sir, dead; and he were dead for a long time. So there was nothin' to do but to wrap th' poor man safe in th' things that were there, an' bring back th' papers an' other things, sir."

We kept silent, we five men, until Donald added:

"We saw a place when right handy to th' tent where you'd had a fire by a brook, sir."

"Yes," I said; "I built that fire—so that really was the brook near our tent!"

"'Twere th' mercy of God, sir," said Allen, "that you didn't know th' poor man were there dead; you would ha' given up yourself, sir."

Having a superstitious horror of the dead, Donald would not touch the body, and without assistance Allen had been unable to place it on a stage as I wished. However, he arranged it carefully on the ground, where, he assured me, it would be perfectly safe. He suggested that I permit them to bury the body where it was, as it would be quite impossible to transport it over the rough country for weeks to come, or until Grand Lake had frozen solid and the ice on the Susan River rapids become hard enough to bear the weight of men with a sled. Both Donald and Allen were willing to go back to the log house on Grand Lake, and get the tools necessary for digging the grave.

But it would be bad enough for me to return home without Hubbard alive, and I felt that I simply must get the body out and take it with me. And, although the trappers could not understand my reasons, I refused to consent to its burial in the wilderness. In spite of their superior knowledge of the country and the weather conditions, I felt that the body could be taken down to the post later, but recognized the impracticability, if not impossibility, of undertaking the task immediately.

When Donald and Allen turned over to me the papers they had found in the tent, I took up Hubbard's diary wondering if he had left a last message. In the back part of the book was a letter to his mother, a note to his wife, the evident attempt again to write to his wife, and the letter to the agent at Missanabie written on George's behalf. From these I turned hastily to the diary proper. Yes, there was an entry written on the day George and I had left him, and this is what it read:

"Sunday, October 18th, 1903.

"Alone in camp, junction Nascaupee and some other stream—estimated (overestimated, I hope) distance above head of Grand Lake 33 miles.

"For two days past we have travelled down our old trail with light packs. We left a bit of flour—wet—about 11 miles below here—12 miles (approx.) below that about a pound of milk powder—4 miles below that about 4 pounds of lard. We counted on all these to help us out in our effort to reach the head of Grand Lake where we hoped to find Skipper Tom Blake's trapping camp and cache. On Thursday, as stated, I busted. Friday and Saturday it was the same. I saw it was probably hopeless for me to try to go farther with the boys, so we counselled last night and decided they should take merely half a blanket each, socks, etc., some tea, tea pail, cups and the pistols, and go on. They will try to reach the flour tomorrow. Then Wallace will try to bring a little and come back to me. George will go on to the milk and lard and to Skipper Blake's, if he can, and send or lead help to us. I want to say here that they are two of the very best, bravest and grandest men I ever knew, and if I die it will not be because they did not put forth their best efforts. Our past two days have been trying ones. I have not written my diary because so very weak. Day before yesterday we caught sight of a caribou, but it was on our lee, and winding us got away before a shot could be fired. Yesterday at our old camp we found the end we had cut from a flour bag. It had a bit of flour sticking to it. We boiled it with our old caribou bones, and it strengthened the broth a little. We also found a can of mustard we had thrown away. Mina gave it to me as we were coming away, saying she had no use for it and it might be good for plasters here. I sat and held it in my hand a long time thinking how it came from Congers and our home, and what a happy home it was, and what a dear, dear girl presided. Then I took a bite of it and it was very good. We mixed some in our bone soup and it seemed to stimulate us. We had a bit of caribou skin in that same pot. It swelled up thick and was very good. Last night I fell asleep while the boys were reading to me. This morning I was very, very sleepy. After the boys left—they left me tea, the caribou bones and another end of a flour sack found here, a rawhide caribou moccasin and some yeast cakes—I drank a cup of strong tea and some bone broth. I also ate some of the really delicious rawhide (boiled with bones) and it made me stronger—strong to write this. The boys have only tea and ½ pound of pea meal. Our parting was most affecting. I did not feel so bad. George said: 'The Lord help us, Hubbard. With His help I'll save you if I can get out.' Then he cried. So did Wallace. Wallace stooped and kissed my cheek with his poor, sunken bearded lips—several times—and I kissed his. George did the same, and I kissed his cheek. Then they went away. God bless and help them.

"I am not so greatly in doubt as to the outcome. I believe they will reach the flour and be strengthened, that Wallace will reach me, that George will find Blake's cache and camp and send help. So I believe we will all get out. My tent is pitched in open-tent style in front of a big rock. The rock reflects the fire, but now it is going out because of the rain. I think I shall let it go and close the tent till rain is over, thus keeping out wind and saving wood. Tonight or tomorrow perhaps the weather will improve, so I can build fire, eat the rest of my moccasins and have some more bone broth. Then I can boil my belt and oil-tanned moccasins and a pair of cowhide mittens. They ought to help some.

"I am not suffering. The acute pangs of hunger have given way to indifference. I'm sleepy. I think death from starvation is not so bad. But let no one suppose I expect it. I am prepared—that is all. I think the boys will be able, with the Lord's help, to save me."

Bravo, Hubbard! nothing could down your spirit for long, could there? So high was your spirit that you could not know it was impossible for your poor old body to hold it any longer. Your hand was firm when you wrote, b'y, speaking eloquently of that which most of all was you. "It is a man's game," you said one day, in referring to our desperate struggle to reach those we loved. Well, you played it to the limit, b'y, and it was a man's death. My friend, I am proud of you.

\*   \*   \*

Putting down the coverless book in which Hubbard's brave last words had been written, I sat and thought. The tea, the bones and the other things we had left with him had been found in the tent with the body. The tent was closed as he said he was going to close it, and the snow, which began to fall that Sunday night, had not been disturbed. He had been found well wrapped in the blankets, as if sleeping. Yes, it was quite evident that after making that last entry in his diary on the day we left him, he had lain down, and there all alone amid the solitudes of desolate Labrador, there in the wild that had called to him with a voice to which he must needs harken, had gone to sleep, and sleeping had not awakened.

# CHAPTER TWENTY-ONE

# *From out the Wild*

Donald and Allen returned at once to the log house on Grand Lake, leaving with the boys and me their tent and tent-stove. Donald also gave me a pair of high sealskin boots with large, soft moccasin bottoms. It was their expectation that we should remain in camp until they got back with other things to aid my journey out; but, although I was still very ill, and the heated tent was comfortable, I found waiting irksome, and at daylight the next morning (Sunday, November 1) the boys and I pulled up stakes. To protect my hands during the journey I made a pair of mittens from a piece of blanket duffel that had been brought back from the tent where Hubbard was.

A pretty good path had been trodden in the snow by the trips of my rescuers up and down the valley, and following along it, with Duncan and Gilbert on their snowshoes ahead of me packing it down still further, I did not sink very deeply; nevertheless, such was the condition of my feet that every step I took was painful. As the boys carried all that was to be carried, I managed, however, to walk about ten miles during the day. We camped at a place where the four trappers on their journey in had cached a fat porcupine. For supper I ate a bit of meat and drank some of the broth, and found it very nourishing.

On the following day we met Donald and Allen as they were returning to aid us. Allen brought with him a pair of trousers to cover my half-naked legs. At sunset we reached the rowboat, which had been left near the mouth of the Susan, and as we approached Donald's log house something more than an hour later a rifle was fired as a signal that we were coming. When we landed, George was there on the starlit shore to welcome us. I hardly knew him. His hair had been cut, he had shaved off his ragged beard, and he was dressed in clean clothing that Donald had lent him. He, of course, had heard of Hubbard's death from Donald and Allen, and when he clasped my hand in a firm grip to help me from the boat, he said:

"Well, Wallace, Hubbard's gone."

"Yes," I said, "Hubbard's gone."

He was good enough to say he was glad I had escaped, and then in silence we followed the trail up to the house—the first human habitation I had seen for months. There was only one room in the house, and there all of us, men and women alike, slept as well as ate; but it was scrupulously clean—the floor, table, chests and benches had been scoured until they shone—and to me it seemed luxurious. The family did everything for me that was within their power. Donald gave me fresh under-clothes, and his wife made me drink some tea and eat some rice and grouse soup before I lay down on the bed of skins and blankets they had prepared for me on the floor by the stove.

My two-days' walk had completely exhausted me, and I had a severe attack of colic and nausea. George then told me of his sufferings. Mrs. Blake, it appeared, had baked a batch of appetizing buns, and George, not profiting by his experience after his indiscretion on the night of his arrival, had partaken thereof with great liberality, the result being such as to induce the reflection, "Have I escaped drownin' and starvin' only to die of over-feedin'?"

The women of the household slept in bunks fastened to the wall, and while they prepared themselves for their night's rest the lamps were turned low and we men discreetly turned our backs. Just before this incident we had family worship, which consisted of readings from the Bible and the Anglican Book of Common Prayer, in accordance with the usual custom of the household. Donald, our host, professed not to be a religious man, but never a day passed that he did not offer thanks to his Maker, he regularly subscribed one-tenth of his income to the support of the Methodist Mission, he would not kill a deer or any other animal on Sunday if it came right up to his door, his whole life and his thoughts were decent and clean, and he was ever ready to abandon his work and go to the rescue of those who needed help. It may be thought strange that he should observe the forms of the Anglican Church in his family worship and subscribe to the Methodist Mission. The explanation is, that denominations cut absolutely no figure in Labrador; to those simple-hearted people, whose blood, for the most part, is such a queer mixture of Scotch, Eskimo, and Indian, there is only one church—the Church of Jesus Christ—and whenever a Christian missionary comes along they will flock from miles with the same readiness to hear him whatever division of the Church may claim his allegiance.

So accustomed had I become to living in the open that I soon found the atmosphere of the closed room unendurable, and several times during the night I had to go out to breathe. I was down on the shore of Grand Lake for a breath of the crisp winter air when the sun rose. It was glorious. Not a cloud was there in all the deep blue vault of the heavens, and, as the sunbeams peeked over Cape Corbeau, the lake was set a-shimmering and the snow on the surrounding hills radiated tiny shafts of fire. It was to me as if the sun were rising on a new world and a new life. Our hardships and their culminating tragedy seemed to belong to a dim and distant past. What a beautiful world it was after all! and how I thanked God that I lived!

Allen Goudie had offered George and me the use of his sailboat in returning to Northwest River Post, and it was agreed that he and Duncan should row us over to his tilt on the Nascaupee. So after breakfast George and I said good-bye to Donald and the rest of his household, and three hours later were welcomed by Allen's wife. Again we received every attention that kindly hearts could suggest. We remained at Allen's two days while he and Duncan made a pair of oars and fitted up the sailboat for our trip to the post. With the soap and warm water and bandages provided by Mrs. Goudie I was able to dress my feet. One foot especially had been affected, and from it I cut with a jackknife much gangrenescent flesh.

It was on Thursday morning, November 5, that George and I, warmly dressed in Donald's and Allen's clothes, set sail in a snowstorm for the post through the thin ice that was forming in the river. Upon reaching Grand Lake we found the wind adverse and the snow so thick we could not see our course, but after we had hovered about a fire on the shore until well into the afternoon, the wind shifted to the west and the storm abated, enabling us to proceed a little farther on our journey, or until signs of approaching night compelled us to take refuge in a trapper's tilt near Cape Blanc on the southern shore. This was the tilt that George, in his struggle out, had supposed he would have to reach to get help. It was about six by seven feet, and as it contained a tent-stove we were able to make ourselves comfortable for the night after our supper of tea and bread and butter and molasses thoughtfully provided by Mrs. Goudie.

The next morning was clear and beautiful, and although there was scarcely wind enough to fill the single sail of our little craft, we made an early start. Towards noon the wind freshened and soon was blowing furiously. The seas ran high, but George and I had become so used to rough weather and had faced danger so often that we ran right on in front of the gale, I at the tiller, and he handling the sail rope and bailing the water out when occasionally we shipped a sea. The rate at which we travelled quickly brought us to the rapid at the eastern end of the lake, and through this we shot down into the Little Lake, and thence through the strait known as the Northwest River out into Groswater Bay. It was about 3:30 in the afternoon when, turning sharply in below the post wharf, we surprised Mackenzie, the agent, and Mark Blake, the company's servant, in the act of sawing wood close down by the shore.

That they were astonished by the sudden appearance of the boat with its strange-looking occupants, was evident. They dropped their crosscut saw, and stood staring. In a moment, however, Mackenzie recognized George, who, having had a haircut and a shave, looked something like his old self, and came to the conclusion that the other occupant of the boat must be I. He came quickly forward, and, grasping my hand as I stepped from the boat, asked abruptly:

"Where's Hubbard?"

"Dead," I said. "Dead of starvation eighty miles from here."

Mark Blake, a breed but not related to Donald, took charge of George, and as Mackenzie and I walked to the post house, I gave him a brief account of Hubbard's death and my rescue. He had been warmly attracted to Hubbard, and his big heart was touched. I saw him hastily brush away a tear. Taking me into the kitchen, he instructed his little housekeeper, Lillie Blake, Mark's niece, to give me a cup of cocoa and some soda biscuit and butter, while he made a fire in the dining-room stove. Lillie cried all the time she was preparing my lunch.

"I feels so sorry for you, sir," she said. "An' 'tis dreadful th' poor man's starvin', an' he were such a pretty man. In th' summer I says, before you went t' th' bush, sir, he's sure a pretty man. 'Tis wonderful sad, 'tis wonderful sad t' have he die so."

Oh, that pleasant kitchen, with the floor and all the wood-work scrubbed white and the rows of shining utensils on the shelves! And the comfort of the great wood-burning stove roaring out a tune to us on that frosty winter evening! As I sat there sipping the deliciously rich cocoa, Mackenzie joined me, and while Lillie cooked the dinner I must tell him over and over again my story. And in spite of herself the tender-hearted little housekeeper would cry and cry.

The dinner, which consisted of grouse, potatoes, marmalade, bread, and tea, was served in the dining room, which was also the living room. Mackenzie sat at the head of the table, I at the foot, and on a lounge to one side sat Atikamish, a small Mountaineer Indian hunting dog, gravely alert for the bones his master would occasionally toss to him. Atikamish had very good table manners. He caught the bones neatly and deftly, and he invariably chewed them up without leaving his seat or changing his position. My appetite was returning, and I ate well; but it was fully two weeks before I could eat without experiencing distress later. When that blessed time arrived, I never could get enough; Lillie was always pressing me to eat, and for a time I had at least six meals a day.

After dinner Mackenzie got Mark Blake to cut my hair and shave off my beard. Then he took me to my room upstairs, where a stove was crackling out a welcome and a big tub of warm water had been prepared for me. After my bath, he again came up to rub my legs, which were much swollen from frostbite, and to dress my foot with salve. In a suit of Mackenzie's flannel pajamas I then went to my soft bed, and lay snug and warm under the blankets. It was the first real bed I had lain in for nearly four months, and oh, the luxury of it!

It is impossible for me to express the gratitude I feel towards those good friends. They nursed me with the tenderest care. Mackenzie's big Scotch heart and the woman's sympathetic instinct of the little housekeeper anticipated my every want, and he and she never could seem to satisfy themselves with doing things for my comfort. When I left the post with Hubbard I weighed 170 pounds; a week after my return I weighed 95. But with the care they took of me my general health was soon restored, and I rapidly put on flesh.

My difficulties, however, were not yet ended. Hubbard's body was still to be recovered from the wild and repatriated, and during the long months that ensued before it could be reached I lived in constant dread lest it should be destroyed by animals, until at length the dread amounted almost to an obsession. Moreover, the gangrene in my foot became worse, and if it had not been for the opportune arrival in that dreary land of an unfortunate young medical student, it in all likelihood would have killed me.

CHAPTER TWENTY-TWO

# A Strange Funeral Procession

The young medical student was George Albert Hardy,
of Prince Edward Island. Everybody called him "Doctor," and for all practical purposes he was a regular physician
and surgeon; for if he had been able to do two or three months'
more hospital work he would have received his degree. The
reason he had hastily abandoned his studies and sought profes-
sional service with the lumber company that maintains camps
at the western end of the Hamilton Inlet was that he had fallen
a victim to consumption. He arrived at Northwest River Post on
November 8 on a small schooner that brought supplies from
Rigolet for Mackenzie and the Muddy Lake lumber camp at the
mouth of the Grand River.

The schooner remained only an hour at Northwest River,
and Dr. Hardy had to continue on to Muddy Lake with her, but
he found time to operate on my left foot, which was badly affected, and advise me how to continue its treatment myself. The
doctor said that the mail boat, the *Virginia Lake*, which had carried
him to Rigolet, would return there within three weeks for her
last trip to Newfoundland of the season, and he urged me to
take advantage of that opportunity to go home, and get proper
treatment for my feet. The temptation was great, but I felt it
was my duty not to leave Labrador without Hubbard's body.

It was my plan to engage dog teams and start with the body
for the coast as soon as it could be brought to the post. Everybody
agreed that it could not be recovered before January, and Mackenzie argued strongly against the practicability of transporting
it with dogs, suggesting that we place it in the old post mission
chapel until navigation opened in the spring, when it could be
sent home on the mail steamer. But I knew I must get home as
soon as possible, and my mind was made up to take the body with

me, if I had to haul it all the way to Quebec.

The great toe on my left foot growing steadily worse, it became necessary for me again to see the doctor. Groswater Bay and Goose Bay by this time were frozen solid, and on December 4 I travelled to Muddy Lake, where Dr. Hardy was stationed, by dog team and komatik, Willie Ikey, an Eskimo employed by Monsieur Duclos, the manager of the French trading post across the Northwest River, acting as my driver. Upon my arrival I was cordially welcomed by Mr. Sidney Cruikshanks, the lumber "boss"; Mr. James McLean, the storekeeper, and Dr. Hardy. It was arranged that I should stop and sleep with the doctor at McLean's house. The doctor did some more cutting, and under his careful treatment my foot so improved that it was thought I could with safety return to the post on December 15, to prepare letters and telegrams for the winter mail, which was scheduled to leave there by dog team for Quebec on the eighteenth. It was the twentieth before the mail got away, and with it went the first news of Hubbard's death to reach his relatives and friends.

My dispatches, forwarded from Chateau Bay, the outpost of the Canadian coast telegraph service, were received in New York on January 22, the letters two months later.

Immediately upon my return to Northwest River, my feet began to trouble me again. Word was sent to Dr. Hardy, who, regarding it as a call of duty, arrived on December 31. I very much regret to say, that in responding to the call, Dr. Hardy received a chill that hastened, if it did not cause, his death. After examining my feet upon his arrival, he advised me to return with him to Muddy Lake. So it was arranged that George, with Mackenzie's dogs and komatik, should drive Dr. Hardy and me to the Kenemish lumber camp, twelve miles across Groswater Bay, where there was a patient that required attention, and that from there Hardy and I should go on to Muddy Lake with other dogs. Alas! the doctor never saw Muddy Lake again.

Before starting, I learned from Allen Goudie and Duncan McLean, who came from the interior to spend New Year's Day, that Grand Lake was frozen hard and an attempt might be made to bring out Hubbard's body. Accordingly, I engaged Duncan

McLean and Tom Blake, also a breed, to undertake the task with George, and to recover, so far as possible, the photographic films and other articles we had abandoned at Goose Camp and Lake Elson. Blake was the father of Mackenzie's housekeeper, and lived at the rapid at the eastern end of Grand Lake. As he had, at the request of friends, frequently prepared bodies for burial, it was arranged that he should head the expedition, while George acted as guide, and the agreement was that, weather permitting the party should start inland on January 6. A coffin, made by the carpenter at Kenemish, was all ready to receive the body when it should arrive at the post.

George was to have driven Dr. Hardy and me to Kenemish on January 3, but as there was a stiff wind blowing and the thermometer registered 40 degrees below zero, we postponed our departure until the following day. The morning was clear, and the temperature was 34 below. The dogs, with a great howling and jumping, had hardly settled down to the slow trot which with only fair travelling is their habitual gait, when we observed that the sky was clouding, and in an incredibly short time the first snowflakes of the gathering storm began to fall. Soon the snow was so thick that it shut us in as with a curtain, and eventually even old Aillik, our leader, was lost to view.

"Bear well t' th' east'ard, an' keep free o' th' bad ice; the's sure t' be bad ice handy t' th' Kenemish," had been Mark Blake's parting injunction. So George kept well to the eastward as, hour after hour, we forged our way on through the blinding, drifting snow. At length we came upon land, but what land we did not know. The storm had abated by this time, and a fresh komatik track was visible, which we proceeded to follow. On all sides of us ice was piled in heaps as high as a house. We had been travelling altogether about six hours, and the storm had ceased, when we came upon a tilt on the shore of a deep bay, and, close by it, a man making passes with a stick at a large wolf, which, apparently emboldened by hunger, was jumping and snarling about waiting for a chance to spring in upon him.

The noise of our approaching komatik caused the wolf to slink off, and then the man hurried to the tilt, reappeared with a rifle and shot the beast as it still prowled among the ice hills. He proved to be Uriah White, a trapper. Not at all excited by his adventure, he welcomed us to his tilt. In throwing off his mittens to fire his rifle at the wolf, he had exposed his naked hands to the bitter cold, and they had been frostbitten. While thawing out his hands at a safe distance from the stove, he informed us that he had been "handy 'nuf to he [meaning the wolf] to see that he were a she."

The condition of my feet had not permitted me to leave the komatik during our long journey, and I suffered severely from the cold. George and, alas! Hardy, were also thoroughly chilled, though they had occasionally exercised themselves by running behind. Uriah prepared for us some hot tea and hardtack, and gave us our bearings. We were about four miles east of Kenemish, and an hour later we arrived there.

The lumber camp at the mouth of the Kenemish River is composed of a sawmill, a storehouse in which also live the native helpers, a cookhouse, a part of which is given over to lodgings for the Nova Scotian lumbermen, and a log stable for the horses that do the general work about the camp and in the woods. Hugh Dunbar, the engineer, extended a warm welcome to the doctor and me, and his wife, who did the camp cooking, made us comfortable in the cookhouse. I was destined to remain at the camp for many weeks, and I cannot help testifying to the gratitude I feel to those lumber folk, especially Mr. and Mrs. Dunbar; Wells Bently, the storekeeper; Tom Fig, the machinist; and Archie McKennan, Leigh Stanton and James Greenan.

The chill he had received during the trip from Northwest River so affected Dr. Hardy that he was unable to proceed to Muddy Lake. Two days after our arrival he had a severe hemorrhage, and the following day another. They forced him to take to his bed, and thereafter he rose only occasionally for half an hour's rest in a chair. He was a deeply religious nature, and, realizing that he was doomed, he awaited the slow approach of death with calm resignation.

And my feet steadily grew worse. Three days after our arrival at Kenemish I could not touch them to the floor. The doctor and

I lay on couches side by side. I could not even bear the weight of the bedclothes on my feet, and Dunbar built a rack from the hoops of an old flour barrel to protect them. Under the doctor's direction, Mrs. Dunbar every day removed the bandages from my feet, cleansed them with carbolic acid water and rebandaged them. Dunbar and the other men carried me in their arms when it was necessary for me to be taken from my couch. My temperature ran up until it reached 103½. The doctor then said there was only one way to save my life—to cut off my legs.

"And," he added, "I'm the only one here that knows how to do it, and I'm too weak to undertake it. So we're both going to die, Wallace. There's nothing to fear in that, though, if you trust in God."

The doctor was an accomplished player of the violin, but he had left his own instrument at Muddy Lake, and the only one he could obtain at Kenemish was a miserable affair that gave him little satisfaction. So while he lay dying by the side of his patient who he thought was also dying, he, for the most part, gratified his love of music and sought to comfort us both by softly singing in his sympathetic tenor voice the grand old hymns of the church. "Lead Kindly Light" and "Nearer My God to Thee" were his favorites, and every syllable was enunciated clearly and distinctly.

But he was mistaken in thinking that I, too, was to die. Soon there was an improvement noticeable in the condition of both of my feet, and gradually they grew better.

"It's truly a miracle that the Lord is working," said the doctor. "You were beyond human aid. I've prayed from the bottom of my heart that you'd get well. I've prayed a dozen times a day, and now the prayer is answered. It's the only one of my prayers," he added sadly, "that has been answered since I have been in Labrador."

During January and February the cold was terrific. The spirit thermometer at the camp was scaled down to 64 degrees below zero, and on several days the spirit disappeared below the scale mark before eight o'clock in the evening. For a week the temperature never, even at midday, rose above 40 below. The old natives of the bay said there never had been such a winter before. Not a man in the camp escaped without a frozen nose and the cheeks and chins of all of them were black from being nipped by the frost. Bently declared that he froze his nose in bed, and Mrs. Bently bore witness to the truth of the statement. But Bently's nose was frosted on an average of once a day.

Nearly all of this time I lay at the lumber camp worrying about Hubbard's body. One day late in January, when I had been hoping that the body had been safely brought out, Mackenzie and George arrived from Northwest River with the news that the storms had been so continuous it had not been deemed wise to attempt the journey inland. I wished to be removed at once to the post, thinking that my presence there might hasten matters, but Dr. Hardy said there would be no use of having two dead men, and I was forced to be content with promises that the expedition would get under way as soon as possible.

Early in February the doctor said I might try my feet on the floor. The result was the discovery that my knees would not bear me, and that I should have to learn to walk all over again. Recovering the use of my legs was a tedious job, and it was not until February 29 that I was able to return to Northwest River. After leaving Kenemish I never saw the unfortunate young doctor again; for he died on March 22.

Back at Northwest River, I was able to stir things up a bit, and bright and early on Tuesday morning, March 8, George, Tom Blake, and Duncan MacLean, composing the expedition that was to recover Hubbard's body, at last left the post, prepared for their difficult journey into the interior. I regretted much that my physical condition made it impossible for me to accompany them. Their provisions were packed on an Indian flat sled or toboggan, and their tent and other camp equipment on a sled with broad flat runners that I had obtained especially for the transportation of the body from some Indians that visited the post. At the rapid they were to get Tom Blake's dogs to haul their loads to Donald Blake's at the other end of Grand Lake. After that, the hauling was all to be done by hand, as it is quite impossible to use dogs in cross-country travelling in Labrador.

In the course of the afternoon snow squalls developed, and all day Wednesday and Thursday the snow fell heavily. I knew the storm would interfere with the progress of the men, but I hoped they had succeeded in reaching Donald's, and were at that point holding themselves in readiness to proceed. What was my disappointment, then, when towards noon on Sunday Douglas and Henry Blake, Tom's two young sons, came to the post to announce that their father was at home! He had made a start up Grand Lake, they said, but the storms had not permitted the party to advance any farther than the Cape Corbeau tilt.

Douglas had accompanied the men to Cape Corbeau, which point it had taken an entire day to reach, as the dogs, even with the men on their snowshoes tramping a path ahead, sank so deeply in the snow that they could hardly flounder along, to say nothing of hauling a load. It was evident, therefore, that the dogs would retard rather than accelerate the progress of the party on Grand Lake, and when the Cape Corbeau tilt was reached on Tuesday night it was decided that Douglas should take them back to the rapid. On Wednesday morning the storm was raging so fiercely that it was considered unsafe to go ahead for the present. George, moreover, complained of a lame ankle, and said he required a rest. So Tom came to the conclusion that if he remained at the tilt he would be eating the "stock of grub" to no purpose, and when Douglas turned homeward with the dogs he went with him. George and Duncan were to stay at the tilt until the travelling became better, Douglas said, and then push on to Donald's and wait for Tom there.

Douglas' story made it plain that the weather conditions on Grand Lake had been fierce enough to appall any man, but as there had been no snow since Friday night I could not understand what Tom was doing at the rapid on Sunday, and with Mackenzie's consent I had Mark immediately harness the post dogs and drive me up to his house. I arrived there considerably incensed by his inactivity, but I must say that his explanation was adequate. He asked me if I had been able to see anything of Grand Lake, and made me realize what it meant to be out there with a high west wind of Arctic bitterness drifting the snow in great clouds down its thirty-seven miles of unbroken expanse. There was no doubt that the men had done the best they could, and after instructing Tom that, if more provisions were needed, to obtain them at Donald's at my expense, and receiving from him an assurance that he would again start for Hubbard's body as soon as the weather would permit, I returned, mollified, to the post.

It was on this day (Sunday, March 13) that I received my first news from home and the outside world, Monsieur Duclos, who had been on a trip north, bringing me two telegrams from New York. They conveyed to me the comforting assurance that all was well at home, being replies to the dispatches I had sent in December. Received at Chateau Bay, they had been forwarded to me 350 miles by dog teams and snowshoe travellers.

Tom Blake started on Monday morning, the fourteenth, and Tuesday at noon joined George and Duncan at Donald's. On Wednesday the three men began their march up the Susan. The weather continuing fair, they made good progress and had no difficulty in finding the site of our last camp. Hubbard's body, with the tent lying flat on top of it, was under eight feet of snow. Near the spot a wolverine had been prowling, but the body was too deeply buried for any animal to scent it, and in its quiet resting place it lay undisturbed. It was fortunate that it had not been placed on a stage, as I had suggested; for in that event it would undoubtedly have been destroyed.

Continuing on inland, the men recovered the photographic films, the sextant, my fishing rod, and other odds and ends we had dropped on the trail as far back as Lake Elson. Tom and Duncan praised George unstintingly for the unvarying accuracy with which he located the things. With the country and smaller trees buried under a great depth of snow, and no landmarks to guide him, George would lead the other men on, and, with no searching about or hesitancy, stop and say, "We'll dig here." And not once did his remarkable instinct play him false.

"'Tis sure wonderful," said Tom, in telling me about it. "I ne'er could ha' done it, an' no man on Th' Labrador could ha' done it, sir. Not even th' Mountaineers could ha' done it." And Duncan seconded Tom's opinion.

\* \* \*

On Sunday, March 27, I was sitting in the cozy post house wondering where George and the others were, when suddenly George appeared from out the snow that the howling gale was whirling about. My long suspense was ended. The body had been recovered in good condition, George said. Wrapped in the blankets that Hubbard had round him when he died—the blankets he had so gaily presented me with that June morning on the *Silvia*—and our old tarpaulin, which George had recovered farther back on the trail, it had been dragged on the Indian sled forty miles down over the sleeping Susan River, and thence out over Grand Lake to the Cape Corbeau tilt, where the men had been compelled to leave it the day before owing to the heavy snowstorm that then prevailed. From the tilt the men had gone on to Tom's house at the rapid to spend the night, and George had now come down to the post to relieve my mind with the news that the body was safe.

It was arranged that the next morning George and Duncan should take the post dogs and komatik, drive up to Cape Corbeau and bring the body down. The morning was calm and fine, and they started early. It was a strange funeral procession that returned. The sun was setting when, on their way back, with the body lashed to the komatik, they passed over the rapid where Hubbard that beautiful July morning had sprung vigorously into the water to track the canoe into Grand Lake. How full of hope and pleasurable anticipation he had been when we paddled through the Little Lake! Over the snow and ice that now hid the lake the seven dogs that were hauling his corpse strained and tugged, ever and anon breaking into a trot as George and Duncan, running on their snowshoes on either side of the komatik, urged them forward with Eskimo exclamations or cracked their long whip over a laggard. No need to urge any one of them on, however, when they came in sight of the post. Darkness was falling. Knowing that their daily meal was near at hand, the dogs broke into a run, and with much howling and jumping swung around the point and up to the buildings.

# CHAPTER TWENTY-THREE

# Over the Ice

With the body at the post, it was my intention to hire dog teams, and, accompanied by George, start with it at once for home, travelling up Hamilton Inlet to the ocean, and then down along the coast to Battle Harbour, or some port farther south, where we might happen on a ship that would take us away from the land where we had suffered so much. More than three weeks elapsed, however, before we could get away from the Northwest River. It was about 325 miles over the ice to Battle Harbour, and Mackenzie and the others continued to argue against the feasibility of my plan. For a time it did seem as if it would be impossible to carry it out. First of all, I had trouble with Hubbard's coffin. When we received the body, the plain spruce box that had been made for it was found not to be deep enough. I sent over a request to James Greenan, the carpenter at Kenemish, that another one be made as speedily as possible. He replied that the last board they had on hand had been used in making a coffin for poor Dr. Hardy, but said that if I would return to him the coffin we had, he believed he could raise the sides to the requisite height. Mackenzie immediately dispatched Mark with the dogs and komatik to carry the coffin to Kenemish, and on April 4 it was returned with the necessary alterations. The body meanwhile had lain wrapped in the blankets and tarpaulin in a storehouse where the temperature practically was as low as it was out of doors. Now we placed it in the box with salt as a preservative, and everything was ready for our long journey.

Then arose the question as to where I could get dogs. Two teams were needed, one for the body and one for our baggage. Not a dog owner could I find who would undertake the task. I sent imploring messages for twenty-five miles around, but all to no purpose. They would not even undertake the ninety-mile journey to Rigolet. Some, I knew, did not like the idea of travelling with a corpse, and others, like Tom Blake, did not have enough dogs to haul our loads. In despair I went to Monsieur Duclos on April 19 and urged him to lend me his team to take us as far as Rigolet, telling him that Mackenzie was willing to let us have his team for the trip to Rigolet, but that another was needed. The French post dogs had just returned from a long journey, and Monsieur Duclos said they were not fit for travel, but finally, to my great joy, he very kindly consented to let me have them, with Belfleur, a French-Indian, as driver, after they had a couple of days' rest.

It was Mackenzie's custom to make an annual trip to Rigolet on post business, and this usually took place in May; but he expedited his arrangements so as to be able to leave with us and thus save his dogs an additional journey. Belfleur arrived with his dogs early on the morning of April 21. Unfortunately Fred Blake, Mackenzie's driver, was not on hand, but it was decided that Belfleur should go ahead with George and the coffin, and that Mackenzie and I should follow with the baggage the next morning. It was nine o'clock when the eight dogs that were to haul the two men and the coffin got under way. All the natives were sorry to see George go, his genial manners and cheerful grin having made him a prime favorite. Mackenzie's little housekeeper and Mark Blake's wife, who had been George's hostess, wept copiously.

Mackenzie, Fred Blake, and I got off at six o'clock the next morning. Our seven big dogs were howling and straining on the long traces as I said good-bye to all the good friends that had been so kind to me and had gathered to see me leave. It took us until evening of the following day to reach Rigolet. The Eskimo dogs almost invariably leave a house and arrive at one with a great flourish, but between times they settle down to a gentle pace and have to be urged on with exclamations and much snapping of the whip. Ours were much better travellers than those belonging to the French post, and, despite the fact that they had a heavier load to haul and were one less in number, we overtook George and Belfleur on the afternoon of the second day. A part of the time Mackenzie and Fred ran beside the komatik on their snowshoes to get warm, but my knees were still so weak that I had to stick to the komatik all the way. We spent the night at the log cabin of a breed, and before noon the next day came to the cabin of one Bell Shepard, where we learned George and Belfleur had spent their second night.

It is considered a gross breach of etiquette on The Labrador to pass a man's house without stopping for bread and tea, and so we had to turn in to see Bell. As he served us with refreshment, he gave us a startling bit of news, to wit: that there was a great war raging in the outside world, with Great Britain, the United States, and Japan on one side, and Russia, France, and Germany on the other.

"I's sure 'tis true, sir," he insisted, upon observing that Mackenzie and I appeared incredulous. "I's just come from Rigolet, an' Scott, th' trader, had th' word by th' telegraph to Chateau. So 'tis sure true, sir, an' 'tis bad word for us poor folk on Th' Labrador, with th' prices to go up, as they tells me they sure will, on flour an' pork."

We found out later that such a report had really spread up the coast from dog driver to dog driver until it had reached Rigolet, and it was not until I got to Battle Harbour that I learned that its basis was the beginning of the conflict between Russia and Japan.

At Rigolet we were again hospitably received by Fraser, the factor. The news of Hubbard's death had preceded us; in fact it had been carried up and down the coast all the way from Cape Charles to Cape Chidley. Awaiting me was a letter from Dr. Cluny Macpherson, of the Deep Sea Mission at Battle Harbour, who, I was informed, had recently been to Rigolet and had hoped to see me. The letter proved to contain much valuable information as to stopping places and the probabilities of getting dogs between Rigolet and Battle Harbour, as well as the good news that a steamer was expected at Battle Harbour early in May.

I also learned from Fraser that Mr. Whitney, editor of *Outing* magazine, of which Hubbard had been the associate editor, had sent a message to the telegraph operator at Chateau Bay requesting him to lend me every assistance possible and "to spare no expense." Well-meant though the message was, it had the effect of increasing my difficulties. Duly exaggerated and embellished, it had spread up the coast until every dog owner gained the impression that a little gold mine was about to pass through his country. I found this out when I tried to get dog teams to carry me to Cartwright Post, the next stage on my journey. A haughty person named Jerry Flowers, it appeared, had a monopoly just then of the dog-team business in the vicinity of Rigolet, and when we arrived at the post he proceeded to deal with me in the high-handed manner common to trust magnates. The regular rate paid by traders for transportation over the eighty odd miles between Rigolet and Cartwright was from ten to twelve dollars a team, but for the two teams I needed Jerry expected me to pay him sixty dollars.

While I was still arguing with the immovable Jerry, John Williams, an old livyere, fortunately arrived from West Bay, which is halfway to Cartwright, and Fraser used his influence with John to such good purpose that he consented to take us with his dog team at least as far as his home at the regular rate. John had only six dogs, but he told us we should be able to get an additional team at William Mugford's two miles beyond Rigolet.

The strait at Rigolet was open, and when, late in the afternoon of Monday, April 25, we bade Mackenzie and Fraser farewell, George and I, with our baggage and Hubbard's body, were taken across through the cakes of floating ice in one of the Company's big boats, manned by a crew of brawny post servants.

On the other shore we loaded the baggage and coffin on John's komatik, and with him driving the dogs and George and I walking behind on snowshoes, we reached Mugford's at dusk. There we stopped for the night, being served with the meals that the people all down the coast usually eat at that time of the year—bread and molasses and tea. With one or two exceptions we had to sleep on the floor at the places where we stopped; for the houses generally contained only one room divided by a partition. Almost all of the houses had low extensions used as a storage place, and there Hubbard's body would rest overnight. Never did we pay anything for our entertainment; poor as the people are, they would be greatly offended if a traveller they took in offered them money.

Generally speaking, we had good weather for our long journey to Battle Harbour and pretty fair going. Day after day we followed the coast line south, crossing from neck of land to neck of land over the frozen bays and inlets. Sometimes we encountered ridges on the necks of land, and then we would have to help the dogs haul the loads to the top. Resuming our places on the komatiks, we would coast down the slopes, with the dogs racing madly ahead to keep from being run over. If the descent was very steep, a drag in the form of a hoop of braided walrus hide would be thrown over the front of one of the komatik runners, but even then the dogs would have to run their hardest to preserve a safe distance between them and us, and out on the smooth ice of the bays we would shoot, to skim along with exhilarating swiftness. As we proceeded south we were interested in observing signs of spring. Towards the end of our journey we encountered much soft snow and water-covered ice.

Mugford agreed to help us out with his four dogs as far as West Bay. Arriving there, we found that only one team was procurable for the rest of the trip to Cartwright, so John Williams continued on with us all the way. Forty or fifty miles a day is about all that dogs can be expected to accomplish with average going, and we spent two days between Rigolet and Cartwright, reaching the Hudson's Bay Company Post at Sandwich Bay on the evening of Wednesday, April 27, to receive kindly welcome from the agent, Mr. Swaffield. Again at Cartwright we had some difficulty in getting dogs, and it was not until Friday morning that we could push on. These delays were exasperating, for I was bent on catching the steamer that Dr. Macpherson informed me in his letter was due at Battle Harbour early in May.

Our journey resumed, it was a case of fighting dog owners all the way. Seal Islands, about ninety miles farther down the coast, we reached on Saturday night, April 30. There we had the good fortune to be entertained by a quaint character in the person of Skipper George Morris, a native trader. He had been expecting us, and he greeted me as if I had been his long-lost brother.

"Dear eyes!" he exclaimed, wringing my hand in his bluff, cordial way; "Dear eyes! but I'se glad to see you—wonderful glad!"

The skipper's house was far above the average of those on the coast. It had two floors with two rooms each, and his good wife kept everything clean and bright. Soon after our arrival the skipper got out for our edification two shotguns—one single, and the other double-barrelled—each of which was fully six feet long from butt to muzzle and had a bore of one and one-half inches.

"Th' Boers ha' been fightin' England," said he, "an' I got un [the gun] t' fight, sir. Dear eyes! if th' Boers ha' come handy t' us, I thinks I could ha' kept un off, sir. I *knows* I could wi' *them* guns. I'd sure ha' shot through their schooners, sir, if un was big as th' mail boat an' steamers like th' mail boat. I'd ha' shot through un, sir, an' th' mail boat's a big un, sir, as you knows."

The next day was May Day. I knew that at home the birds and the flowers had returned, and that in dear old New York gay parties of children were probably marching to the parks. What a May Day it was on The Labrador! The morning ushered in a heavy snow storm, with a tremendous gale. Thinking of the steamer due at Battle Harbour, I suggested that, despite the storm, we might make a start. But the skipper exclaimed:

"Dear eyes! an' start in this gale! No, no, th' dogs could ne'er face un, sir."

And as George and our drivers thought likewise, we spent the day resting with the old skipper and his wife, warmly housed and faring sumptuously on wild duck, while the storm outside seemed to shake the world to its very foundations.

On May 2 the snow had almost ceased falling and the wind had somewhat subsided, when at eleven o'clock we parted from the quaint old skipper whose "Dear eyes!" continued to lend emphasis to his remarks up to the last that we saw of him. Rounding a point of land soon after leaving Seal Islands, we came suddenly upon two runaway dogs from a team that had been stormbound at Seal Islands like ourselves. The runaways were thoroughly startled by our sudden appearance, and took to their heels, with our teams, composed respectively of ten dogs and twelve dogs, after them. The ice we were on had been swept clear of snow by the wind, the hauling was easy, and our dogs almost flattened themselves out in their effort to get at the strangers and chew them up. The pace became terrific, but there was nothing to do but hold on tight and trust to luck. For perhaps five miles our wild ride lasted, and then, the strange dogs turning to the snow-covered land, our teams abandoned the race and condescended to pay some heed to their masters' excited observations. Fortunately the chase had carried us in the direction for which we were bound.

Early in the afternoon we reached a cache of cod heads, and stopped while the dogs were fed one each. Poor brutes! they had had nothing to eat since Friday night—this was Monday—and I imagine a rather scant meal even then; for at this time of the year the stock of salt seal meat and fat and dried cod heads and caplin that the natives put up in the summer and fall for dog food is nearly exhausted, and what remains is used very economically. Often the dogs receive only one scanty meal every other day. Our drivers had intended to feed their teams at Seal Islands, but on account of the scarcity of dog food none could be purchased.

At four o'clock in the afternoon we reached Norman Bay, where we found a miserable hut unoccupied save by an abundance of filth, two cats, and one hen. As there were no tracks visible in the snow, the people evidently had been away since the storm began on Saturday night. We built a fire in the stove, made tea and fed ourselves, the cats, and the hen from our grub bag. I invariably insisted that our drivers travel as long as there was light, which at this season lasted until after eight o'clock, and we pushed on until we came to Corbett's Bite, a place that also rejoices in the name of New York, the same having been facetiously bestowed upon it by some fisherman wag, because four small huts had been collected there to make a "city."

The inhabitants of New York had all moved to their fishing quarters farther out on the coast when we arrived, and we took possession for the night of the best of the huts. Filth and slush lay an inch deep on the floor of the single room. A hole in the roof provided a means of escape for the smoke from the fire we built in an improvised fireplace, and, at the same time, a constant source of fear on our part lest some of the dogs which roamed at will over the roof, fall through it and into our fire. An old bench and loose boards taken from a semi-partition in the room served as beds for our party, and we passed a fairly comfortable night.

We were off at daylight, and at half-past eight that morning (May 3) reached Williams Harbour, where I had hoped to engage the teams of John and James Russell and proceed immediately to Battle Harbour, which place was now only a few miles off. But the Russells were away and did not return until night, so that we were unable to proceed until the following morning. With their teams of eight and six dogs the Russells got us away early, however, and at half-past eleven that morning (May 4) we arrived at Fox Harbour, eight miles across the bay from Battle Harbour. Now a new problem presented itself, which was all the more exasperating for the reason that we were in sight of our goal. The ice pack was in the bay, and it was quite impossible to cross it until the wind might shift and blow the pack out. It is true that by a tortuous trail some thirty miles around we could with dogs reach Cape Charles, just below Battle Harbour; but none of the few drivers that knew the trail was anxious to undertake the journey, and as the probabilities were that even if we did succeed in reaching Cape Charles we should be in the same fix there as where we were, our only course seemed to be to remain at Fox Harbour and wait. No vessel, they told us, had yet arrived either at Battle Harbour or Cape Charles.

George Wakeham, an old English fisherman from Devonshire, who had spent forty years of his life on The Labrador and had an Eskimo wife, welcomed us to his house. Near it was an eminence called Watch Hill, from which the general situation of the ice pack could be observed. Day after day I climbed Watch

Hill, and for hours at a time with a telescope viewed the ice and gazed longingly at Battle Harbour in the distance. On the morning of the ninth day the pack appeared to be spreading, and I decided to run the risk of getting fast in the ice, and make at least an attempt to start. So George and I and the five natives that were to row us over got the boat afloat, prepared for a start immediately after luncheon.

Meanwhile George and I ascended Watch Hill for another look at the ice pack. Upon scanning the distant shore line through the telescope we discovered a speck moving in the bay away over near Battle Harbour. A little later we were assured that it was a big rowboat laboriously making its way through the ice. It came nearer and nearer, obviously headed for Fox Harbour. At noon it arrived, and its brawny crew of fishermen said they had come for us. Dr. Macpherson had sent them. The steamer that the doctor had written me was expected had arrived at Cape Charles with a cargo for a new whale factory, and probably would sail for Newfoundland that next day. Having heard we were on our way down the coast, and divining that we were held at Fox Harbour by the ice, Dr. Macpherson had sent the boat so that we might be sure to get the steamer. I marvelled greatly at these evidences of the doctor's thoughtfulness for us who were absolute strangers to him, and was deeply touched.

We placed the coffin in the boat, together with our baggage, and started at once. The men had instructions to take us directly to the ship as she lay off Cape Charles, and after a row of about thirteen miles we reached her at five o'clock in the afternoon. She was the *Aurora*, one of the Newfoundland sealing fleet. It was like reaching home to be on shipboard again, and I felt that my troubles were ended. The mate, Patrick Dumphry, informed me, however, that her commander, Captain Abraham Kean, was at Battle Harbour, and that the steamer would not sail before the following night. So, wishing to have Hubbard's coffin prepared for the voyage, and to meet and thank Dr. Macpherson, I had the men row me back the five miles to Battle Harbour.

There I learned that, upon receiving the first news of my proposed attempt to bring out Hubbard's body, Dr. Macpherson had made a special trip of twenty-five miles to Chateau Bay, to telegraph to New York suggesting that arrangements be made with Bowering & Co., the owners of the *Aurora*, to have that steamer pick us up at Battle Harbour. Perhaps I should say here that the kindness of the doctor to us was only what might have been expected from a gentleman by birth and breeding who, with his charming wife, buries himself on the desolate coast of Labrador, in order to do his Master's work. Pitiable indeed would be the condition of the poor folk on The Labrador were it not for Dr. Grenfell and his brave co-workers of the Deep Sea Mission. For hundreds of miles along the coast they travel on their errands of mercy, braving the violent storms of the bitter Arctic winter, sleeping in the meanest of huts, and frequently risking their lives in open boats on the raging sea. Many is the needy one for whom they have found work, many is the stricken soul that they have comforted, and many is the life that their medical skill has saved.

At the doctor's house I received my first letters from home, and the first accurate news of what had been transpiring in the outside world. While there I also met Captain Kean. Unfortunately the people in New York had not made the arrangement Dr. Macpherson had suggested, but the captain assumed the responsibility of carrying us to Newfoundland, saying that we should go as his guests. He is a former member of the Newfoundland parliament, and a man of influence as well as initiative, and it was lucky for us that he commanded the *Aurora*, else we, in all probability, should have had to push farther down the coast with dogs, or waited at Battle Harbour for the first appearance of the mail boat.

The next day (Friday, May 13) a firm of traders at Battle Harbour, under Dr. Macpherson's supervision, lined Hubbard's coffin with sheet lead and sealed it hermetically. The body was still frozen and in good condition. In the afternoon we were taken to the *Aurora* by Dr. Macpherson and a crew of his men, and established in the cabin, while Hubbard's coffin was carefully stowed away in the hold, there to remain until it was transferred at St. John's to the *Silvia*, the steamer on which my old friend, so full of life and ambition, had sailed from New York, and which now was to carry him back a corpse.

Because of a delay in getting her unloaded, the *Aurora* did not sail until Saturday evening. The sky was all aglow with a gorgeous sunset when we weighed anchor and steamed out of Cape Charles Harbour down across the Strait of Belle Isle. The night was equally glorious. As darkness fell, the sky and sea were illuminated by the northern lights. There was no wind and the sea was calm. Close to our port side an iceberg with two great spires towered high above us; another large iceberg was on our starboard. Before us Belle Isle and the French shore were dimly visible. Behind us the rocky coast of Labrador gradually faded away.

# CHAPTER TWENTY-FOUR

# Hubbard's Message

O ur voyage from Labrador to Newfoundland was un-
eventful, and on Tuesday morning, May 17, the
*Aurora* steamed into St. John's Harbour. I was on the bridge
with Captain Kean when we passed through the narrows, cagerly
looking to see if the ship was there that was to take us home.
To my great satisfaction the *Silvia* was at her wharf, and George
and I lost no time in presenting ourselves to my old friend
Captain Farrell, her commander, who was engaged on deck when
we arrived. He literally took me to his arms in welcome, and like
everyone in St. John's showed me the greatest consideration and
kindness. Bowring & Company, the owners of *Aurora*, placed at
my disposal their steam launch and such men as I needed, to
aid me in the transference of the body from the *Aurora* to the
*Silvia*, and they would make no charge for either this service or
for our passage from Cape Charles to St. John's.

On Friday morning, May 20, the *Silvia* sailed from St. John's,
and one week later (Friday the twenty-seventh), with her flag at
half mast, steamed slowly to her dock in Brooklyn.

It was a sad homecoming. Scarcely a year before, Hubbard,
light-hearted and gay, filled with hope and ambition and manly
vigor, had stood by my side on that very deck as together we
waved farewell to the friends that were gathered now to welcome
George and me back. I thought of how, when we were fighting
our way across the desolate wilderness, he had talked of, and
planned for, this hour; and thought of his childlike faith that
God would take care of us and lead us safely out. And then I
asked myself why George and I, whose faith was so much the
weaker, had been spared, while Hubbard, who never lost sight
of the religion of his youth, was left to die. I felt that I was the
least deserving. And I lived. And Hubbard died. Why? I had no

215

answer to the question. That was God's secret. Perhaps Hubbard's work, in the fullness of His plan, had been completed. Perhaps He still had work for me to do.

\*   \*   \*

We laid him to rest in a beautiful spot in the little cemetery at Haverstraw, at the very foot of the mountains that he used to roam, and overlooking the grand old Hudson that he loved so well. The mountains will know him no more, and never again will he dip his paddle into the placid waters of the river; but his noble character, his simple faith, a faith that never wavered, but grew the stronger in his hour of trouble, his bravery, his indomitable will—these shall not be forgotten; they shall remain a living example to all who love bravery and self-sacrifice.

The critics have said that Hubbard was foolhardy, and without proper preparation he plunged blindly into an unknown wilderness. I believe the early chapters of this narrative show that these criticisms are unfounded, and that Hubbard took every precaution that could occur to a reasonable mind. Himself a thorough student of wilderness travel, in making his preparations for the journey he sought the advice of men of wider experience as to every little detail, and acted upon it.

Others tell how fishnets might have been made from willow bark "after the manner of the Indians," and describe other means of securing food that they claim men familiar with woodcraft would have resorted to. The preceding chapters show how impracticable it would have been for us to have consumed our small stock of provisions while manufacturing a fishnet from bark; and how we did resort to every method at our command of procuring food. Unfortunately we fell upon a year of paucity. The old men of the country bore witness that never before within their memory had there been such a scarcity of game.

But by far the most serious criticism of all, to my mind, is that against the object of the expedition. It has been said that, even had Hubbard succeeded in accomplishing everything that he set out to do, the result would have been of little or no value to the world. In answer to this I cannot do better than to quote from the eloquent tribute to Hubbard's expedition made by his old college friend, Mr. James A. LeRoy, in the magazine issued by the Alumni Association of their alma mater.

> Editorial wiseacres may preach that such efforts as Hubbard made are of no great immediate value to the world, even if successful. But the man who is born with the insatiable desire to *do something*, to see what other men have not seen, to push into the waste places of the world, to make a new discovery, to develop a new theme or enrich an old, to contribute, in other words, to the fund of human knowledge, is always something more than a mere seeker for notoriety; he belongs, however slight may be his actual contribution to knowledge, however great his success or complete his failure, to that minority which has from the first kept the world moving on, while the vast majority have peacefully travelled on with it in its course. The unpoetical critic will not understand him, will find it easy to call him a dreamer; yet it is from dreams like these that have come the world's inspirations and its great achievements.

Without any trace of the finicality that so often is pure morbidity, Hubbard was the most conscientious man I ever knew, a man who was continually thinking of others and how he might help them. Doubtless some will see in his brave life's struggle only a determination to win for himself a recognized place as a writer and expert upon out-of-door life; but those who were privileged to enjoy his intimacy know that the deep, underlying purpose of the man was to fit himself to deliver to the world a message that he felt to be profoundly true—a message that should inspire his fellow men to encounter the battle of life without flinching, that should make them realize that unceasing endeavor and loyalty to God, their conscience and their brothers are indeed worthwhile. He died before he reached the goal of his ambition, but I do not believe that his message was undelivered.

Only men that have camped together in a lonely, uninhabited country can in any degree comprehend the bond of affection and love that drew Hubbard and me ever closer to each other, as the Labrador Wild lured us on and on into the depths of its desolate waste. "The work must be done," he used to say, "and if one of us falls before it is completed, the other must finish it." His words ring in my ear as a call to duty. I see his dear, brave face before me now. I feel his lips upon my cheek. The smoke of the campfire is in my blood. The fragrance of the forest is in my nostrils. Perhaps it is God's will that I finish the work of exploration that Hubbard began.

*The Lure of the Labrador Wild*
was designed by Quad Left Graphics.

It was typeset in Baskerville by Bateman & Slade, Inc.